THE DEUS ARMAARUSS

An Explanation of the Mars 360 Legal and Economic System

Anthony of Boston

© 2023 Anthony Moore. All rights reserved.

All images gathered and attributed to its rightful

owners accordingly.

Astrology charts used with permission from Astrodienst AG

Astrology Chart Images by Astrodienst AG/

www.astro.com

All rights reserved. No part of this book may be reproduced in any form on by an electronic or mechanical means, including information storage and retrieval systems, without permission in writing from the publisher, except by a reviewer who may quote brief passages in a review.

Table of Contents

Volume I - An Explanation of the Mars 360 Legal and Economic System - pg 4

Volume II - Evidence Justifying Faith in Mars Influence - pg 78

Volume III - Confirming Faith in Mars Influence - pg 93

Volume I - An Explanation of the Mars 360 Legal and Economic System

Mars 360, is a formulated and hypothesized global social accord ideally operable under the same principle as the Paris Climate Accord, that attempts to integrate all nations into a common cause. The Mars effect on human behavior inclines each individual toward certain predispositions that lend itself to fundamental outlooks which carries with it... a high degree of inflexibility. This inflexibility plays itself out in various political and social stances like socialism, pacifism, capitalism, liberalism, conservatism, libertarianism, etc, but is actually the result of Mars's permanent influence on the human brain. This gives rise to the idea that while certain stances are different in external display, they are at the same time fundamentally backed by the same source(to varying degrees of course)....which is Mars.

This influence manifests differently amongst the human population. Mars influences some to be antagonistic to different groups, others to be antagonistic to different individuals. It influences some to be antagonistic to change and others to stagnancy. It's all laid out in 6 different categories and allows for a wider perspective of the human condition, thus opening the door to understanding and improvisation. This construct allows the individual to navigate through life accordingly, adjusting his own behavior to the situation he faces.... catering to the human archetypes in his space according to the Mars number they wear.

Historically humanity has fostered a race-driven ethnocentric perspective. Mars 360, however, introduces the idea of the cosmic-driven perspective. Unlike qualities of ethnicity or nationality which bind peoples and groups together, Mars 360 introduces a way for humans to become cosmically driven, dividing themselves based on natal astrological factors such as where Mars was situated at the time they were born. This outlook fragments the entire human population into 6 cosmic races that are all defined by their natal astrological Mars position, putting humans into a segment in which everyone within that segment would share a similar personality trait and outlook. This ideally would override the ethnicity and nationality factors and bring the world under one construct and legal system, dissolving the boundaries of nationality.

Under Mars 360, laws and privileges are granted based on the general character and personality disposition of a person as defined in the Mars 360 Religious and Social System. This outlook even changes the US Constitution, because under Mars 360, for example, freedom of speech would only be applied to the Mars-4 personality. Everyone else would have restrictions there. Essentially, each group would have laws and privileges that are exclusive to their respective Mars-based personality characteristics. These laws would be enforced by restricting buying and selling to those that have joined the Mars 360 system.

This system divides the entire human race into six categories. A person 's astrological birthchart and the location of Mars thereof is used to determine how the law will be applied to that individual. The law under Mars 360 is not applied uniformly across the population, but is based on where Mars was situated at the time a person was born, along with the personality characteristics that define that position. This would take precedence over race and nationality and could be used to implement a one world government, with people now primarily identified based on Mars factors. Other aspects of identity, such as nationality and race would take a backseat

The Mars 360 social/financial theory takes aspects related to an individual's astrological Mars placement—according to how it is explained in "The Mars 360 Religious and Social System", and has it displayed within a social environment, and combines that with the aspect of buying and selling within that framework. This means that in order for this currency system to work, a person has to believe that Mars influences human beings. And one does not have to call it faith-based. It can simply be hypothesis-based or theory-based, no different than how quantum theory is fostered in the scientific community. This currency system is similar to how private currencies are issued within local communities to encourage spending and economic development within that community. As a contingency plan in the case of obtuseness toward the impact of inflation, a small community would develop as a scientific study. Within that community, each person would calculate where Mars was at the time they were born according to the framework laid out in the book "The Mars 360 Religious and Social System" which divides the astrology chart into 6 sections. The community would then see to it that the individual's rights under their own Mars influence is not violated....meaning that the characteristics associated with the negative Mars influence (according to where it's positioned in the chart) would be allowed some healthy expression(healthy meaning enough to where humans can still co-exist).

Mars is responsible for negative habits dispersed amongst the 6 possible positions:
1. poor face- to-face communication/interaction
2. hyperactivity/reckless thoughts
3. debauchery
4. hyper-opinionated/cultural bias
5. laziness/disobedience
6. introversion/sillyness.

The reason the idea of an outward display of Mars's position in an individual's birthchart is presented is because it would precipitate "understanding," allowing people to prepare or know in advance how to deal with the individual and vice versa without having to go through any extended learning phase, which oftentimes gives rise to contention.

The commercial aspect allows for a dynamic that would encourage buying and selling amongst those who carry some outward form of insignia related to Mars's position at the time they were born, or simply has Mars indicated on their driver's license. This doesn't necessitate issuing a private currency, but due to discrimination laws, issuing a private currency within a local community would be a more feasible legal option. The currency is called the Mars Redback and its growth would follow that old Facebook model, which centered around the private community before slowing branching out into the global sphere. The Mars Redback—backed by a working model that supports the belief that the planet Mars influences human nature—could be used within communities of people who have the position of Mars in their birthchart indicated outwardly in some way. In order to gather how interest rates would be managed, one can read the book "The Mars Hypothesis" which hypothesizes that the Federal Reserve could have set interest rates based on the movements of the planet Mars. The book also lays out future dates of when interest rates should be either raised or lowered.

Here is a diagram of the Redback currency: 200 of these private notes can be found in the book "200 Private Mars Redback Notes"

On the next page is the basis of the law for the Mars 360 system. Unlike the Abrahamic construct, which prioritizes the needs of God the Father over those of man, the Mars 360 construct prioritizes the needs of man over the God of Abraham. The world is divided into six categories of Mars-based personality and character inclinations and all laws will fall subject to that framework. In addition, man is no longer defined only terms of race and nationality, but is now also define in terms of negative personality charcteristics This opens the door for a cohesive one world government, whereby the Mars 360 element adds another dimension to the dynamic regarding how people perceive their positive and negative interactions. This keeps all triggers for separatism in check.

Figure 1d

1st Seal	2nd Seal	3rd Seal	4th Seal	5th Seal	6th seal
Face to face communication. Other people's feelings, rights, property, loved ones within the immediate environment. Siblings, neighbors, relatives. co-workers Visual perception	Listening skills and mental thoughts. Other people's health one on one relationships. Spouse and kids. Homeland, Home government. culture of early upbringing	Physical bodily maintenance. Diet, exercise, sexual attractiveness. sex and home. Doctors, personal trainers. consumption of healthy products	Indirect communication. Choice of words, other people's cultural standards, one's own sense of discipline, restraint, integrity, self denial, God within, Soul, the less fortunate	Servitude, worship. Work, respect for authority, respect for status figures, obedience, skill ethics. work effort	Individual Identity, EGO, distinct persona, DNA. Regard for personal appearance, rectitude, how others view us. Facial & cultural expressions, and tone of voice.

----Mars opposes all of these things and has a lack of energy to engage in any of the behaviors above---

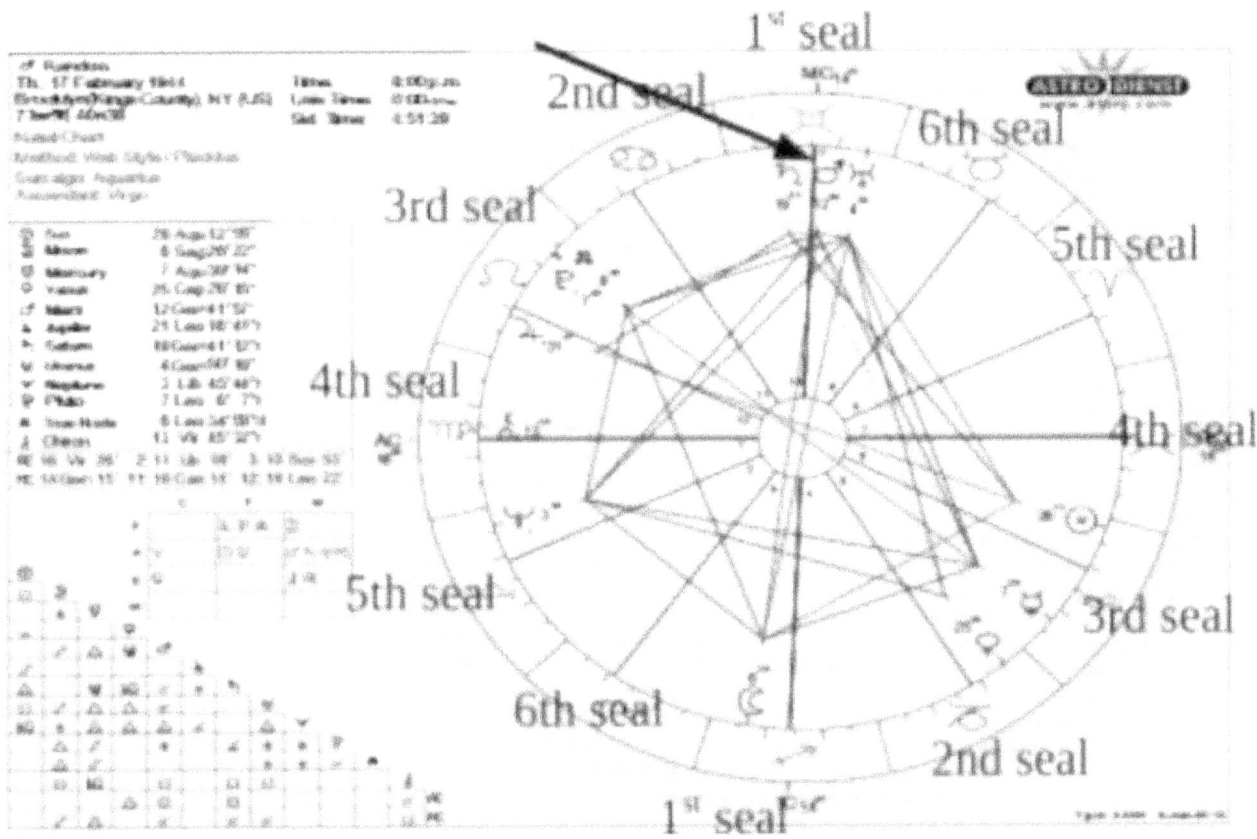

In calculating this chart using western Astrology, we can reference the description of each seal in Figure 1d, and then apply it to this random chart. In the above chart, we find Mars in the 1* seal. (arrow is pointing to it) So in going back to Figure id, its determined for the 1* seal to represent immediate environment, co-workers, neighbors, face to face direct communication, and the right hand. With Mars here we interpret this position as a natural inborn hostility and lack of energy toward neighbors, co-workers, and ace to face communication. Therefore, this person is categorized for that placement and conferred for all the services designated to deal with that placement. Throughout this person's life, he will be entitled to leniency with regard to working with other people, and face to face communication. Mandates will be passed so that this person doesn't have to over-exert himself in situations involving the careful handling of co-workers, neighbors, siblings, and face to face communication. These types would be marked as having capitalist conservative leanings[with "Mars-1" on the ID card]

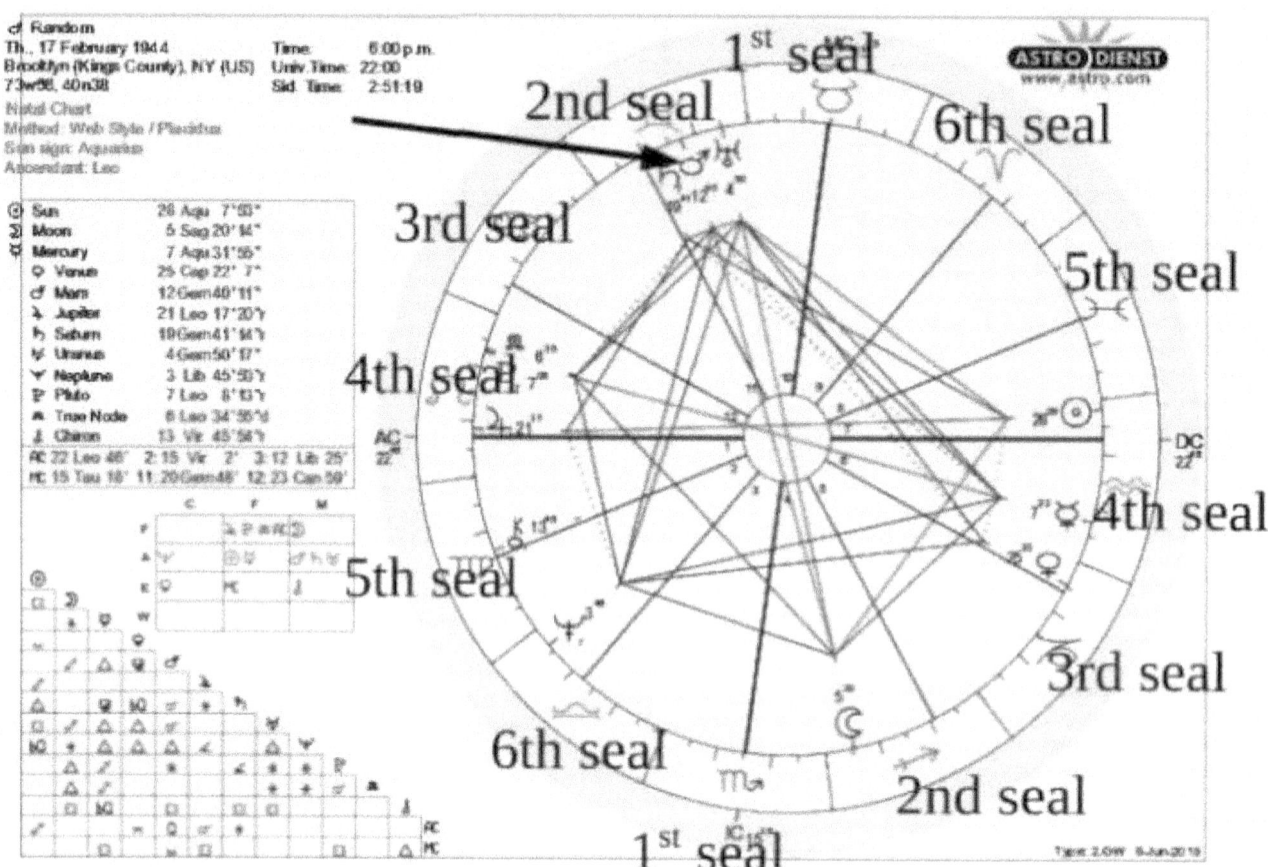

In calculating this chart using western Astrology, we can reference the description of each seal in Figure 1d and then apply it to this random chart. In the above chart, we find Mars in the 2nd seal. (arrow is pointing to it) So in going back to Figure 1d, its determined for the 2nd seal to represent homeland, home government, spouse, one's own children, rest, and listening. With Mars here we interpret this position as a natural inborn hostility and lack of energy towards homeland, home government, spouse, one's own children, rest, and listening. Therefore, this person is categorized for that placement and conferred for all the services designated to deal with that placement. Throughout this person's life, he will be entitled to leniency with regard to dealing with homeland, home government, spouse, one's own children, and listening. Mandates will be passed so that this person doesn't have to over-exert himself in situations involving the extended and methodical valuing of those things. An example of the mandates issued to serve this placement would be passport privileges, time away from family not being full grounds for penalization in divorce court, longer recess hours for inmates, extended time away from classroom learning, and quiet time in places of work designated by law, roaming privileges in one's homeland. Free thought would also be applied here. These types would be marked as having anti-government conservative leanings [with "Mars-2 on the ID card]

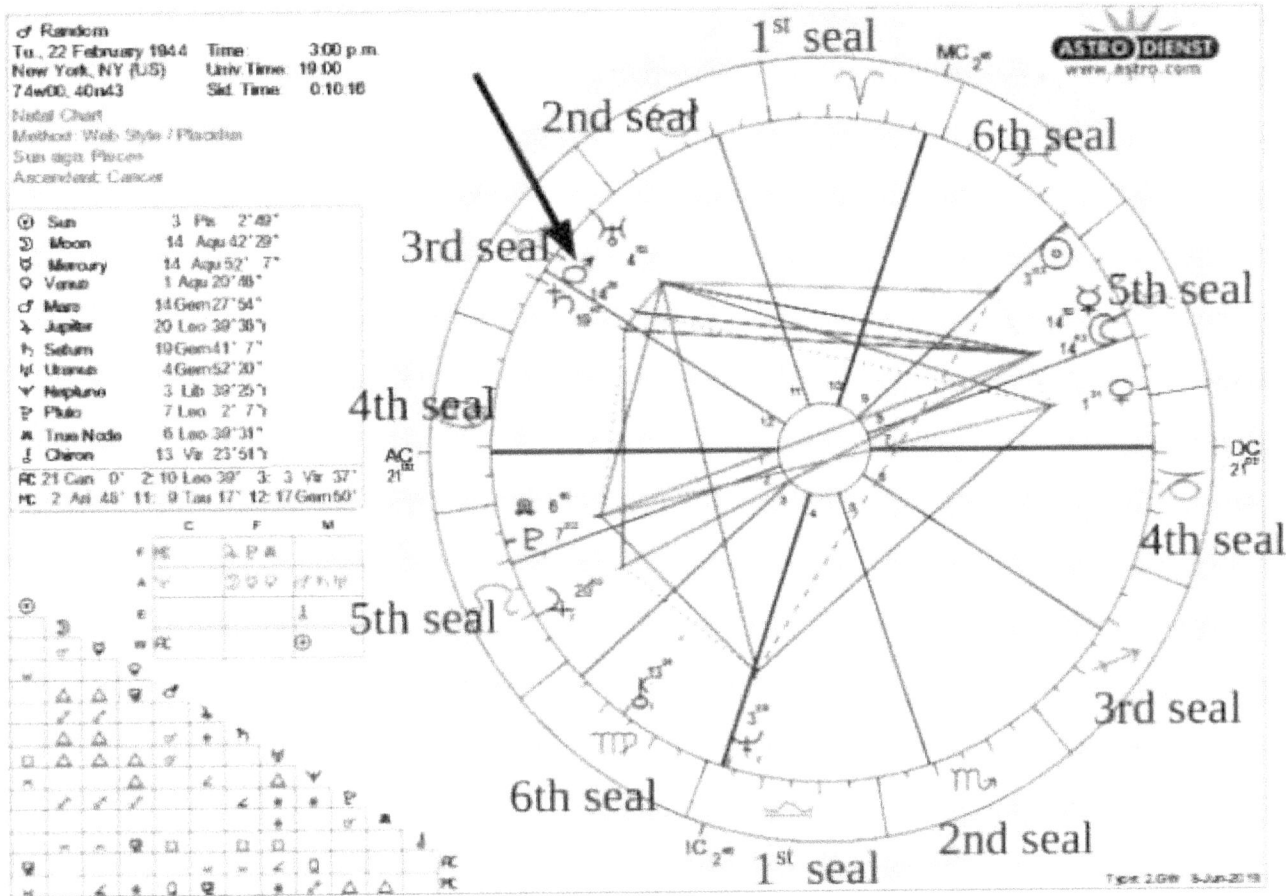

In calculating this chart using western Astrology, we can reference the description of each seal in Figure 1d, and then apply it to this random chart. In the above chart, we find Mars in the 3rd seal. (arrow is pointing to it) So in going back to Figure 1d, its determined for the 3rd seal to represent physical bodily maintenance, exercise, home, diet, sex and physical attractiveness. With Mars here we interpret this position as a natural inborn hostility and lack of energy towards physical bodily maintenance, exercise, diet, sex, home and physical attractiveness. Therefore, this person is categorized for that placement and conferred for all the services designated to deal with that placement. Throughout this person's life, he will be entitled to leniency with regard to dealing with physical bodily maintenance, exercise, diet, sex, staying at home, and physical attractiveness. Mandates will be passed so that this person doesn't have to over-exert himself in situations involving the extended and methodical valuing of those things. An example of the mandates issued to serve this placement would be the person being given less restriction on what he/she can put inside his/her own body. Laws making it illegal to be forced or intimidated into diet and exercise to lose weight would be considered. More leniency regarding pleasure seeking opportunities, such as the ones involving recreational drug use and consensual non-harmful sexual freedom. Bisexuality would get some protection. Also, rights to a sedentary lifestyle will be highlighted here. Because the physical body and its maintenance is tied to being sheltered or in a safe physical dwelling, freedom from having to be stuck at home or stuck at a geographical location would be granted to these types. These types would be marked as having Libertarian leanings and anti-government sentiments[with "Mars-3" on the ID card].

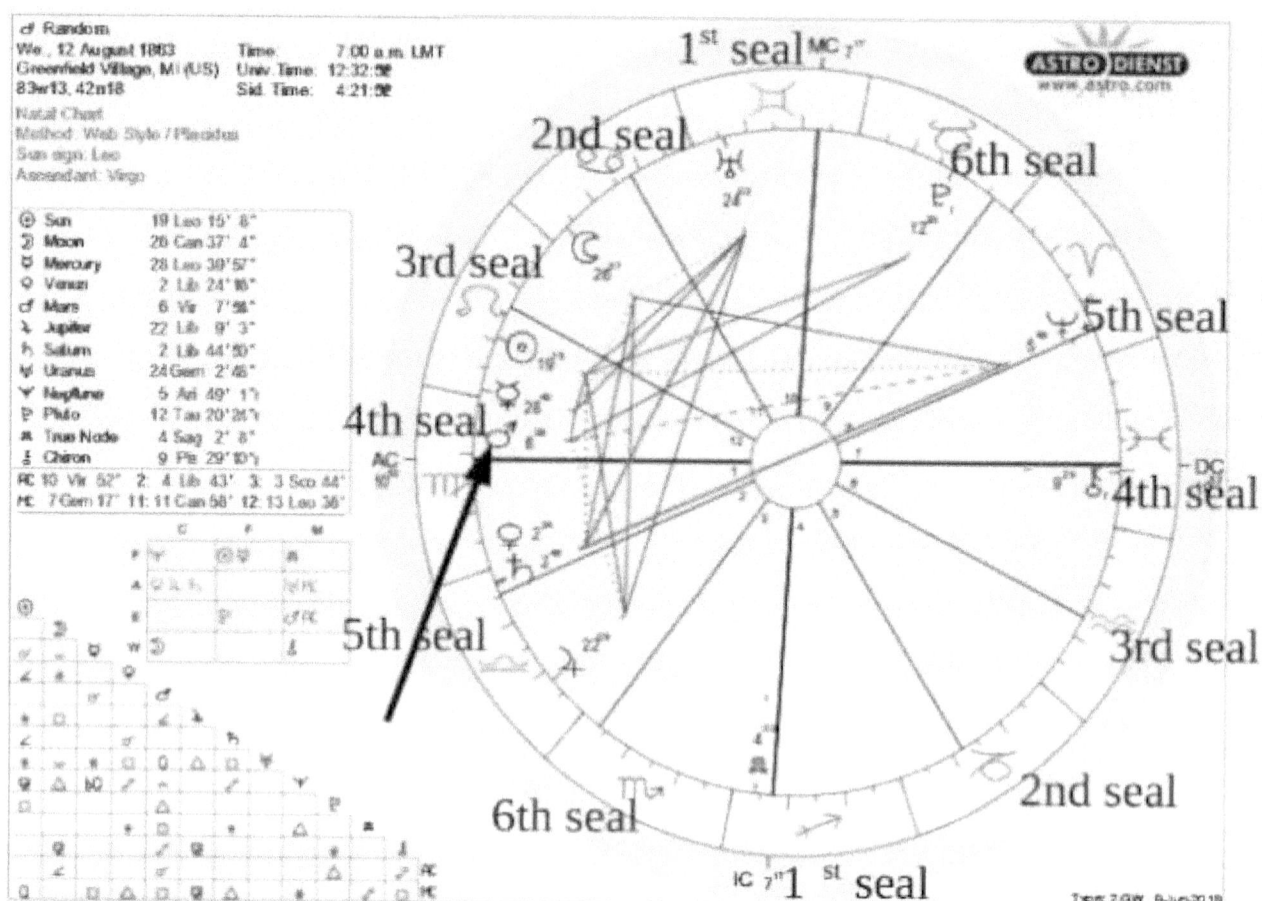

In calculating this chart using western Astrology, we can reference the description of each seal Figure 1d and then apply it to this random chart. In the above chart, we find Mars in the 4th seal. (arrow is pointing to it) So in going back to Figure 1d, its determined for the 4th seal to represent indirect communication, choice of words, other people's cultural standards, discipline, restraint, integrity, self denial, God within, Soul, and the less fortunate. With Mars here we interpret this position as a natural inborn hostility and lack of energy towards those aforementioned. Therefore, this person is categorized for that placement and conferred for all the services designated to deal with that placement. Throughout this person's life, he will be entitled to leniency with regard to dealing with indirect communication, choice of words, other people's cultural standards, discipline, restraint, integrity, self denial, God within, Soul, and the less fortunate. Mandates will be passed so that this person doesn't have to over-exert himself in situations involving the extended and methodical display of those things. An example of the mandates issued to serve this placement would be the person being given less restriction on matters related to indirect speech through various forms of media. Freedom of speech would be more applicable to this placement. Services would be sensitive to material ambition arising from a lack of energy to self-denial, which would lead to top priority for business loans. This placement would be granted some protection from over-exertion of cultural sensitivity regarding cultures not his own. Lies would be understood as Mars influenced and also be given a bit more leniency upon discovery. Also there would be limits on reading material as this placement points to dyslexia. These types would be marked as having nationalist conservative leanings[with "Mars-4" on the ID card].

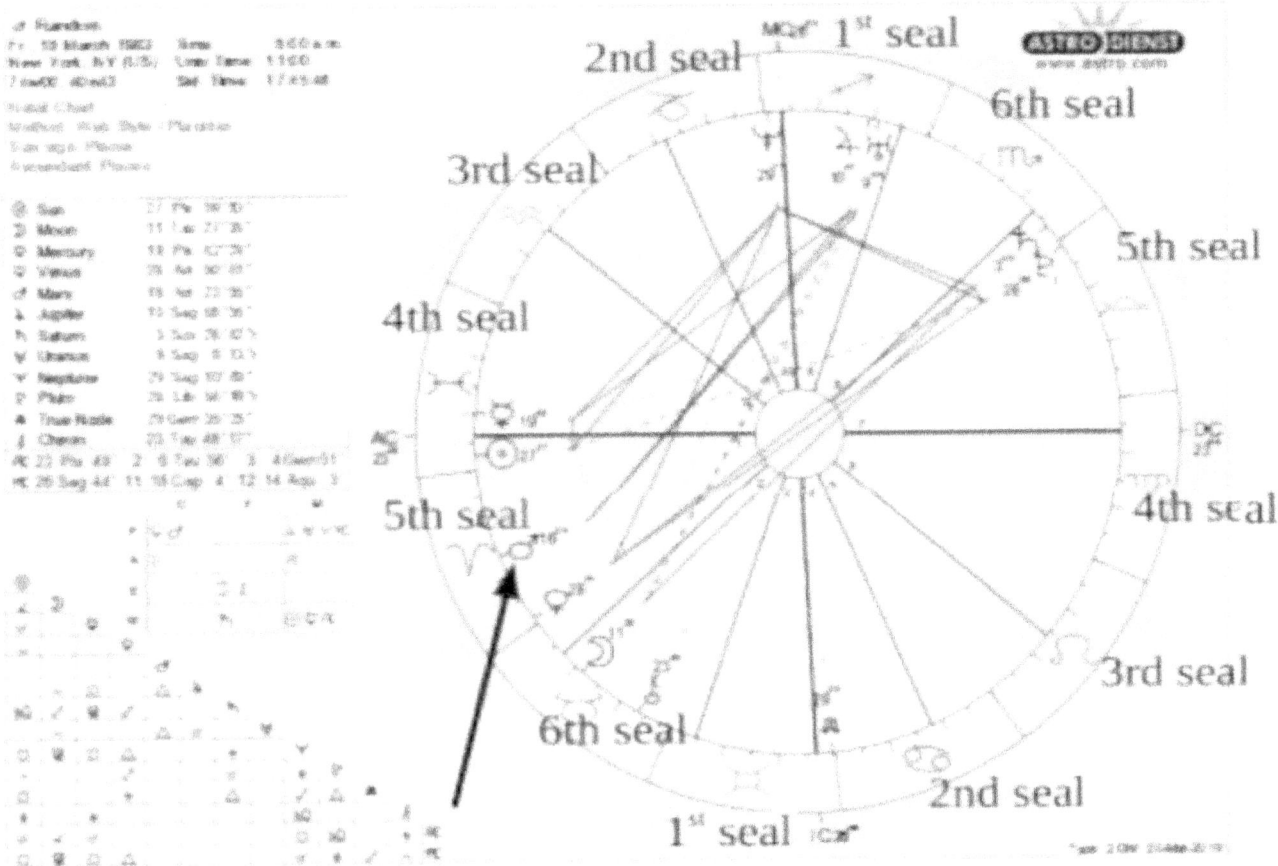

In calculating this chart using western Astrology, we can reference the description of each seal Figure 1d, and then apply it to this random chart. We look for Mars, and find it in the above chart in the 5" seal. So in going back to Figure ad, its determined for the 5" seal to represent authority figures and work. With Mars we interpret this position as a natural inborn hostility and lack of energy toward authority figures and work, so he's categorized for that placement and conferred for all the services designated to deal with that placement. Throughout this person's life, he will be entitled to leniency with regard to work under supervision and will have certain privileges when it comes to addressing status figures. These types would be marked as having Democratic Communist leanings[with "Mars-5" on the ID card].

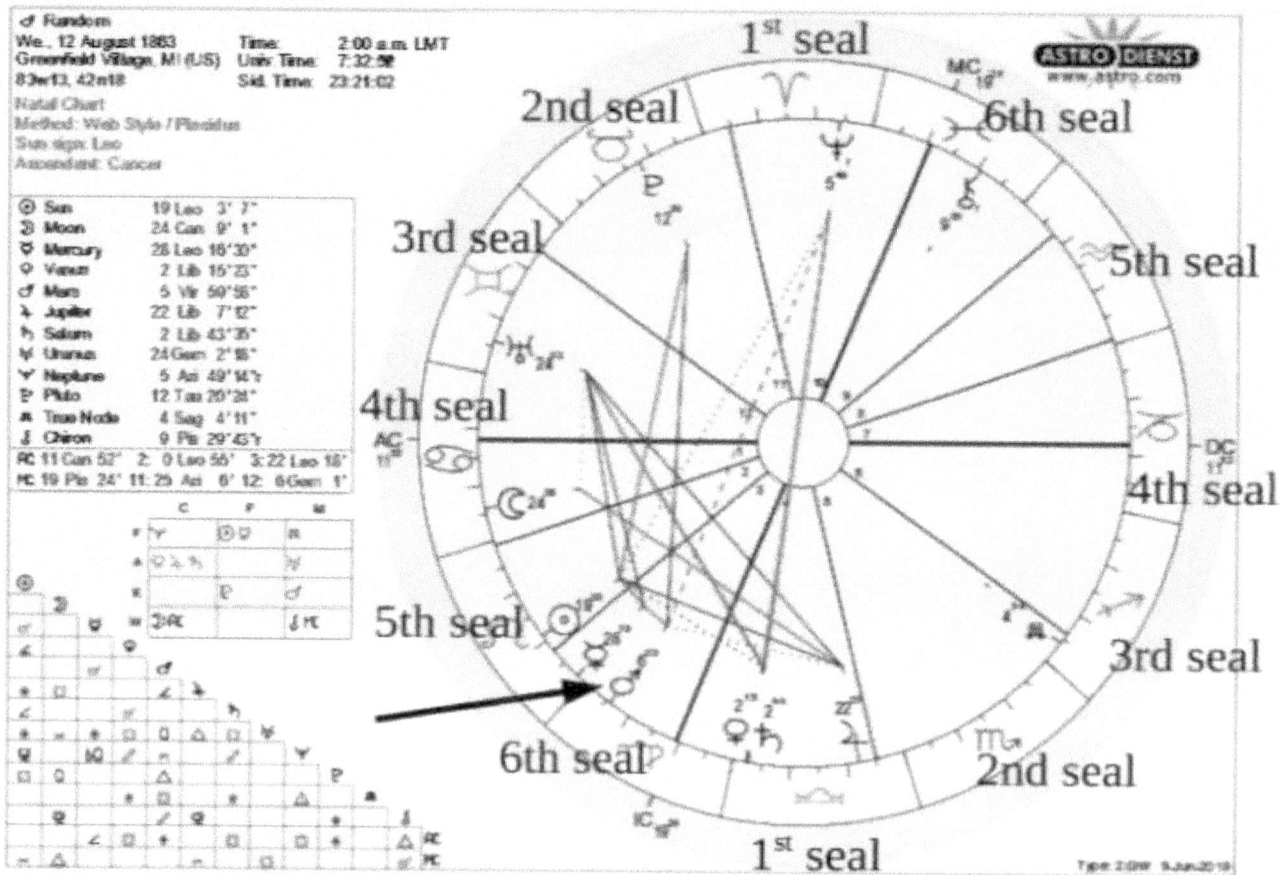

In calculating this chart using western Astrology, we can reference the description of each seal in Figure 1d, and then apply it to this random chart. In the above chart, we find Mars in the 6th seal. (arrow is pointing to it) So in going back to Figure 1d, its determined for the 6th seal to represent individual identity, EGO, distinct persona, DNA, regard for personal appearance, rectitude, and how others view them. With Mars here we interpret this position as a natural inborn hostility and lack of energy towards those aforementioned. Therefore, this person is categorized for that placement and conferred for all the services designated to deal with that placement. Throughout this person's life, he will be entitled to leniency with regard to dealing with individual identity, EGO, distinct persona, DNA, regard for personal appearance, rectitude, and how others view them. Mandates will be passed so that this person doesn't have to over-exert himself in situations involving the extended and methodical display of those things. An example of the mandates issued to serve this placement would be the person being given less restriction on matters related to personal appearance. Extended time away from being seen would be required by law. It would be illegal to label these people in any way in terms of race, religion, creed, etc. All privacy laws would be protecting them to the fullest. Cultural identity exemptions would somehow be in effect. By law, these types would be not accountable to prevailing cultural identity standards related to their DNA and ethnicity. These types would be marked as having Democrat non-nationalist Liberal leanings[with "Mars-6" on the ID card].

Here is an example of how the Mars 360 system would work for the Mars-1 demographic. Here is a sample of charts below, all of which would be classified as Mars-1. First notice the layout of the seals and apply that to the charts below.

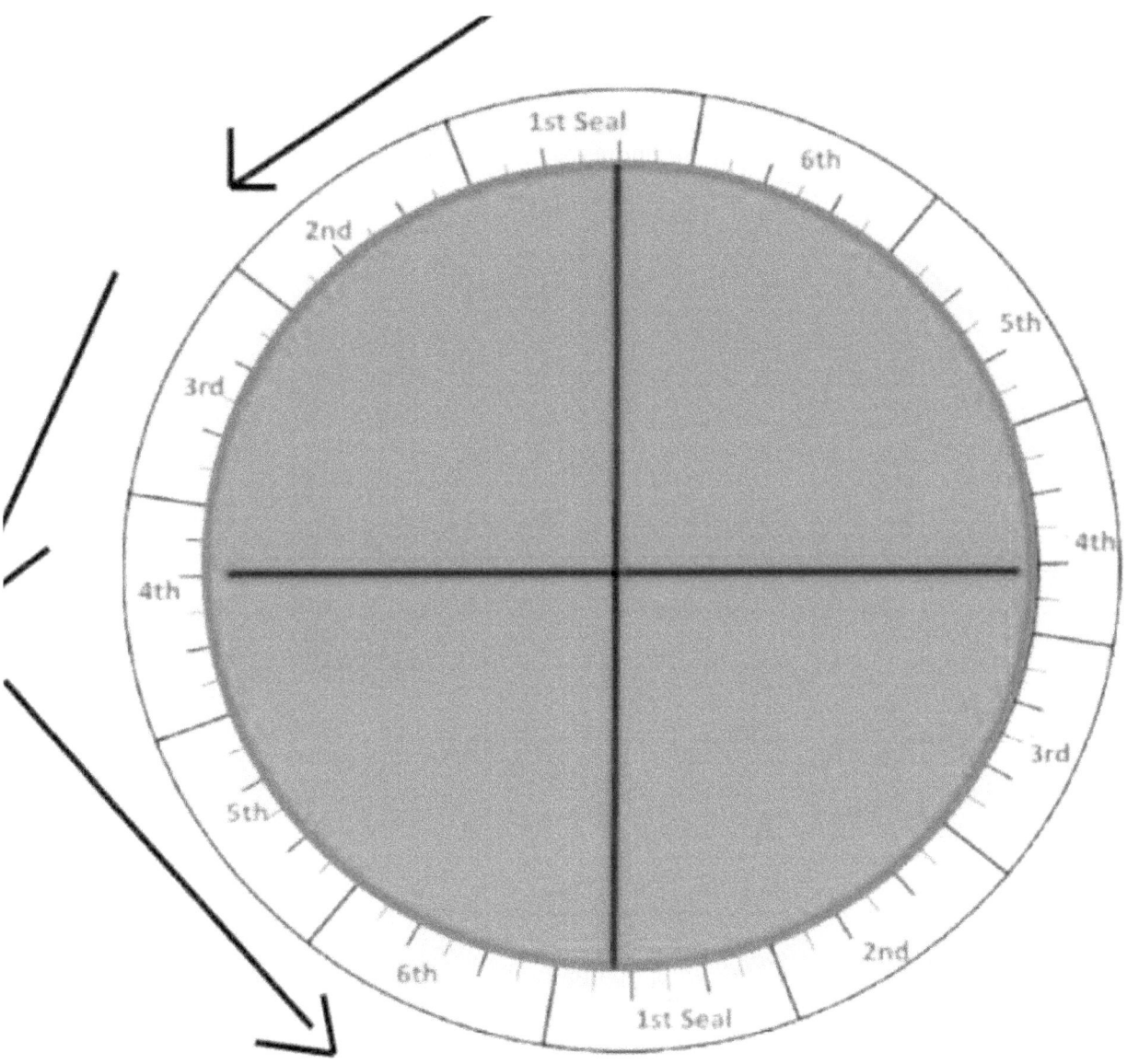

Notice where the 1st seal is located. The 1st seal is designated as causing a person to lack the energy to concern himself with normal standards of face to face communication and other people's money. This person is often blunt and triggers people when communicating directly. These types do not like small talk, but are often ranked high in law enforcement and business. These types are usualy pro-war and verbally abusive, but good as business. These types also lack control over the right hand. They also don't get along with collegues and associates.

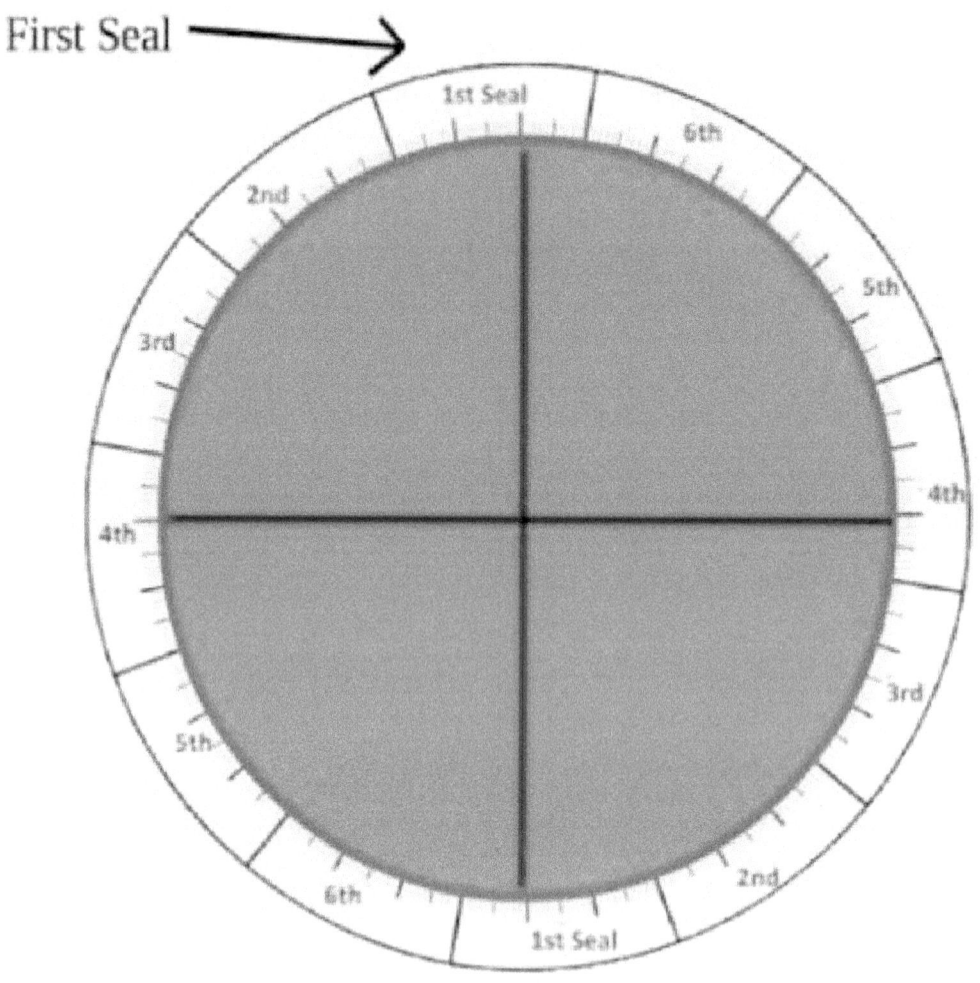

This archetype lacks the energy to concern himself with matters concerning other people's money and proper face to face comunication. The result is that this archetype becomes the most self-centered and corrupt. These types do not do well having to communicate face to face. However, their blunt direct style is can be a virtue in law enforcement, military and business. One of the worst expresions of this archetype came in the form Bernie Madoff. Yet this archetype is one of the major components of the Mars360 system, because their open designation as a Mars-1 could allow for society to accommodate their blunt verbally abusive manner. This means that if you see a Mars-1 walking down the street, he may have some liberty to use foul language in most scenarios, with legal protection. If you have a boss that is a Mars-1, you will know what to expect in terms of communication. These types also use racial slurs often to someone's face. A black, chinese, european, arab, or jewish Mars-1 will be likely to directly call another person a derogatory racial term. However, under the Mars 360 system, this would be understood as a result of Mars influence on the individual and not as a subset of racial animosity from another demographic. Very important. Under Mars 360, the Mars-1, along with his inclinations, will be protected. The people who represent this archetype are Bernie Madoff, Kevin Hart, Bill Gates, Snoop Dogg, Dr. Dre, Sam Bankman Fried, Ken Lay, George Patton, Mitt Romney, and Muhammad Ali

So now, here are the charts

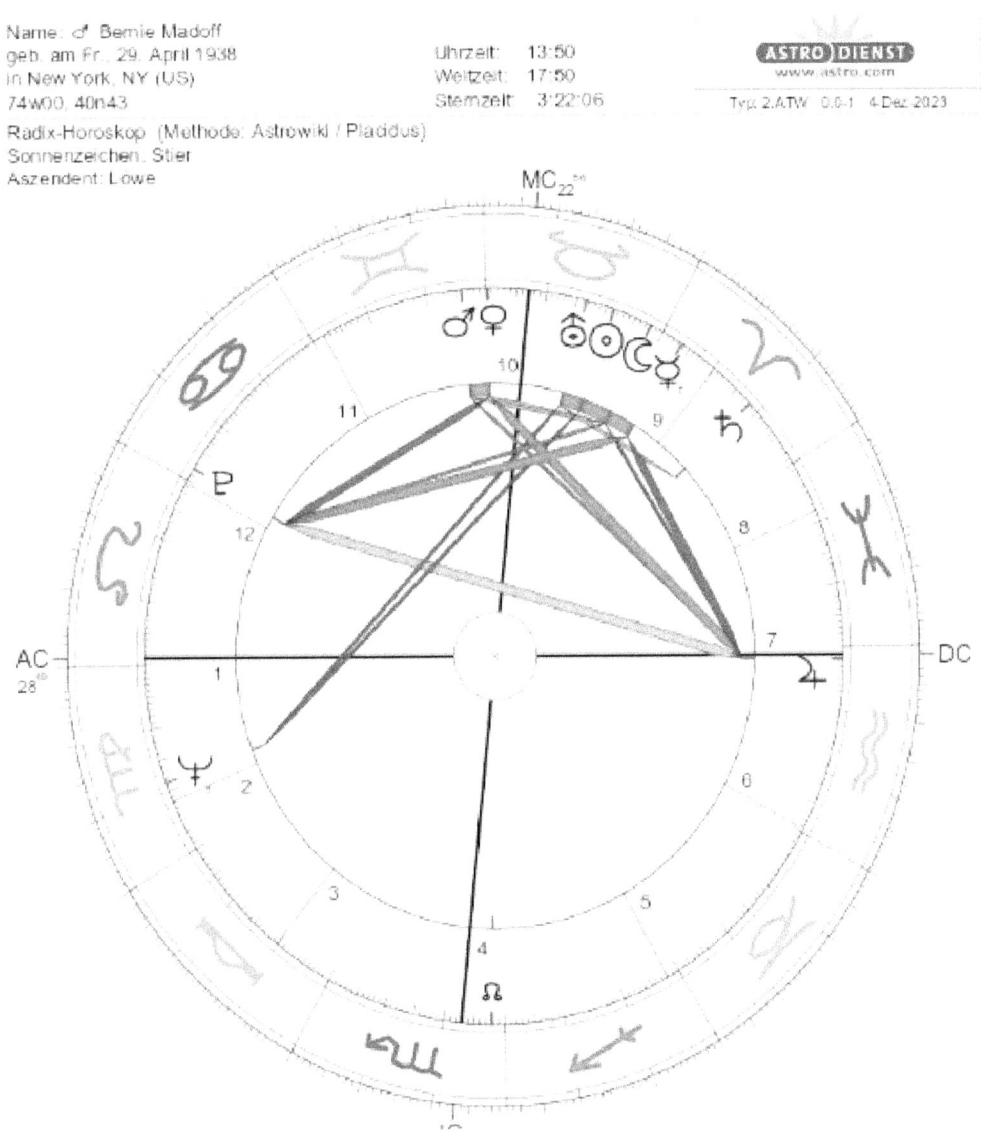

This is Bernie Madoff, convicted fraud, who defrauded millions of dollars from his clients in a massive Ponzi Scheme. Under Mars-360, he would have been designated a Mars-1 at birth and a potential fraud in the future and danger to other people's money. However, his freedom of face to face communication would have been protected and he would given priority when it comes to business grants.

This is the chart for Sam Bankman Friend, the CEO of the cryptocurrency exchange FTX, charged with wire fraud, commodities fraud, securities fraud, money laundering, and campaign finance law violations. Under the Mars 360 system, he would have been marked as a Mars-1 at birth and a danger to other people's money.

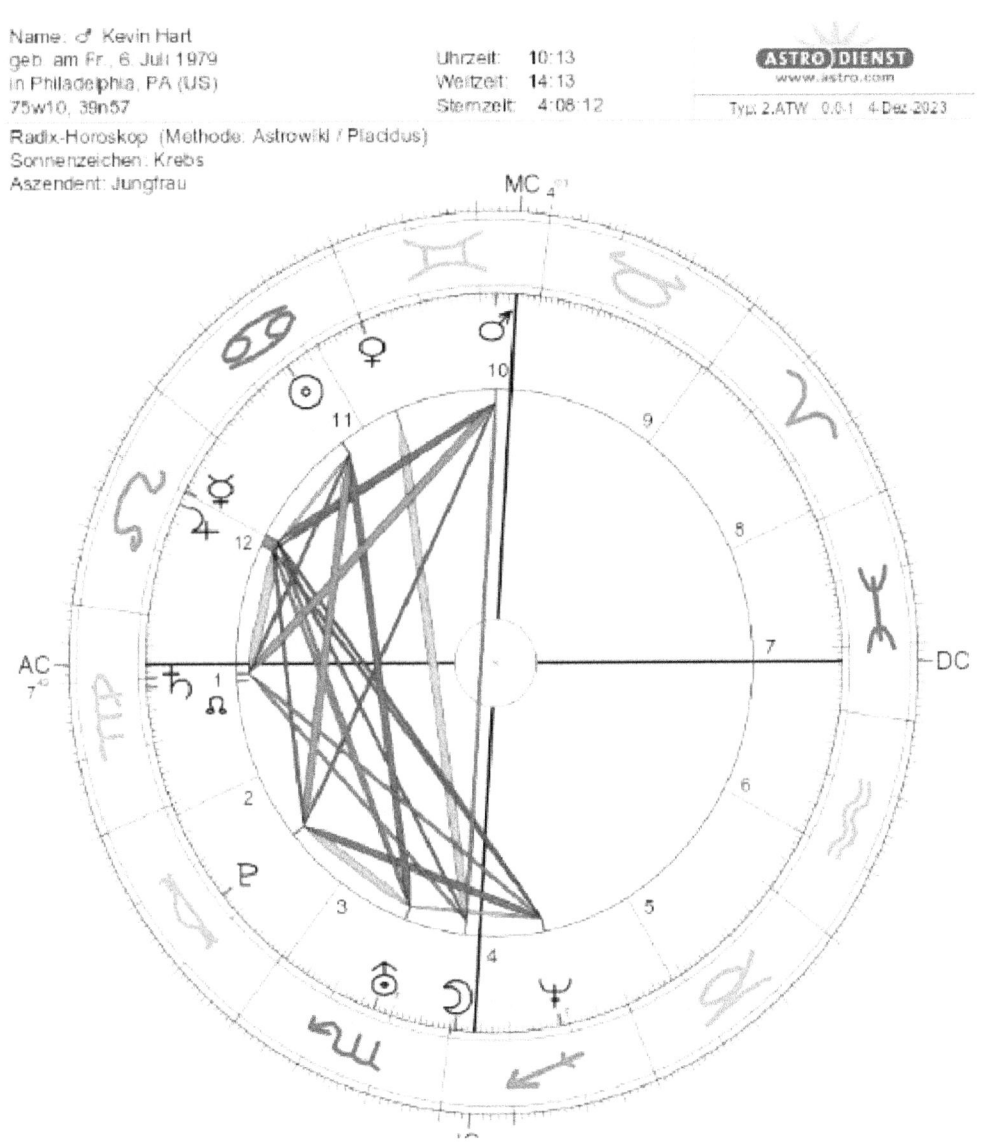

This is the chart of Kevin Hart, a comedian who makes fun of people in his audience directly to their face in typical Mars-1 fashion. Under Mars 360, this would be protected. At birth, however, he would be marked as a Mars-1 and predicted to be verbally abusive in a direct face to face manner

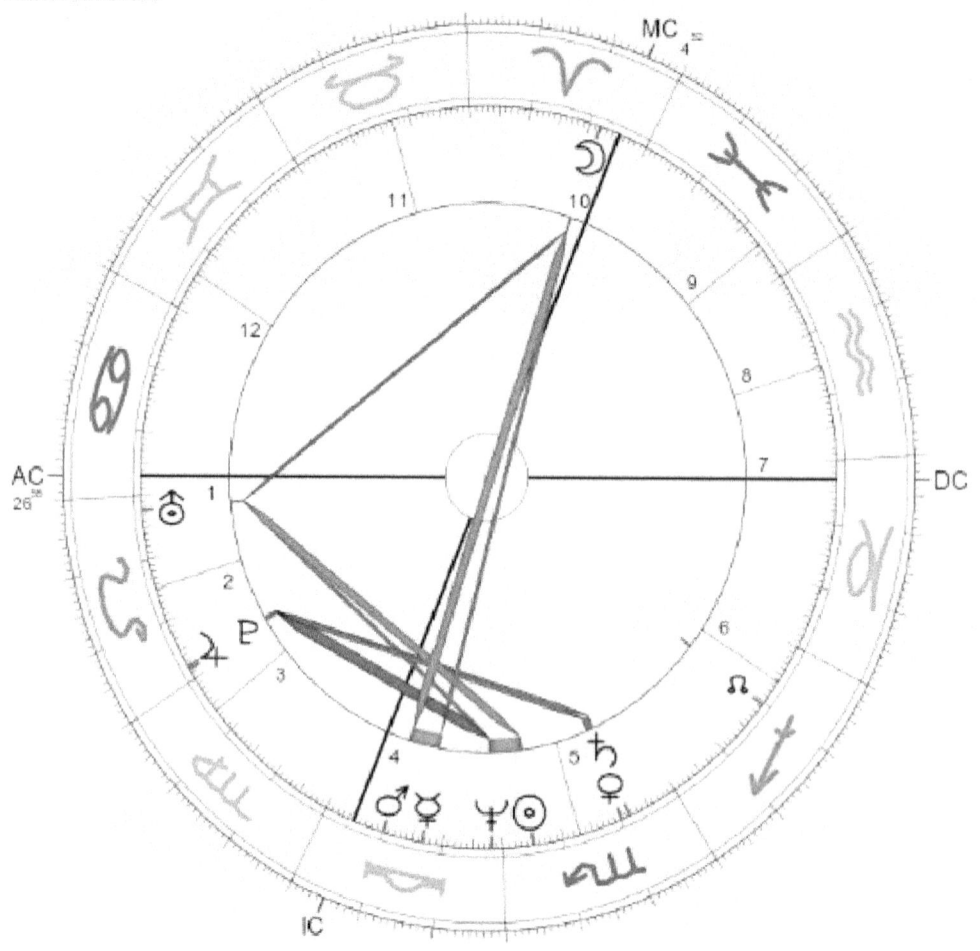

This is the chart of Bill Gates, billionaire CEO of Microsoft, who was known for being a combative figure. Under Mars-360 is direct combative form of communication would be protected. At birth, he would have been designated a Mars-1

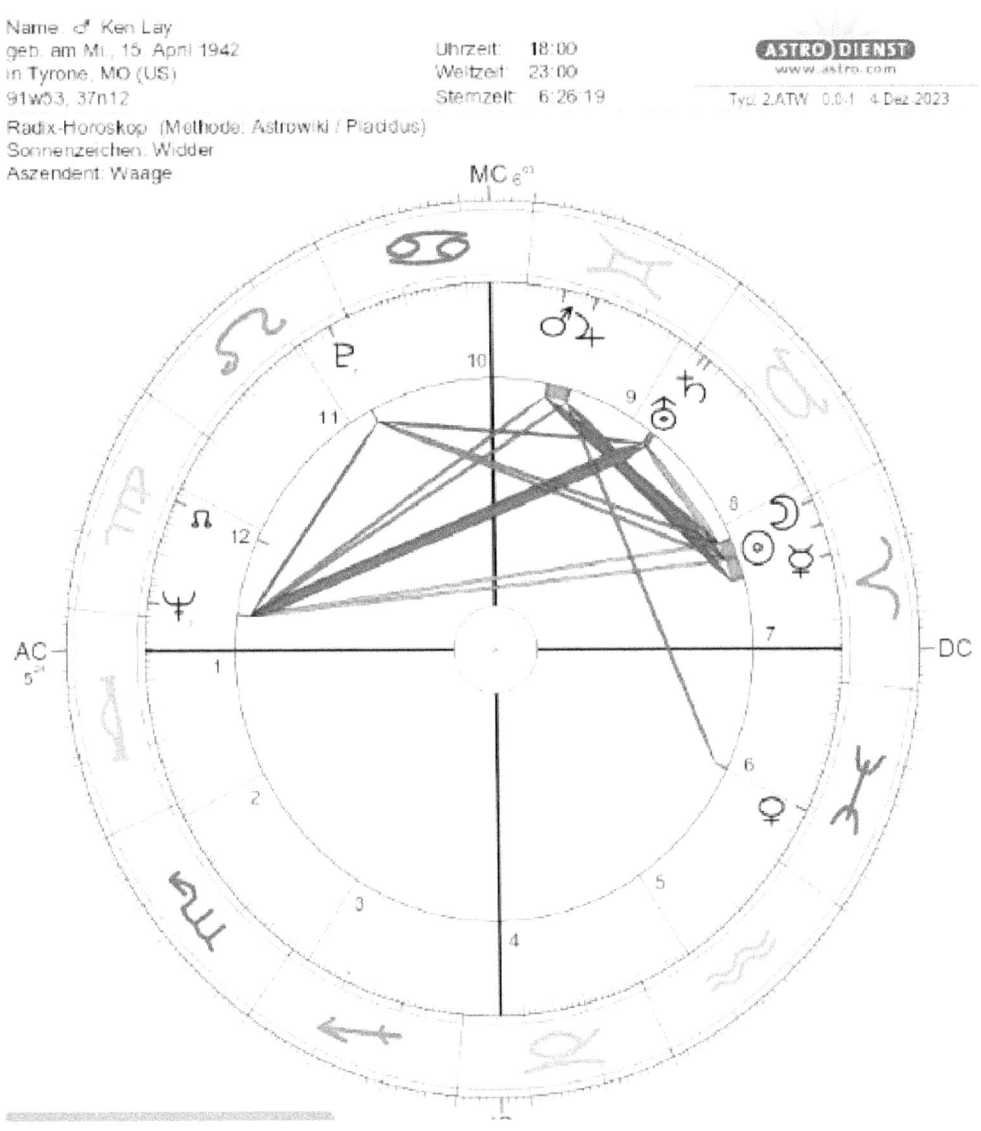

This is the chart of Ken Lay, very close to being a Mars-1. He was the CEO of Enron who defrauded investors of millions of dollars. He was convicted of conspiracy and fraud

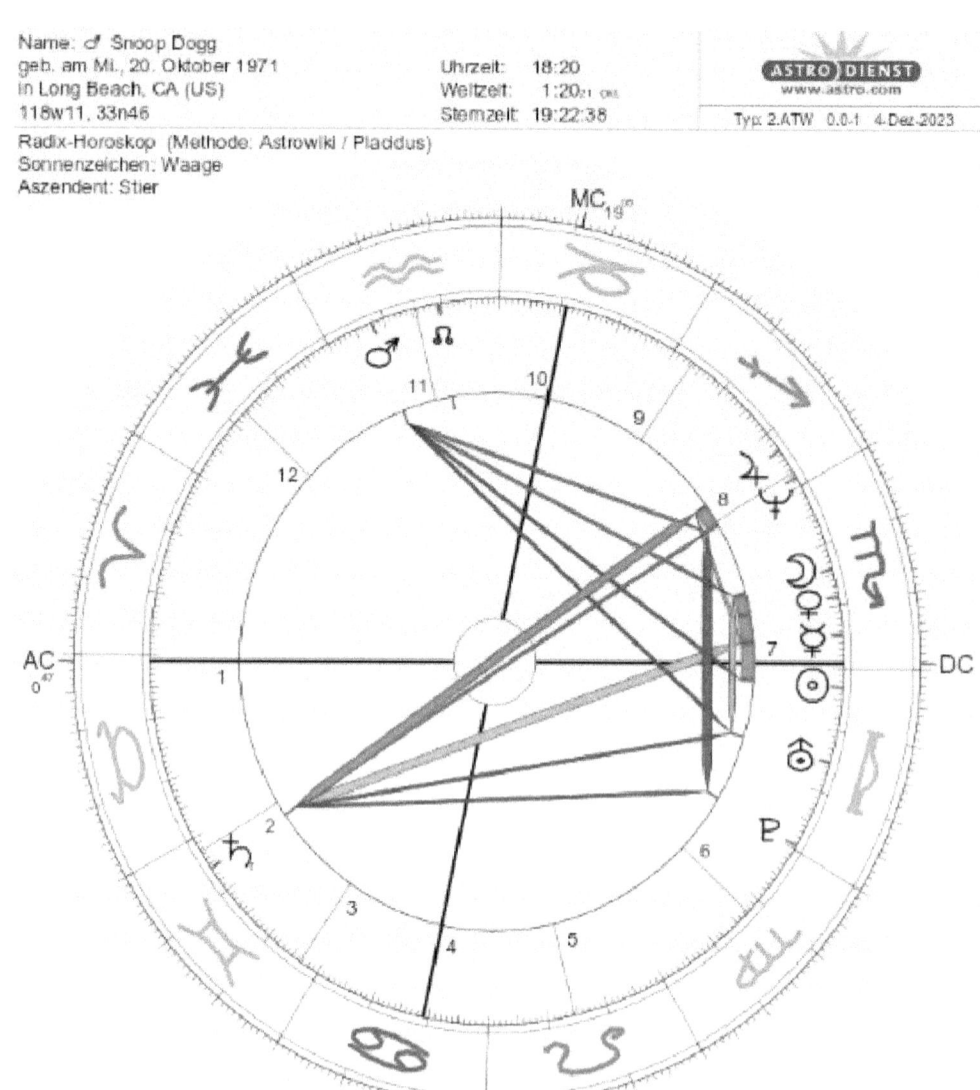

This is the chart for Snoop Dogg, a rapper, who uses foul language in his music and blunt in face to face communication. Most rappers have this placement of Mars. At birth, he would have been assigned to the Mars-1 demographic and been labeled as prone to verbal abuse.

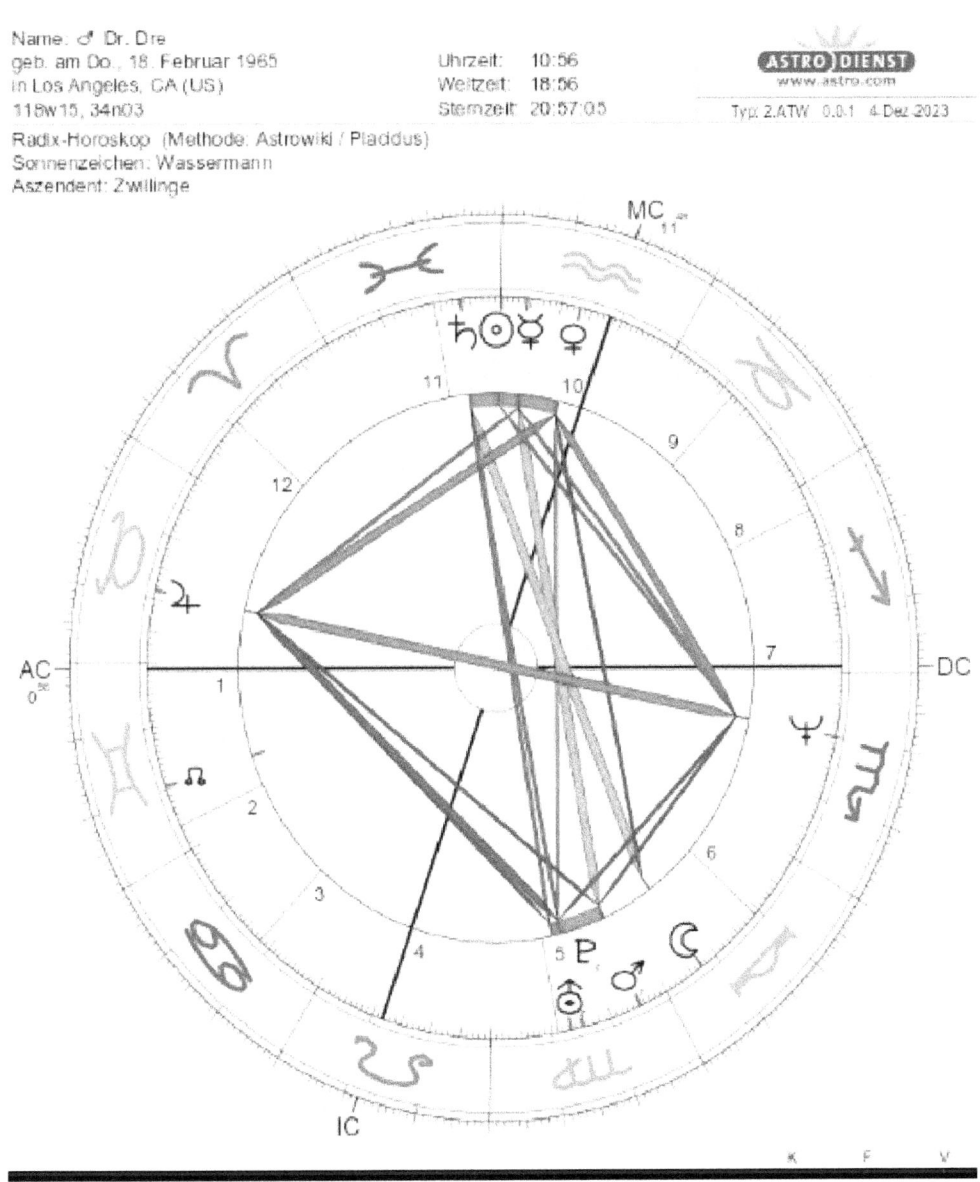

This is Dr, Dre, a billionaire gangster rapper, that made his living using foul language and verbal abuse. Helped foster a culture of rude and abrasive selfish behavior. Under Mars 360, these aspects are protected. He would have labaled a Mars-1 at birth

This is George Patton, one of the most famous generals in World War II. A war hero, George Patton was perhaps one of the most verbally abusive human beings of all time. Was once suspended for slapping a soldier that was injured. Remeber, the Mars-1 has trouble controlling his right hand. Under the Mars 360 system, Patton would have been marked as a Mars-1

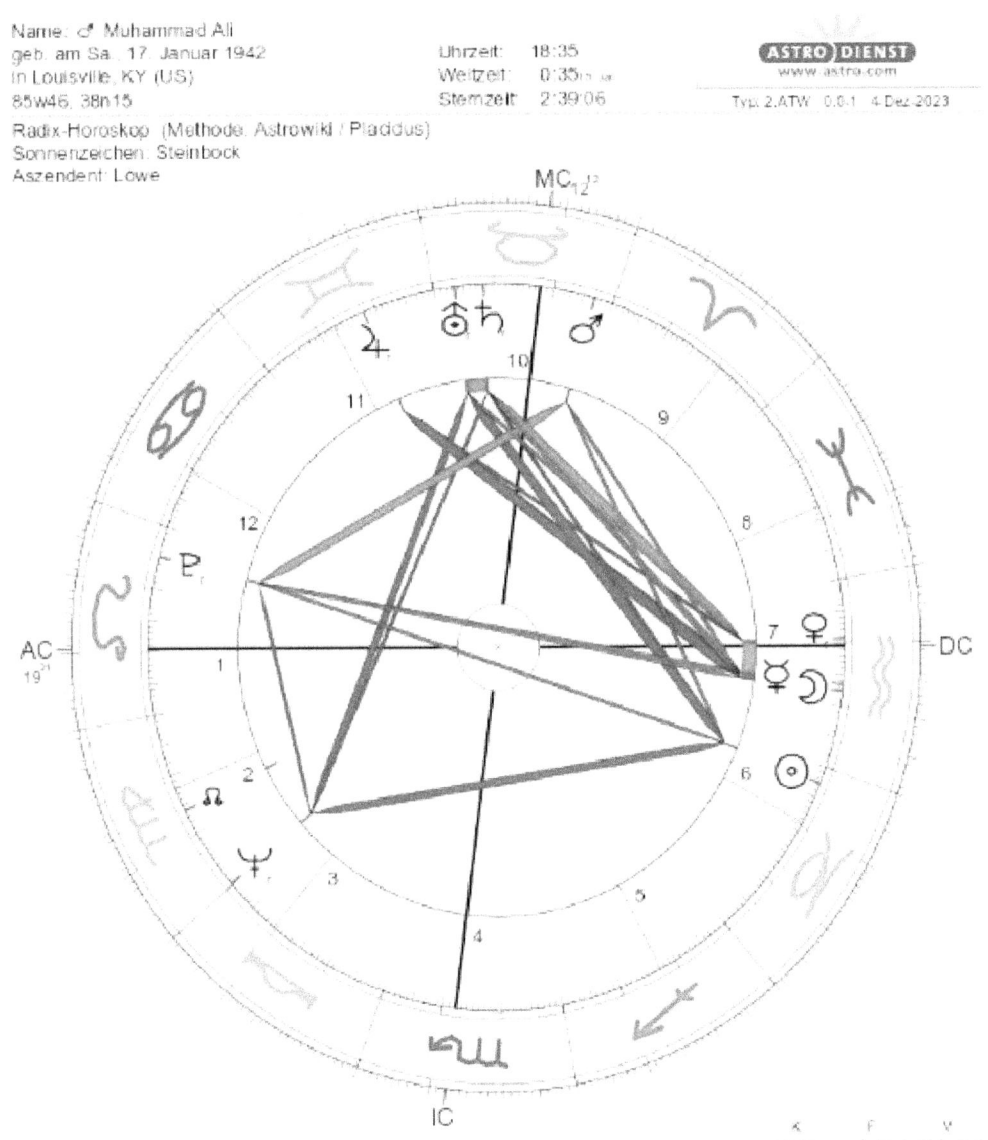

This is the chart for Muhammad Ali, a champion boxer, that was known for verbally abusing his opponents and journalist directly to their face. He is a Mars-1 prototype, with little control over his face to face communication and his right hand. Under Mars 360, he would have been marked as a Mars-1 with the tendency to be verbally abusive

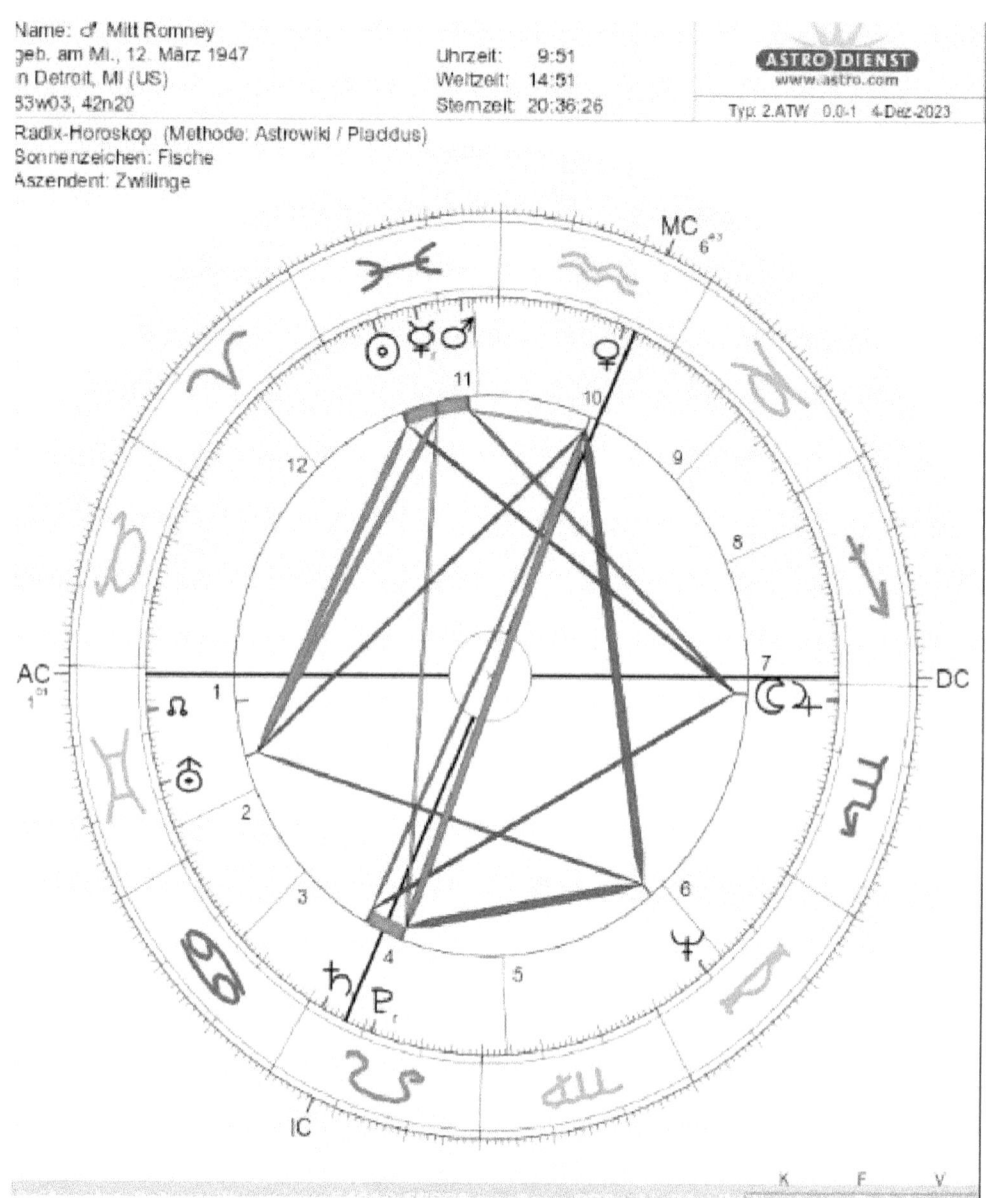

This is the chart for Mitt Romney, a former presidential candidate, that worked as a venture capitalist at Bain Capital. Used leverged buyouts to take over firms, leaving the acquired company with large sums of debt and management fees owned to Bain Capital. Romney is pro-war in typical Mars-1 fashion and under Mars 360 would have been marked as a Mars-1 and a danger to other people's money

Here is an example of how the Mars 360 system would work for the Mars-2 demographic. Here is a sample of charts below, all of which would be classified as Mars-2. First notice the layout of the seals and apply that to the charts below.

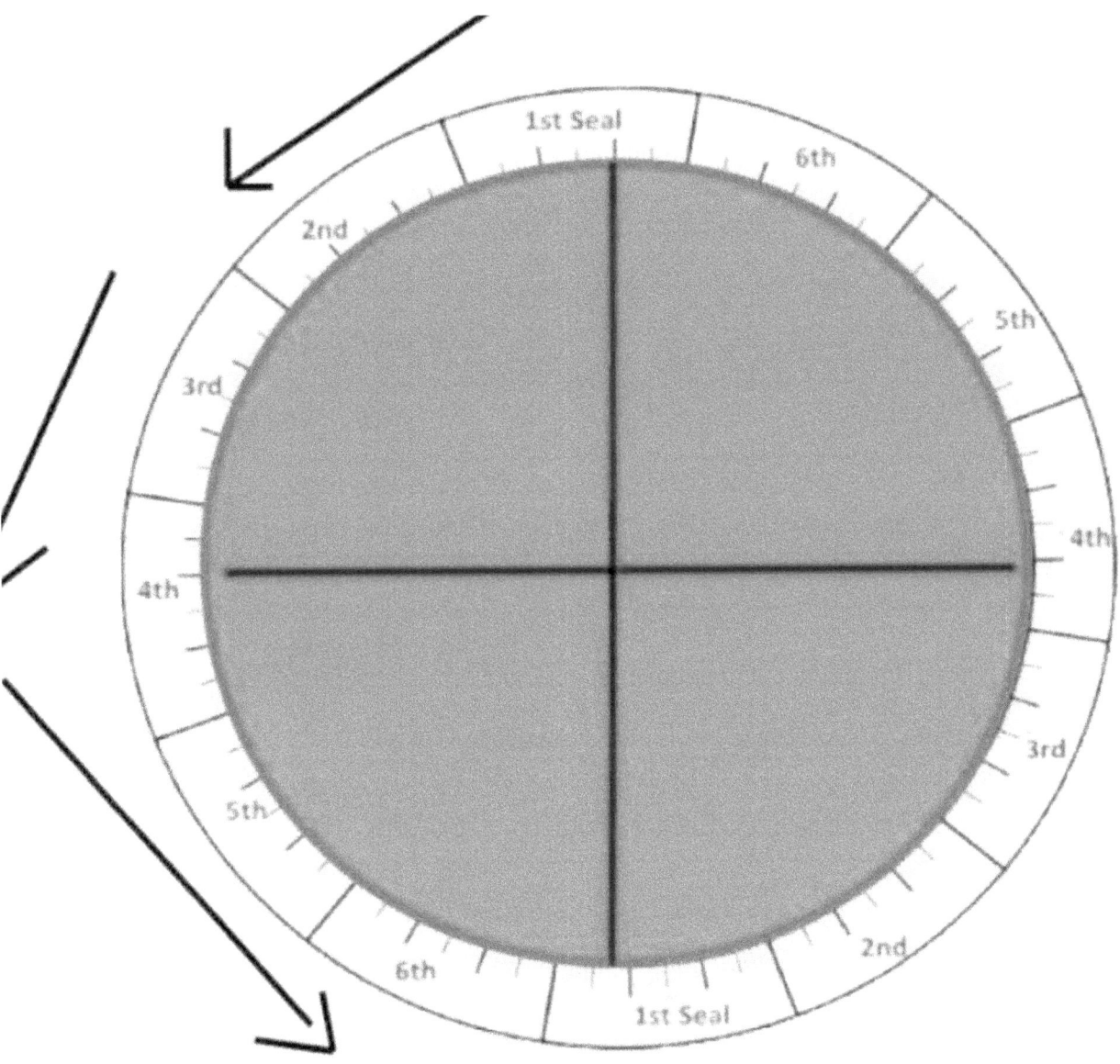

Notice where the 2nd seal is located. The 2nd seal is designated as causing a person to lack the energy to concern himself with normal use of the mind and mood. The result is a natural pessimism about the world and a lack of interest in happiness promoting activities, such as remebering happy times in the past, and developing close one on one relationships. A great deal of dis-trust and skepticism is fostered in this archetype, often leading to wild actions and behaviors, some of which include violence, especialy against women (or the opposite sex)

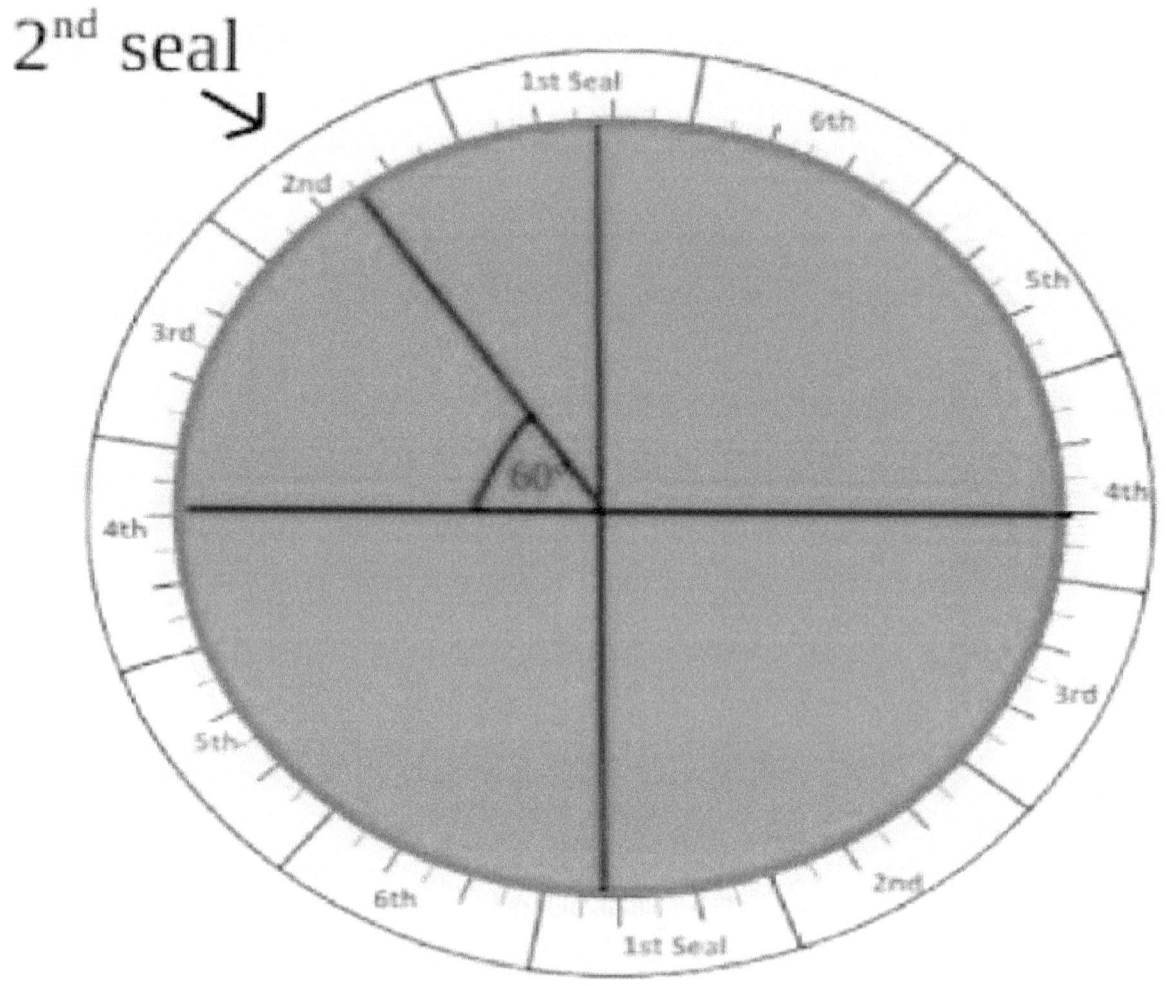

This archetype lacks the energy to concern himself with loved ones, long-term memory, the opposite sex, trust, one on one relationships, getting in touch with one's feelings, and trusting the government. The result is that type often turns to skepticism, nihilism, anti-religion, atheistic, far right conspiracy theories about the government. There is a propensity towards the acquisition of weapons and hightened aggression. This archetype can become sympathetic to extremist groups like Radical Islam, Neo-Nazism or Black Hebrew Israelites. These types are inclined against things taught during their early upbrining. There is a lack of energy towards maintaining a stable mood, leading the archetype to seek anxiety inducing activities. Notables here would be OJ Simpson, Charles Manson, Ted Bundy, Scott Peterson, The Columbine shooters, Timothy McVeigh, Stephen Paddock, Michael Schermer, George Carlin, Richard Nixon and Marshall Applewhite. Under the Mars 360 system, these types would be allowed to think on their own and would not be forced to trust anything. There would be no consensus that would force them to adopt a certain way of thinking. They would not even have to believe in the influence of Mars. Government would stay out of their lives completely

So now, here are the charts

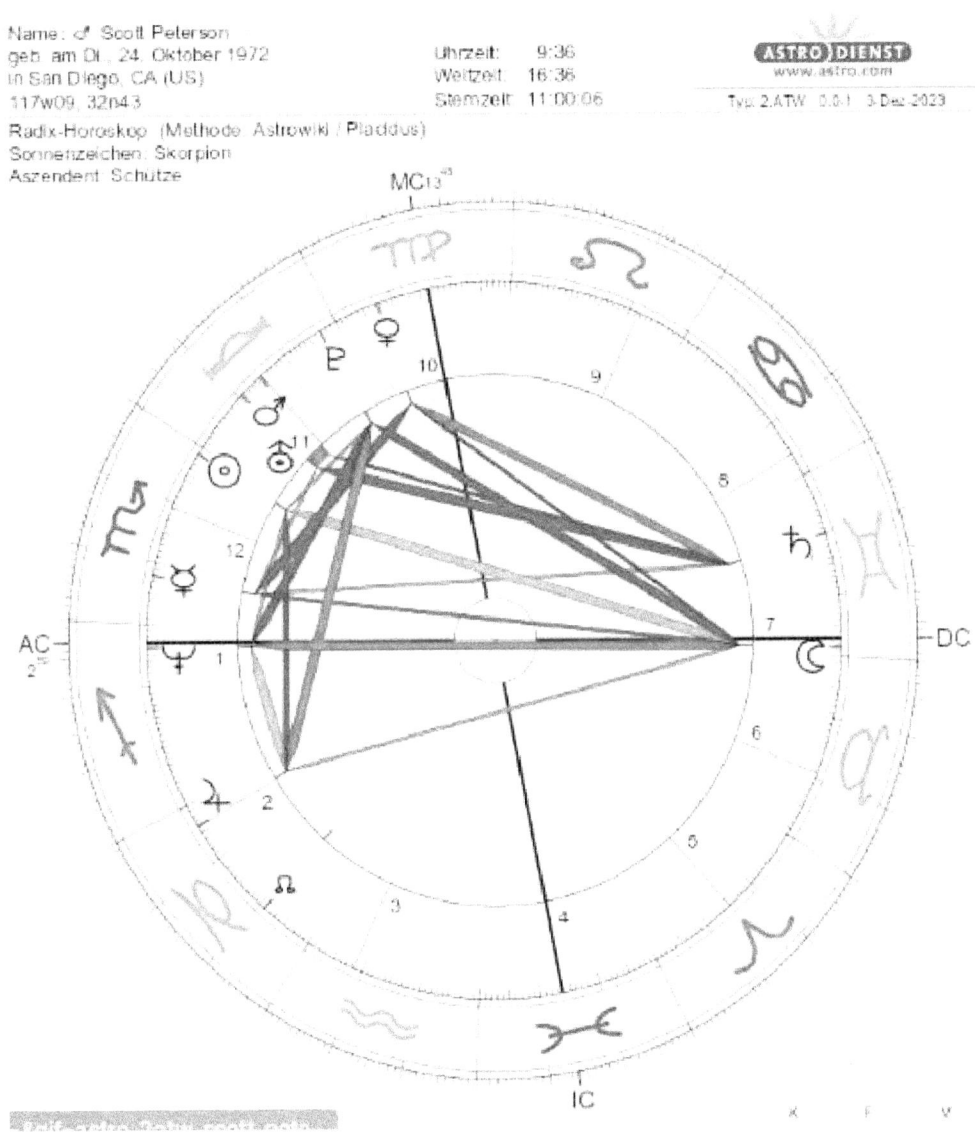

This is Scott Peterson, a convicted murderer, found guilty of killing his pregnant wife and their unborn child. Under Mars 360, he would have been clasified as a Mars-2 at birth and a danger to women

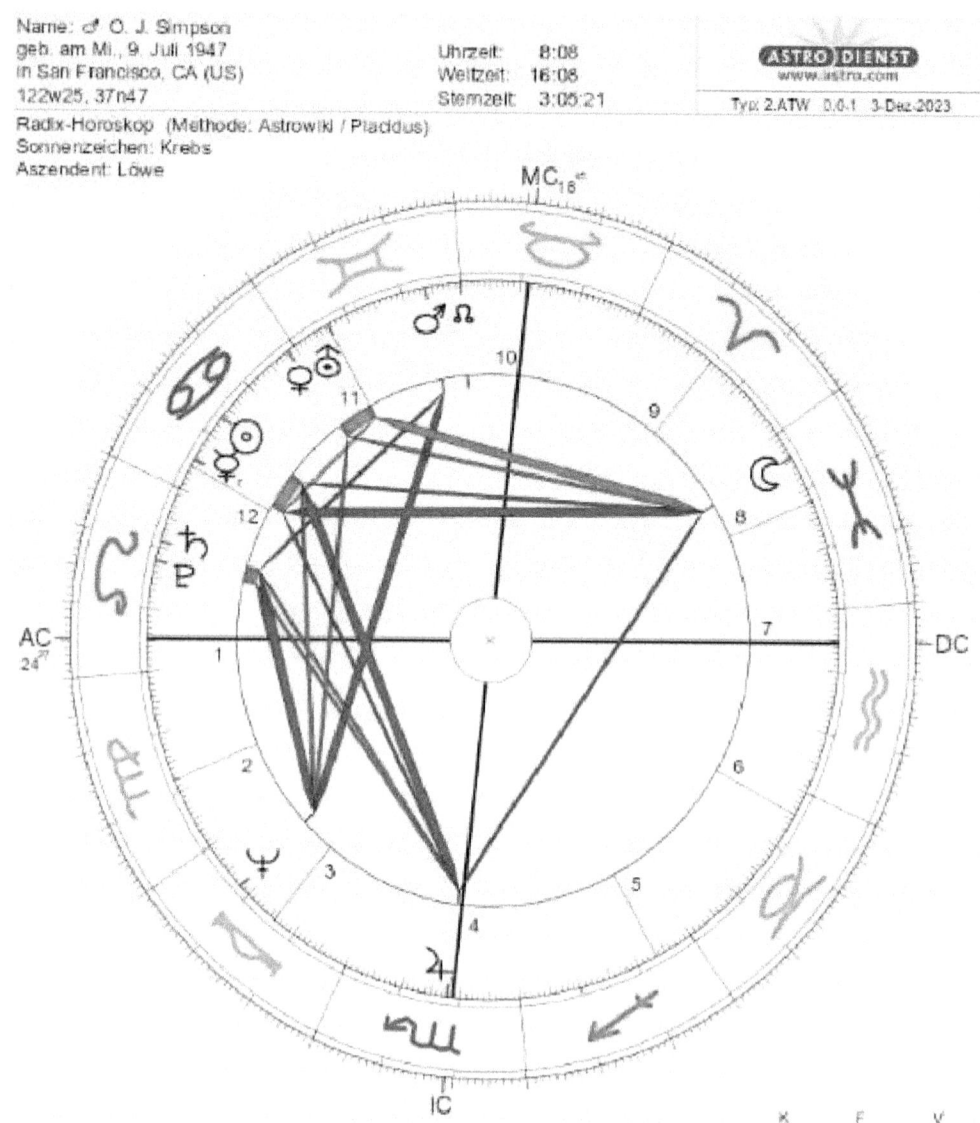

This is the chart for OJ Simpson, former professional football player, who brutally murdered his ex-wife and her boyfreind. At birth, he would have been marked as a Mars-2 and a danger to women.

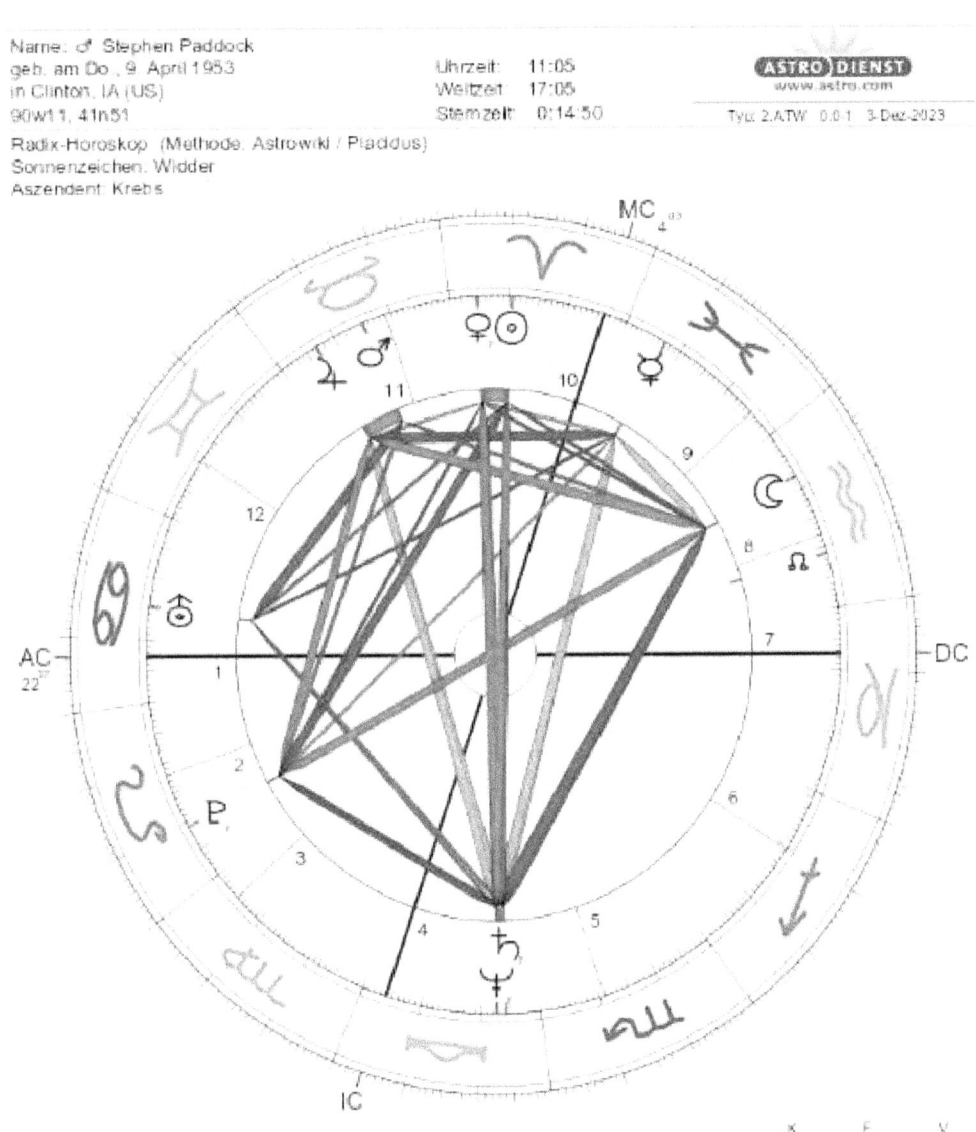

This is Stephen Paddock, the man who carried out the largest mas shooting in US history, killing 58 people at a concert in Las Vegas in 2017. Paranoid about the government, he acquired an arsenal of semi-automatic weapons and murdered scores of people after making multiple noise complaints in the days leading up to the shooting. Under the Mars 360 system, he would haven classified as a Mars-2 and a potential domestic terrorist and misogynist

This is the chart of Timothy McVeigh, who caried out the 2nd largest terorist attack on US soil, bombing a Federal building in Oklahoma City, kiling hundreds of innocent people. He was sympathetic to David Koresh and developed ever growing antipathy towards the government after the ATF laid siege to Koresh's Waco compound, which resulted in the death of David Koresh and his followers. At birth, McVeigh would have been classified as a Mars-2 under the Mars 360 system and possibly given soverign citizenship

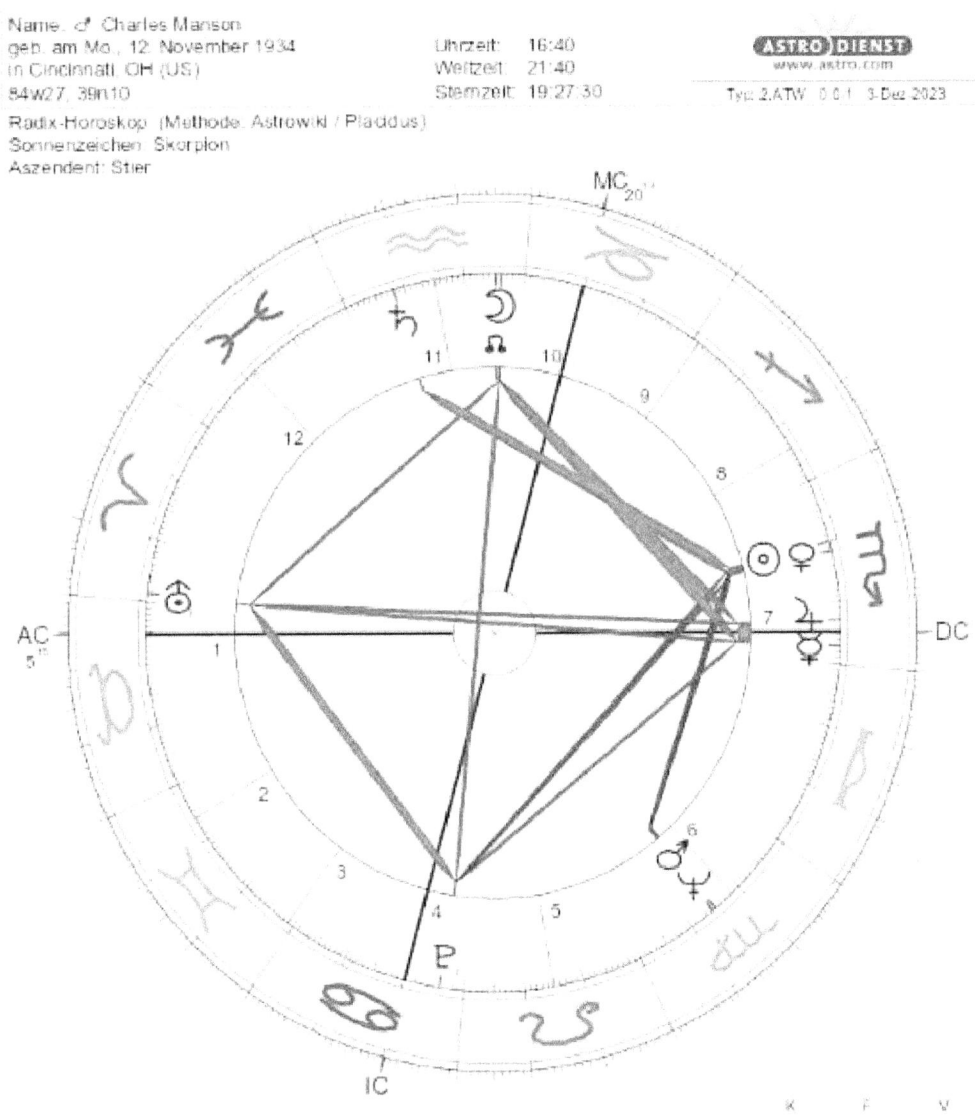

This is Charles Manson's chart. He was a cult leader who drugged and manipulated women to do his bidding, ordering them to cary out multiple kilings, one of which was the murder of Sharon Tate. A self-professed Neo-Nazi, he was known for his wild beliefs and paranoia about a coming race war. Under Mars 360, he would have been labaled a Mars-2 and a threat to women.

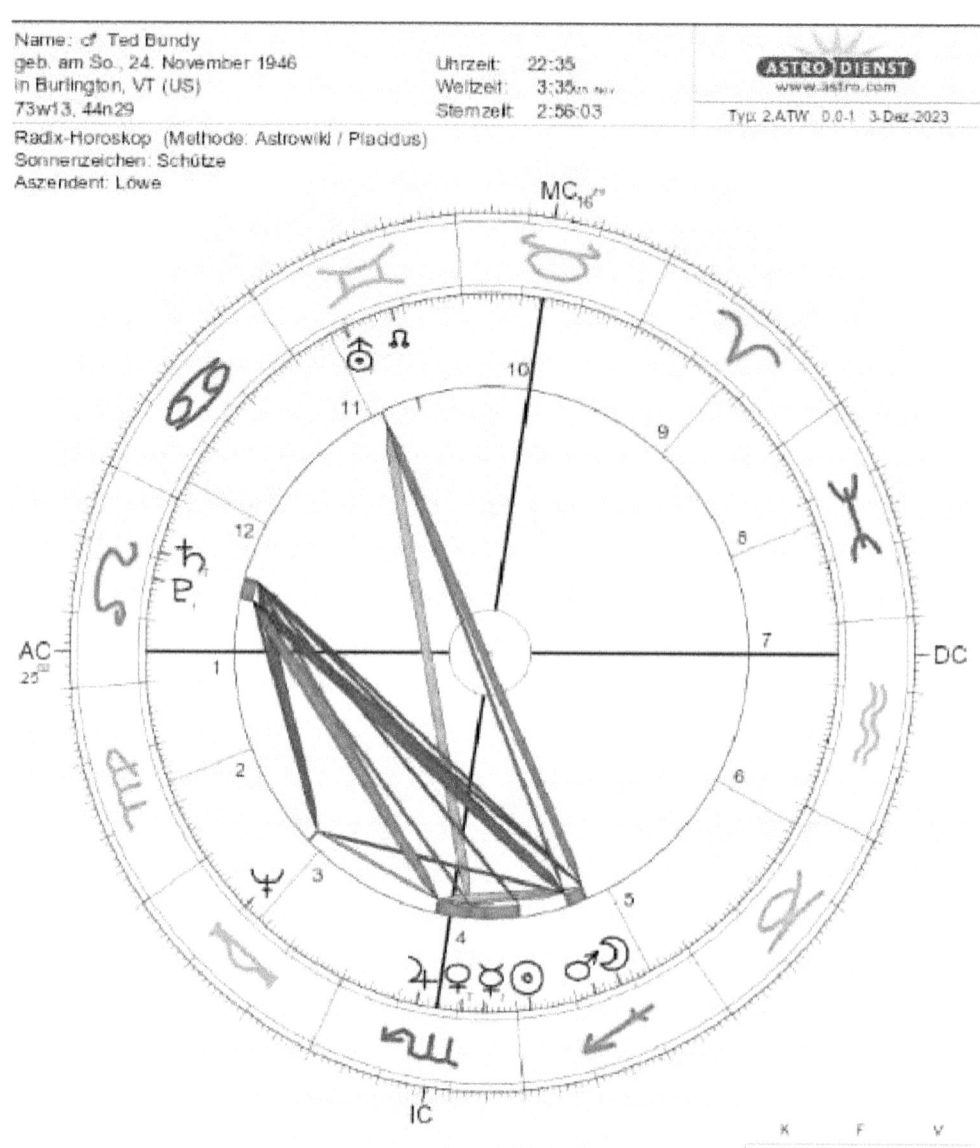

This is the chart of Ted Bundy, a serial killer, that went on a killing spree in Seattle, murdering young college women. He was an aspiring lawyer, btut bitter about his break-up with a previous girlfriend and took his frustration out on any female he could come in contact with. Under the Mars 360 system, he would have labeled a Mars -2 and a potential threat to women.

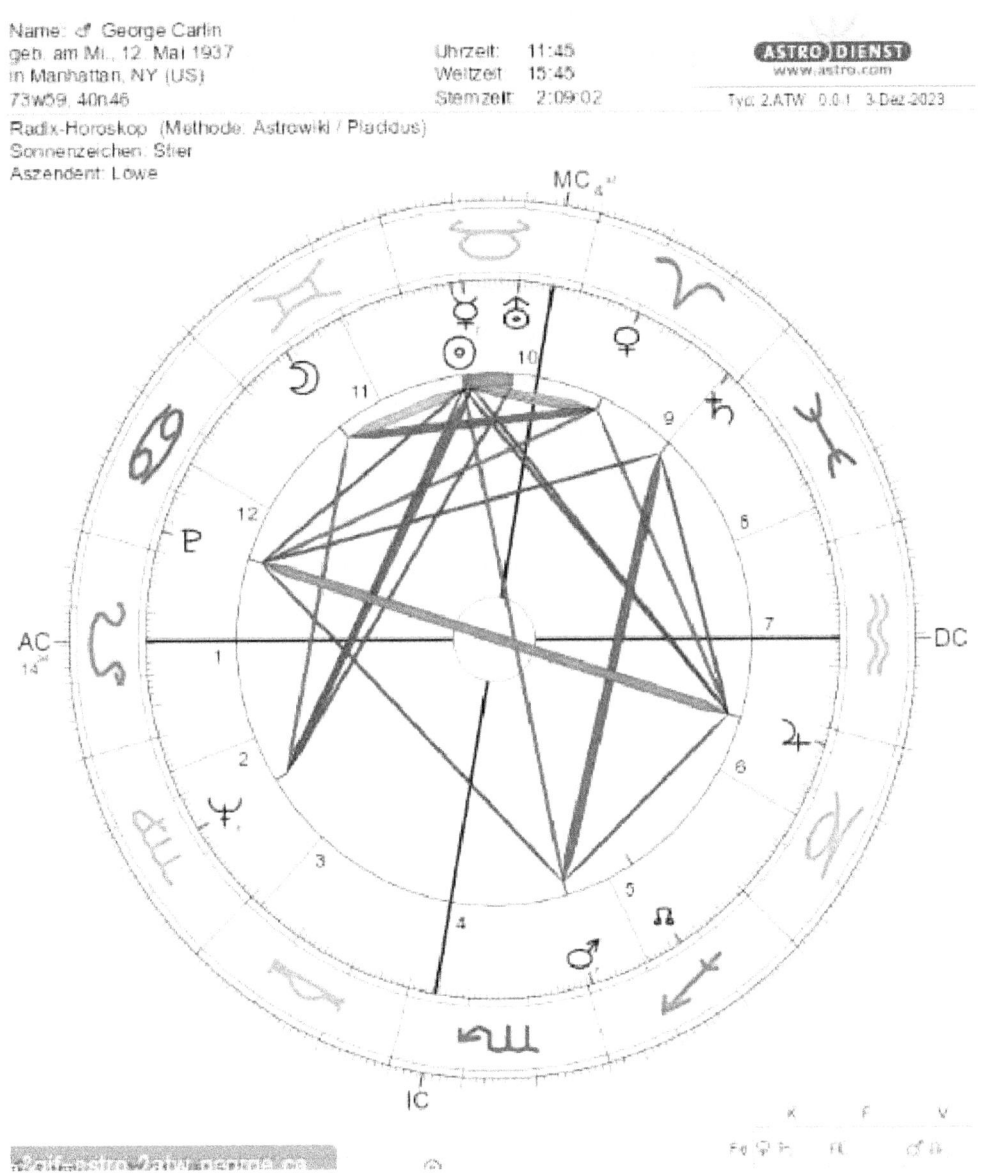

This is the chart for George Carlin, who was a comedian that was anti-religion and didn't belive in God. A free-thinker in typical Mars-2 fashion. Under Mars 360, he would have been classified as a Mars-2 and would have been exempt from much of his early education

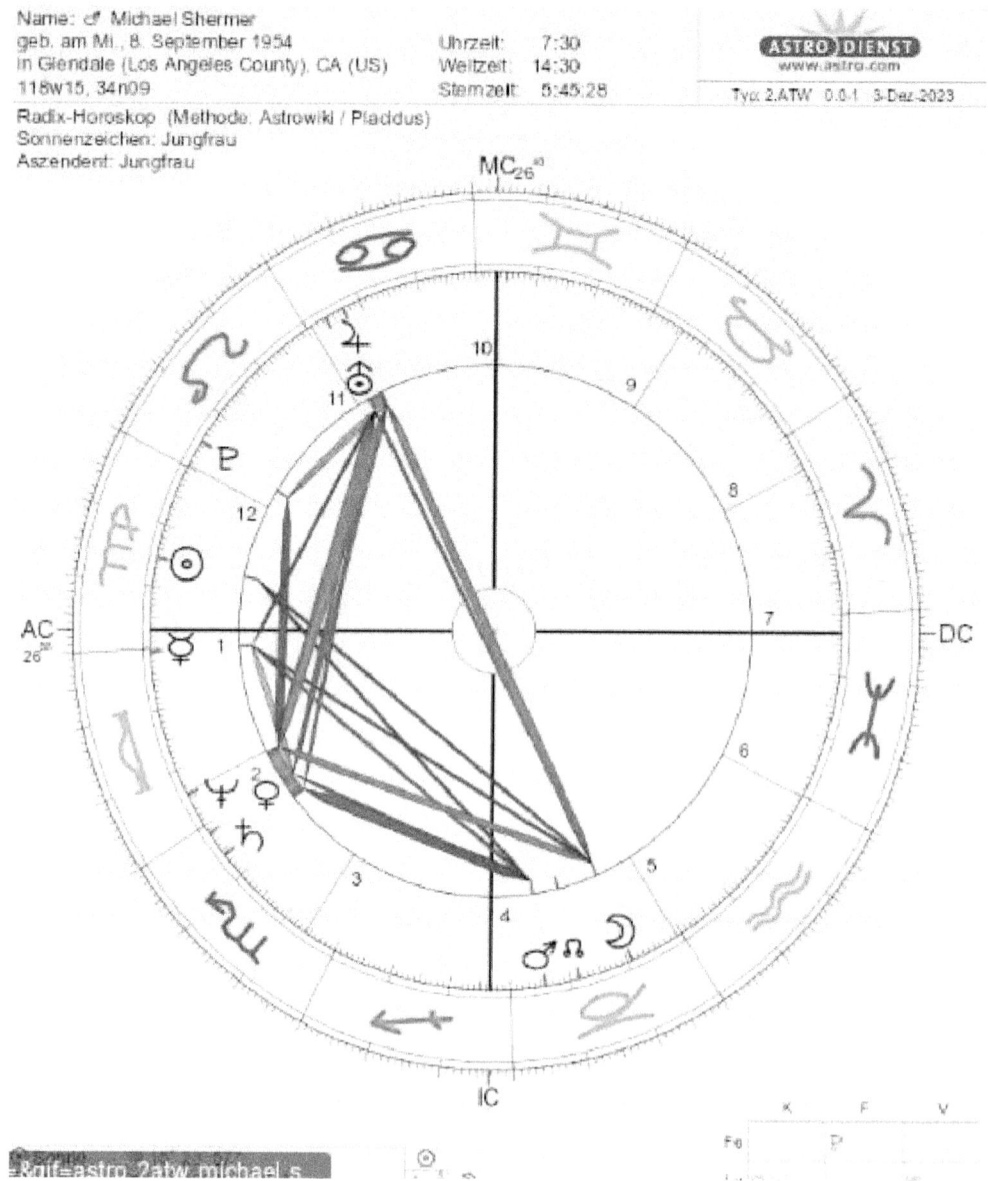

This is Michael Schermer, a notable atheist and fre thinker, who does not believe in God. He is a Mars-2

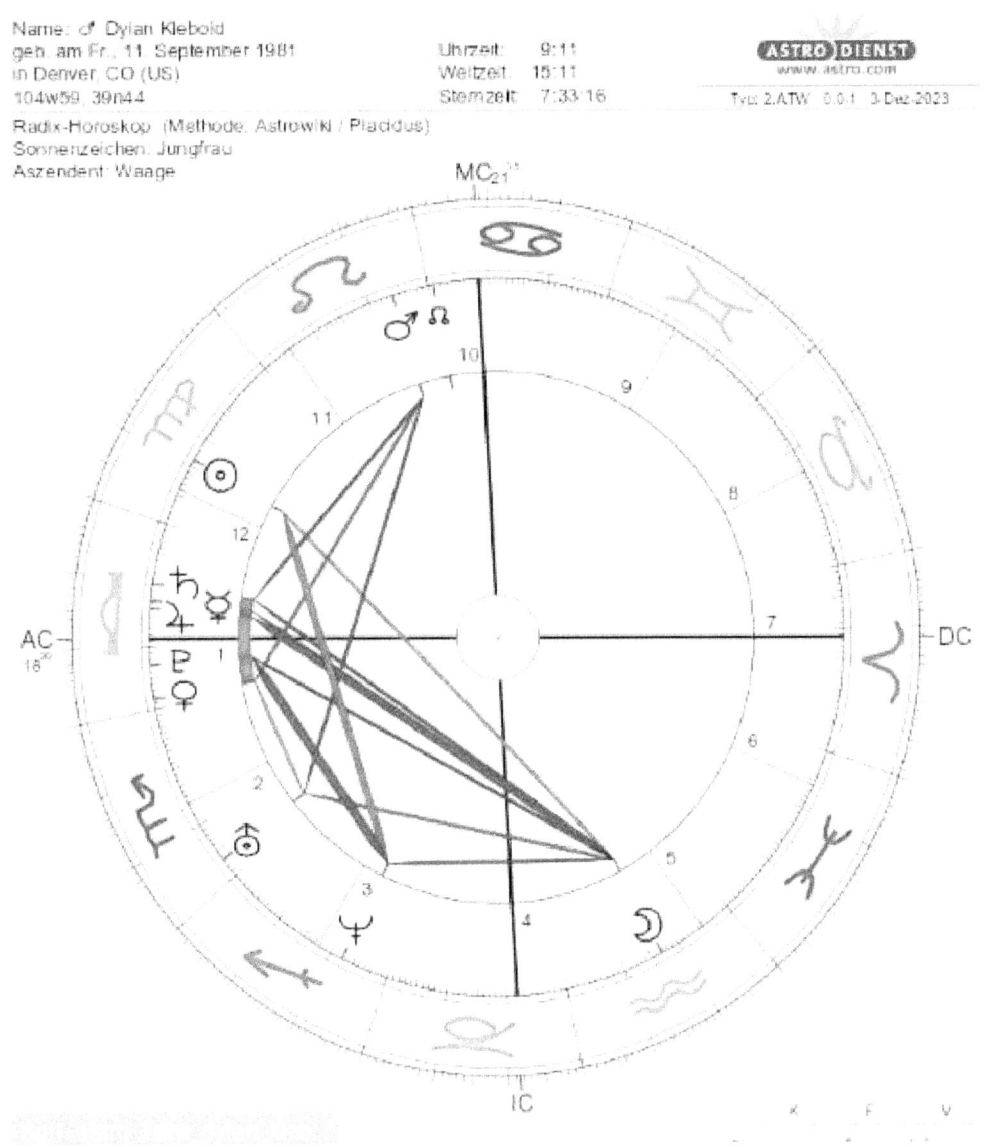

Dylan Klebold, a Mars-2, that shot and killed dozens of classmates at Columbine high school in 1999. He would have ben labeled a Mars-2 under the Mars 360 system

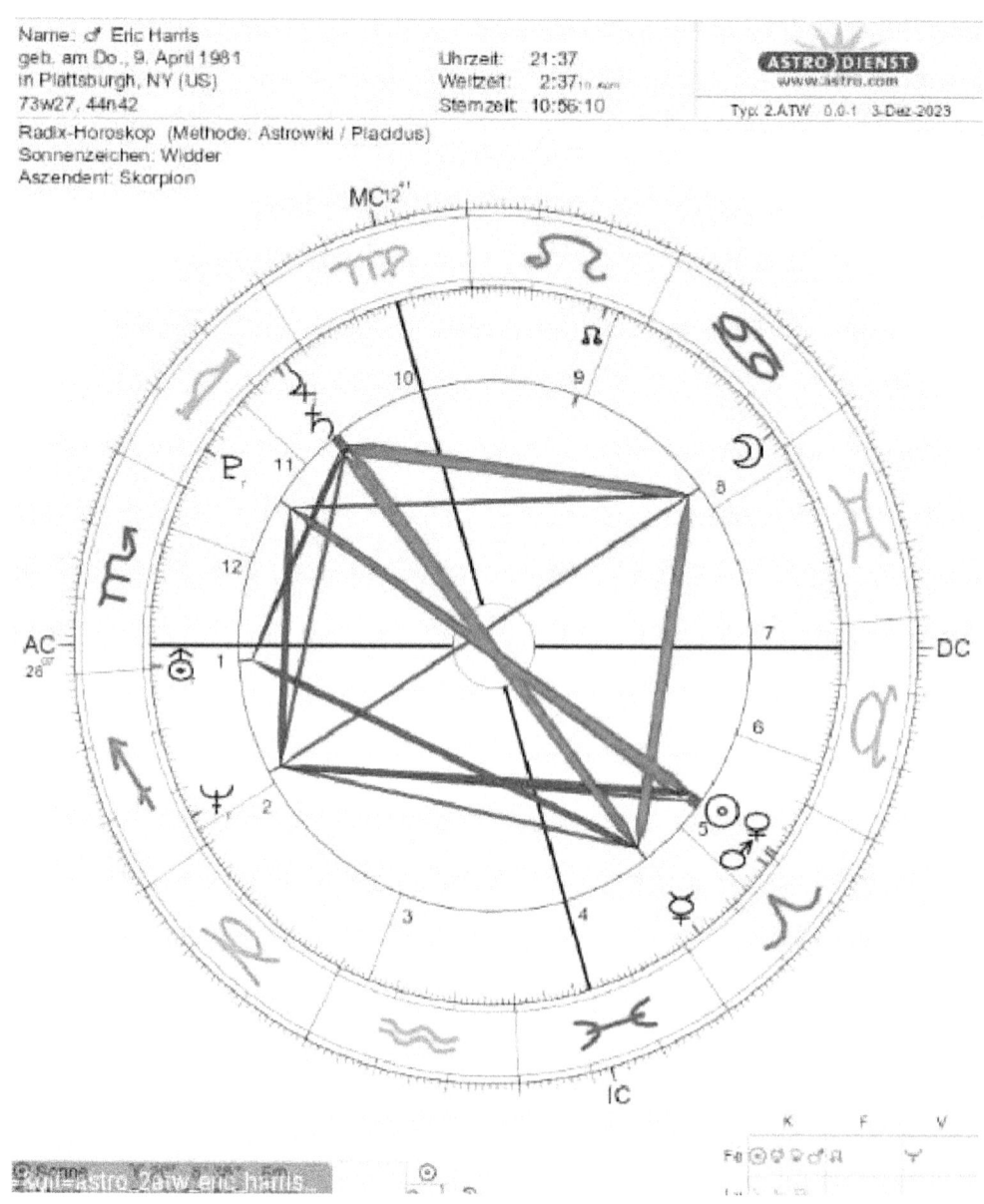

Eric Harris a Mars-2, that shot and killed dozens of classmates at Columbine high school in 1999. He would have ben labeled a Mars-2 under the Mars 360 system

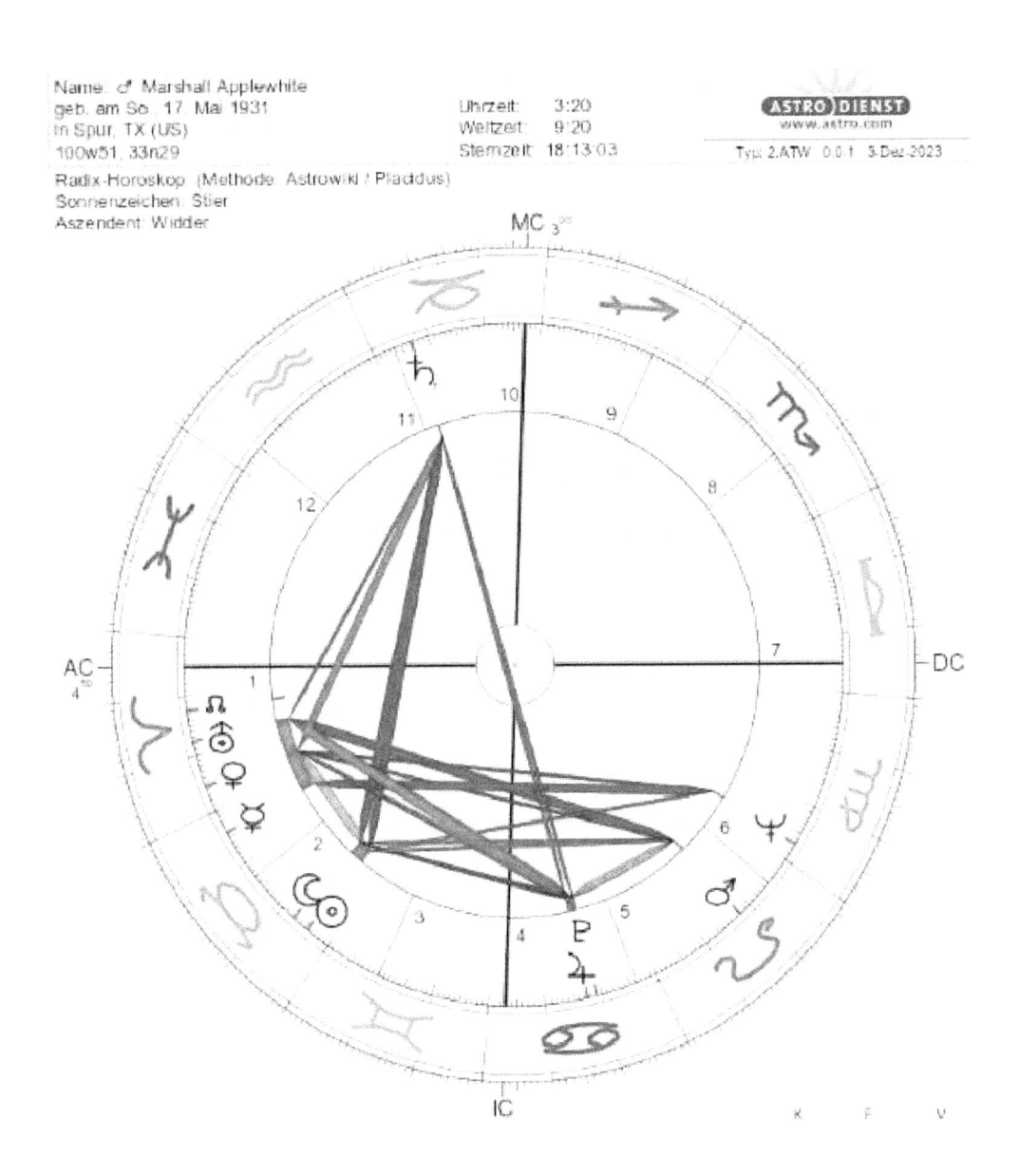

Here is the chart for Marshall Applewhite. He was a cult leader that directed the mass suicide of his followers, believing that a UFO would take their souls to another plane of existence. He would have been classified as a Mars-2 at birth and prone to bizarre belief system.

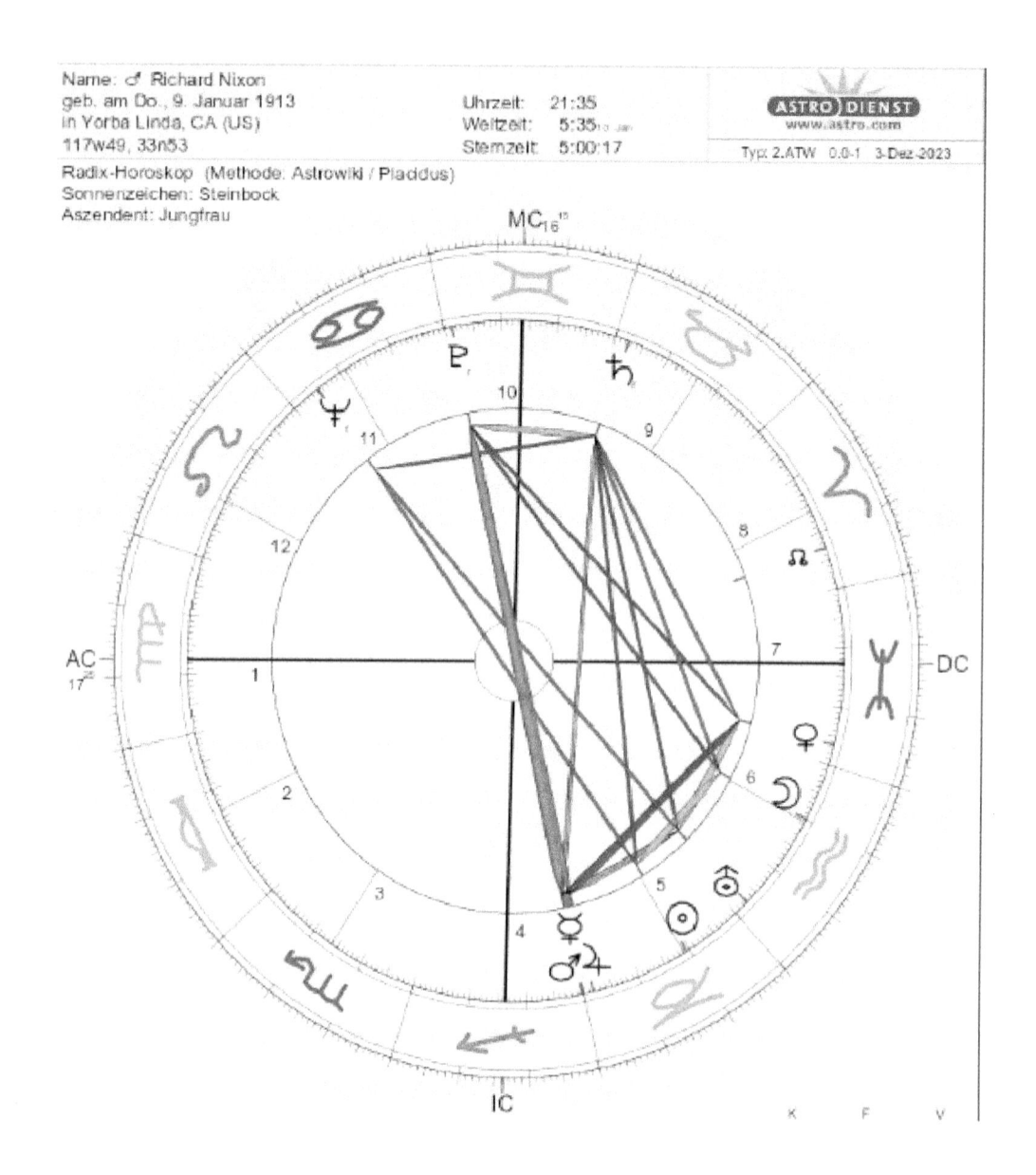

This is the chart for Richard Nixon, former President of the United States, who was known for his paranoia and desire to keep tabs on his collegues and opponents. He was an example of a Mars-2 archetype

Here is an example of how the Mars 360 system would work for the Mars-3 demographic. Here is a sample of charts below, all of which would be classified as Mars-3. First notice the layout of the seals and apply that to the charts below.

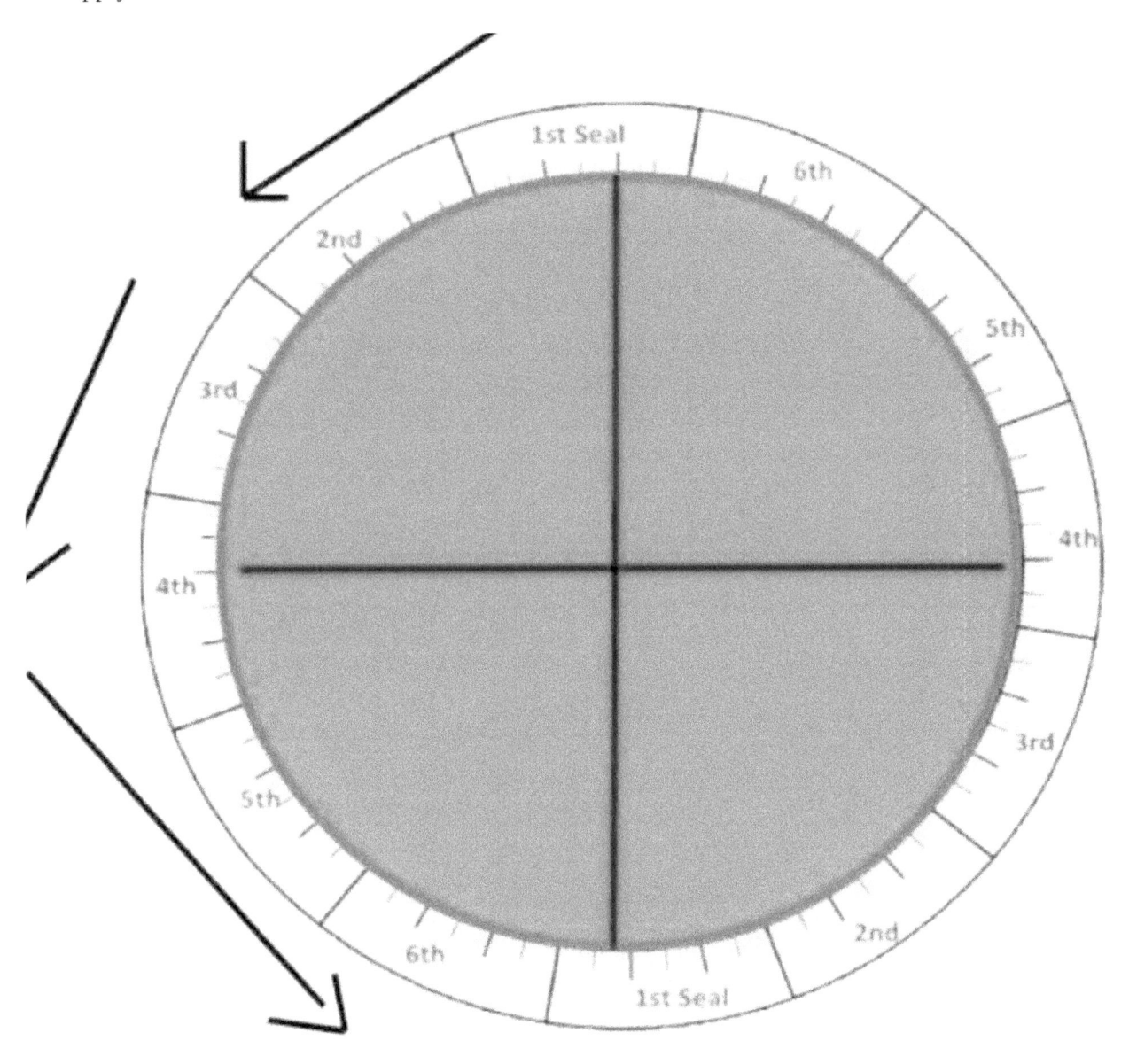

Notice where the 3rd seal is located. The 3rd seal is designated as causing a person to lack the energy to concern himself with his home and physical safety or places that are safe. These are physically restless people and under Mars 360, these types would have free access to pasport priveledges. At birth, however, these archetypes would be designated libertarian and unpatriotic anti-government domestic political dissidents as well as potential sexual perverts/sex addicts. If the military draft was reinstated, these archtypes would be at the top of the list. A standout characteristic of these types is an inability to stay home, hence why many of these are active in sports. The people on the list are David Koresh, Joe Biden, Arnold Schwarzenneger, Sigmund Freud, Aleister Crowley, Michael Moore, Michael Douglas, Charlie Sheen and Karl Marx

3rd seal

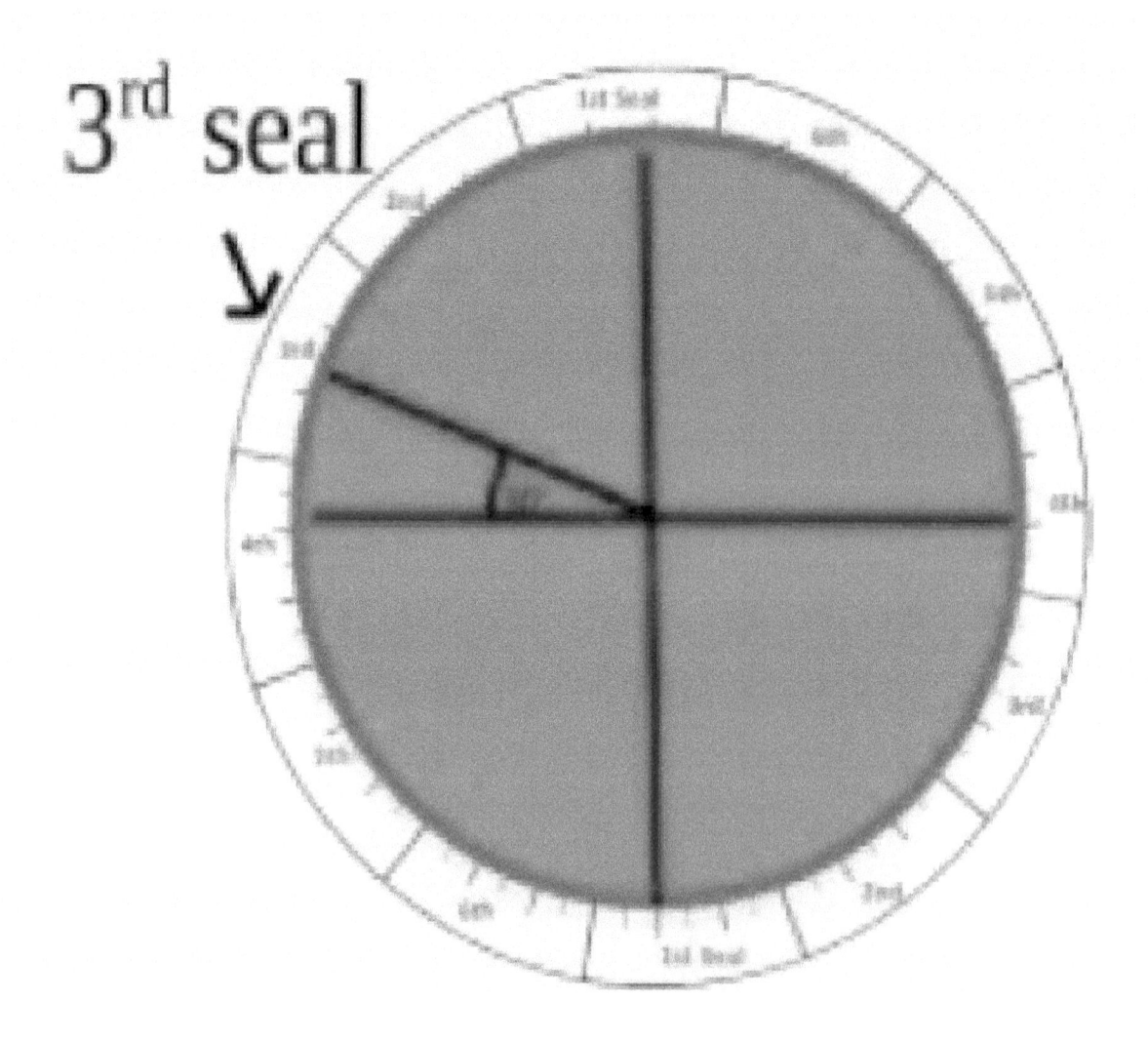

This archetype lacks the energy to concern himself with the basic necesities of everyday survival, such as staying safe, sheltered, eating the right foods, and remaining confined. The result is that these types expend a lot of energy being away from home. They also engage in activities that could be risky and hazardous. These are also inclined to extreme anti-patriotic leanings. Under Mars 360, freedoms regarding the body, physical consumption and travel would be granted to those born with this placement. Also, Mars 360 may have to drop the age of consent for these archetypes. These archetypes may also be exempt from religious laws regarding the use of the body.

So now, here are the charts

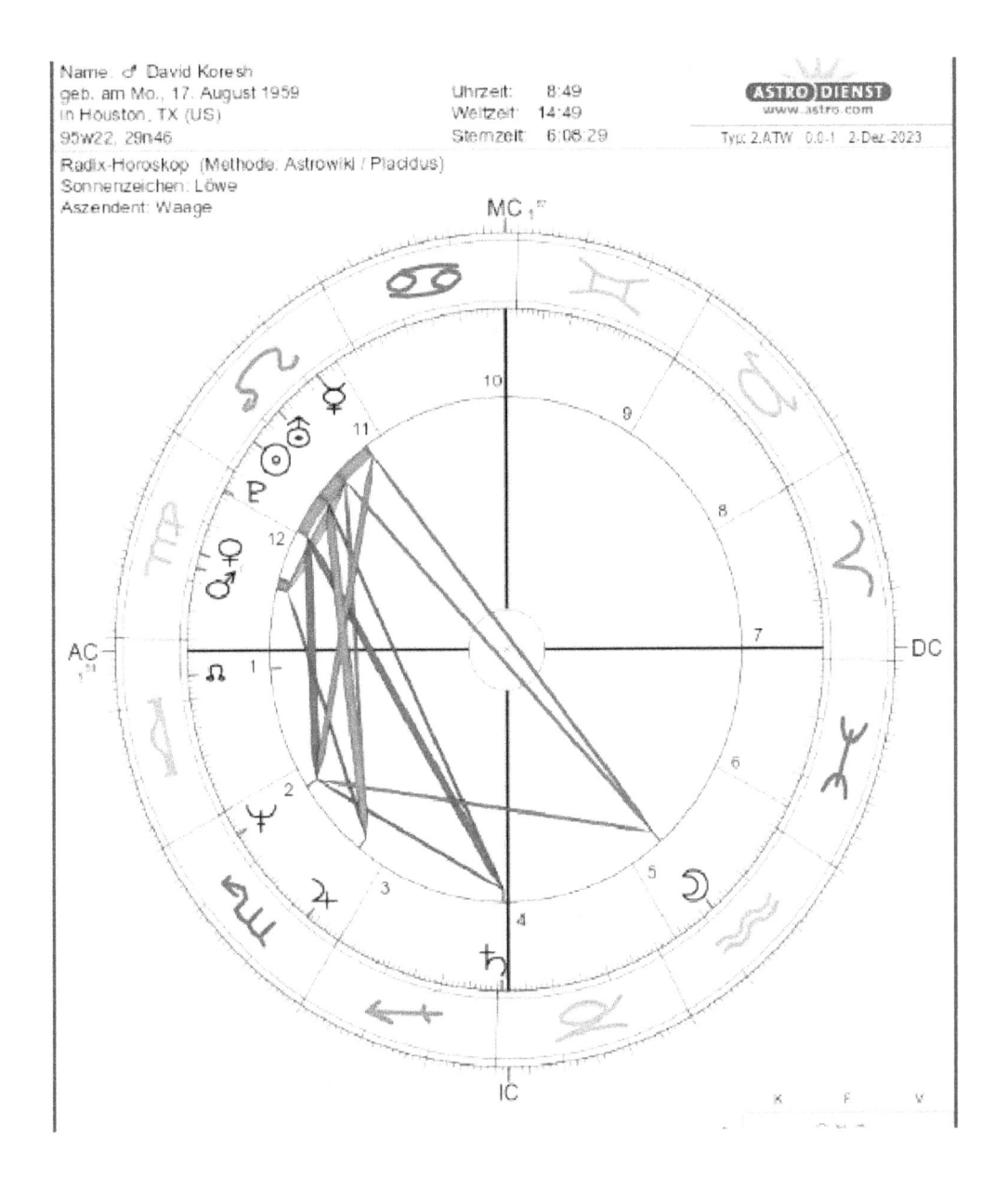

This is David Koresh, who was a polygamist preacher for the Branch Davidian Sect of the Davidian Adventist Church. He was accused of sexual perversion, and also held anti-government views, acquiring a large arsenal of weapons, which led to a standoff with the ATF and his eventual death. As leader of the movement, he held his followers to strict standards of consumption, while he remained free in this manner, taking liberties with food and drink, as well as sex, all in libertarian fashion.

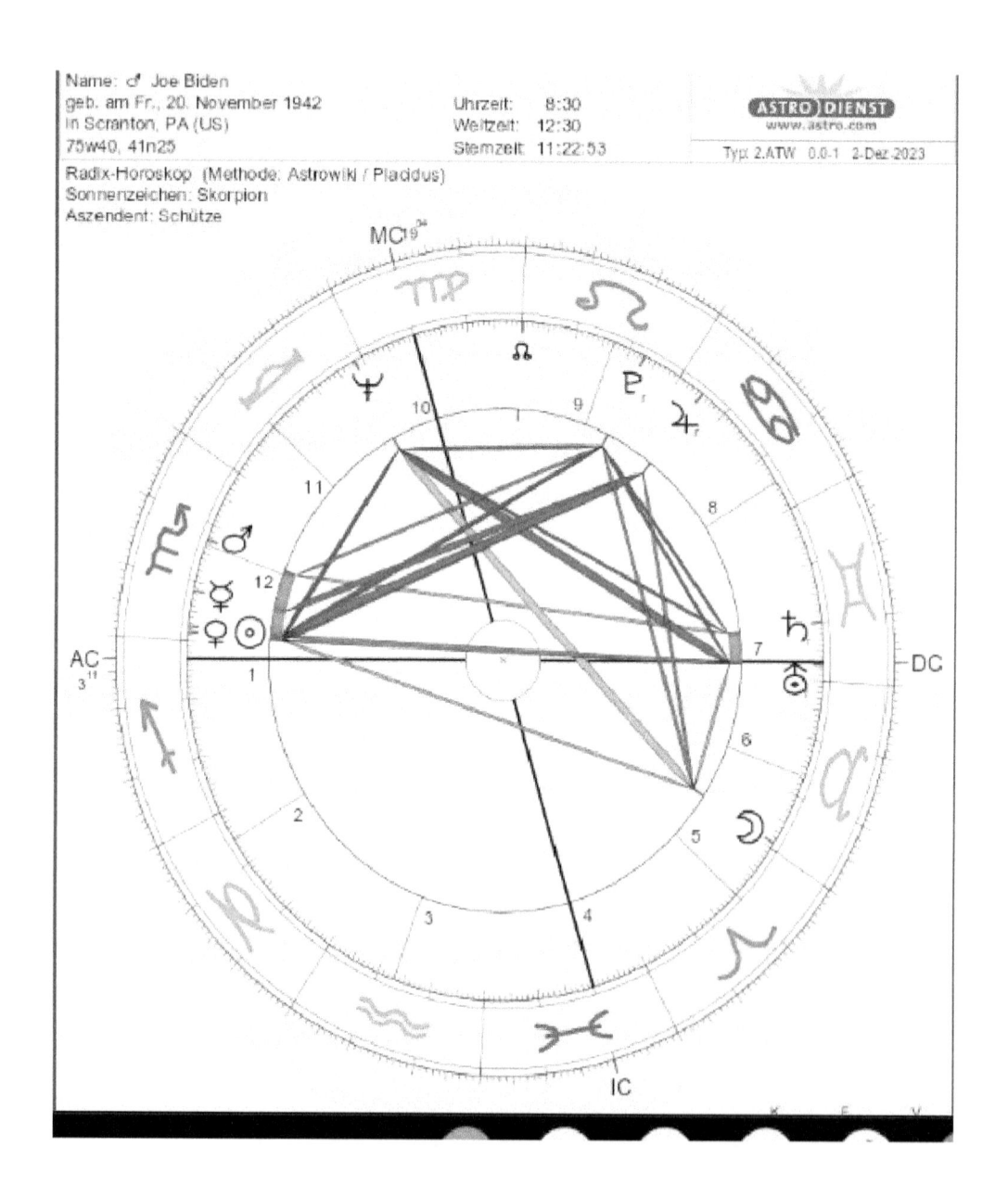

Joe Biden, president of the United States, is believed by many to be driving his own country into the ground with policies that are anti-domestic and un-patriotic. Many of his detractors consider him to possess an anti-domestic, America-last outlook. This could be the result of his Mars location in the 3rd seal. Unable to retire, his restlessnes, keeps him active in politics, despite his age

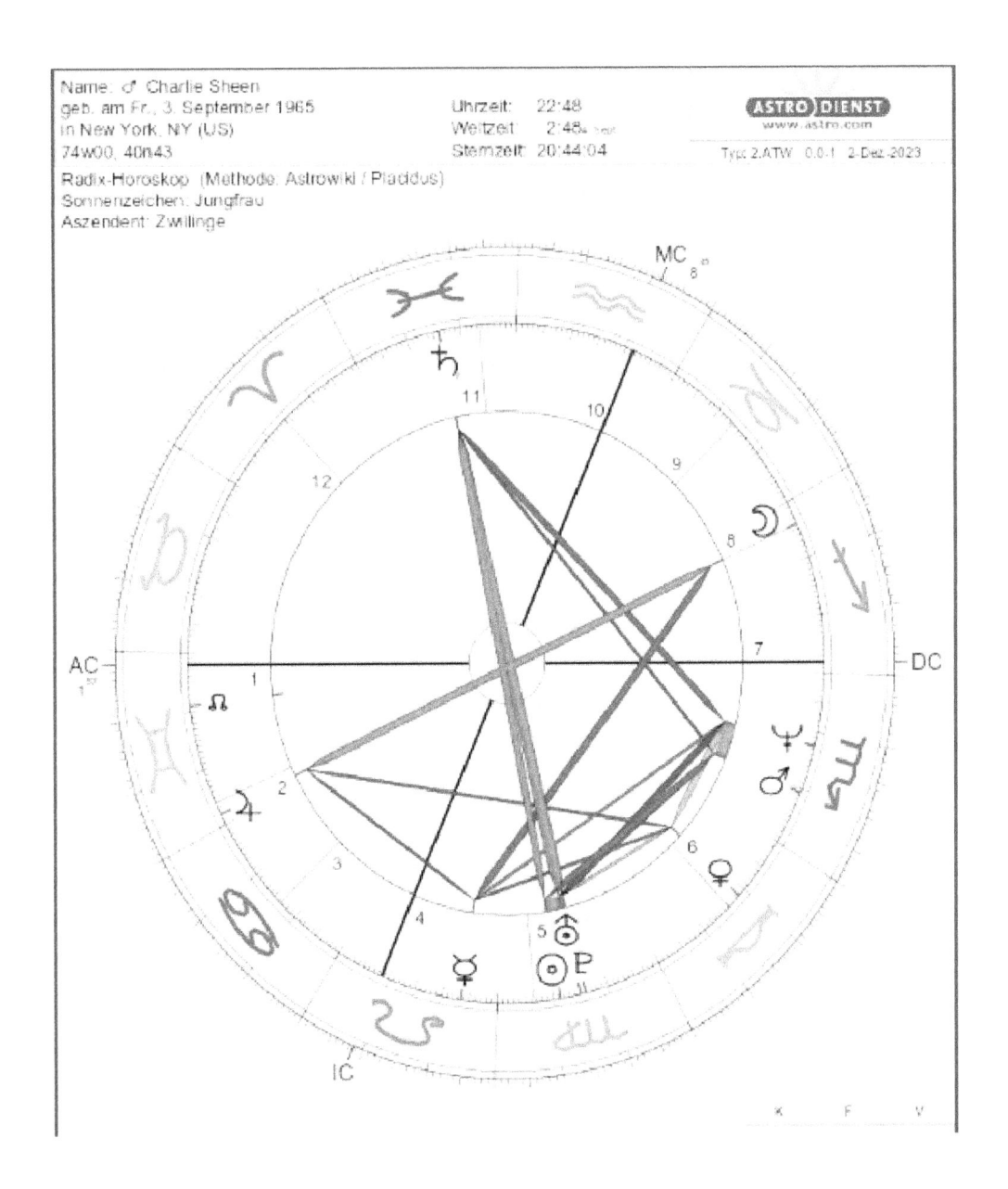

Charlie Sheen is a classic Mars-3, having led a life of sexual addiction, acquiring HIV in the process. He has also consumed whatever he pleased in classic libertarian fashion. His anti-government side came out after the 9/11 terror attacks in which he accused his own government as having played a role in orchestrating the atttack.

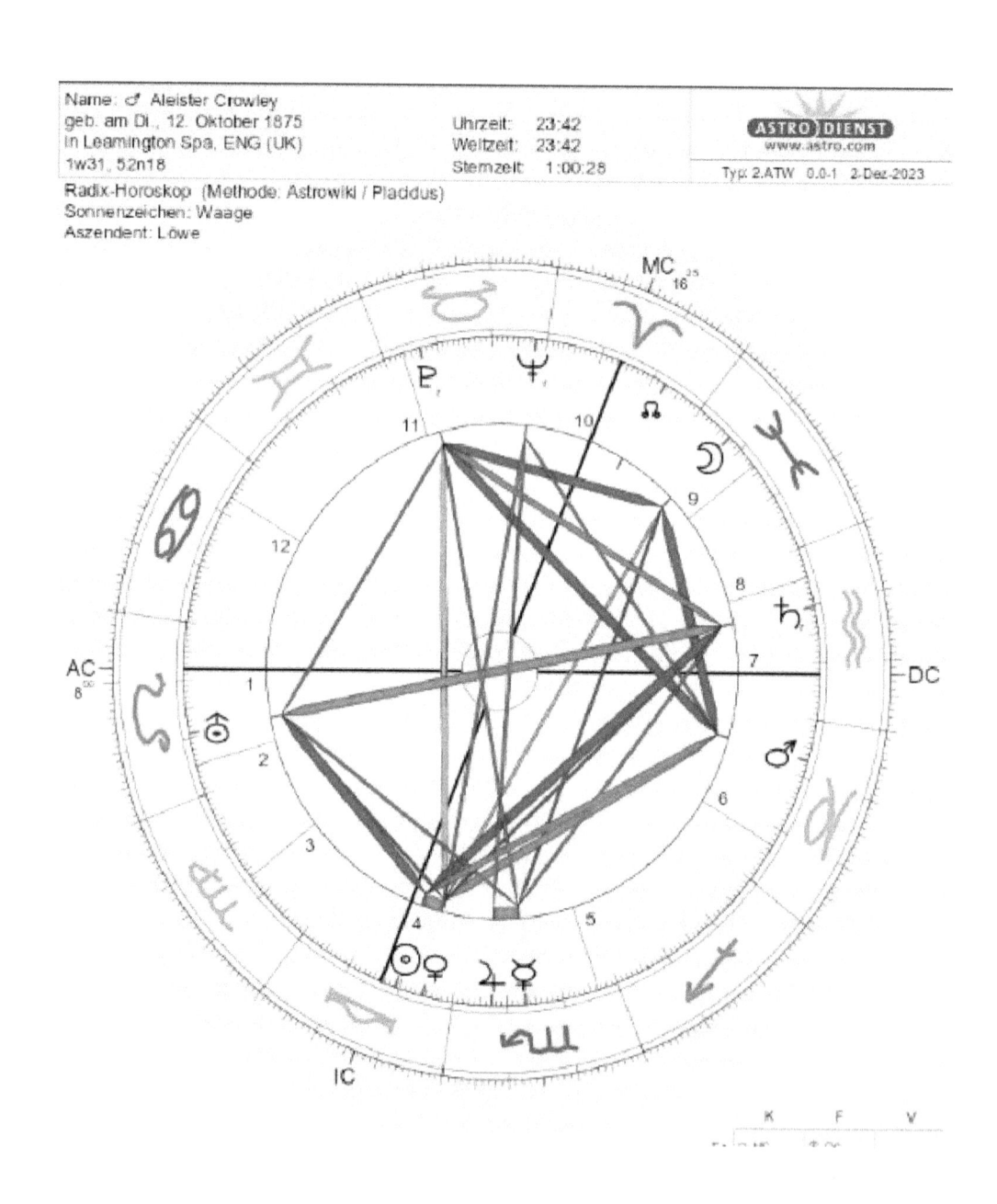

Aleister Crowley is another Mars-3 archetype, leaving a legacy of sexual perversion/addiction and being a drug fiend

Arnold Schwarzennegger, a Mars-3, is an example of how the restless energy regarding this placement can lead to success. Unable to stay home, he has had success in many endeavors, like bodybuilding, acting, and politics. He has also had numerous run-ins with accusations of sexual perversion.

45

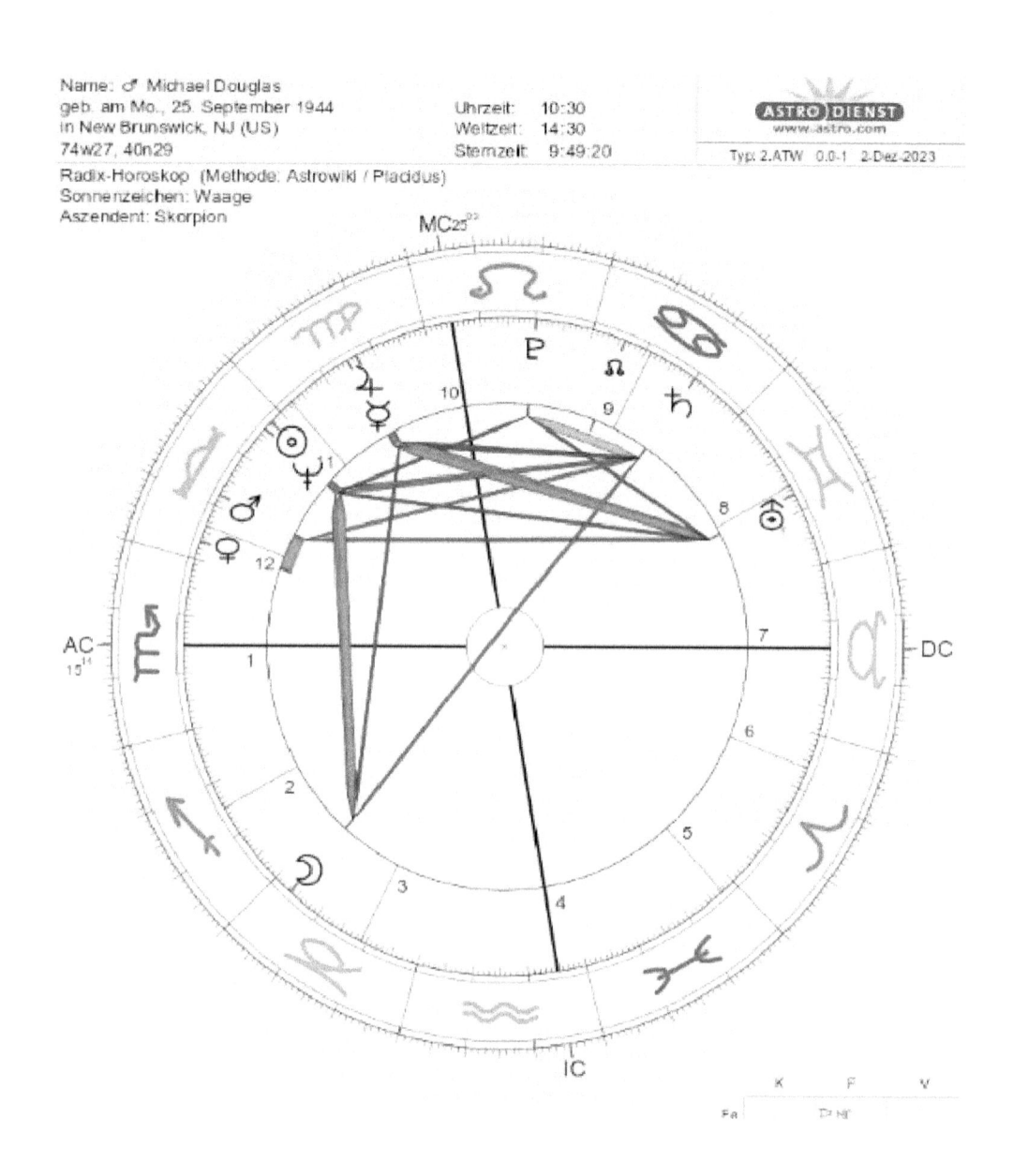

Michael Douglas is a Mars-3 archetype, valuing freedom, and placing career over home life. Was accused of being hospitalized for sex addiction in the early 90s

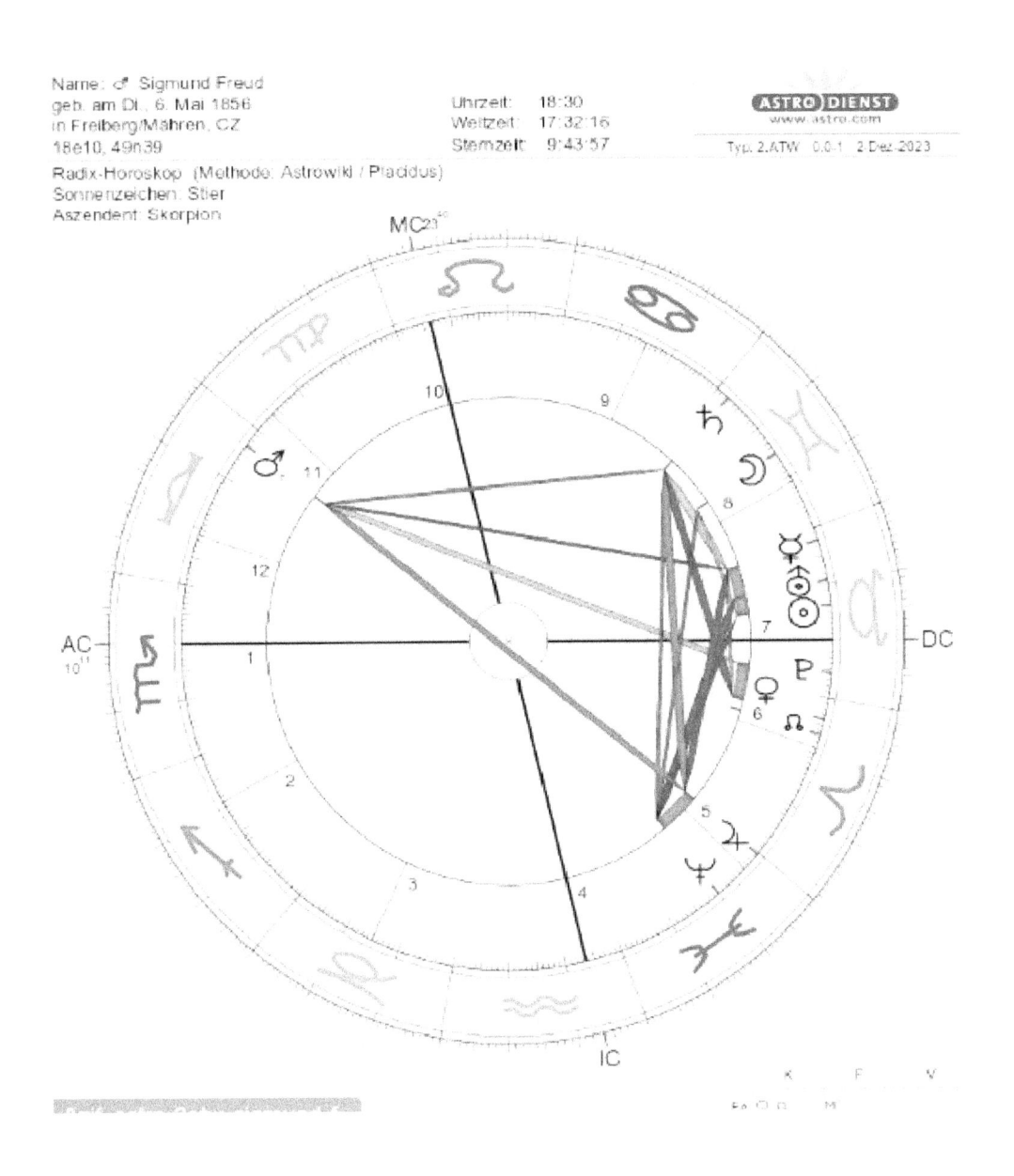

Sigmund Freud, the father of moden psychology and a Mars-3 archetype, was obssesed with sex and cocaine.

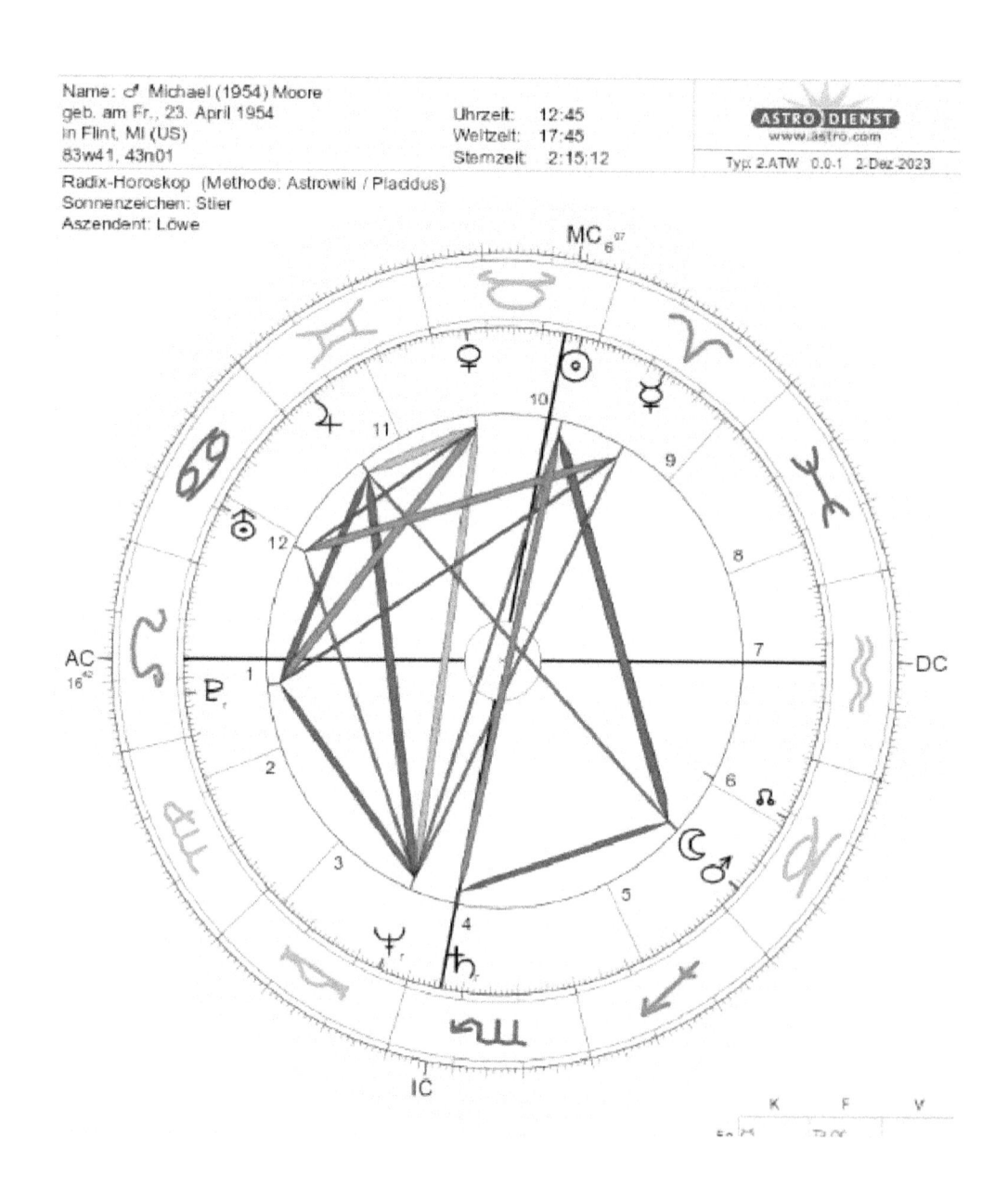

Here is the chart for Michael More, a Mars-3, who is very anti-government, especially during the Bush administration. He often criticized the government for the war in Iraq. He is also a strong proponent of freedom of consumption and physical movement. He doesn't care about his diet

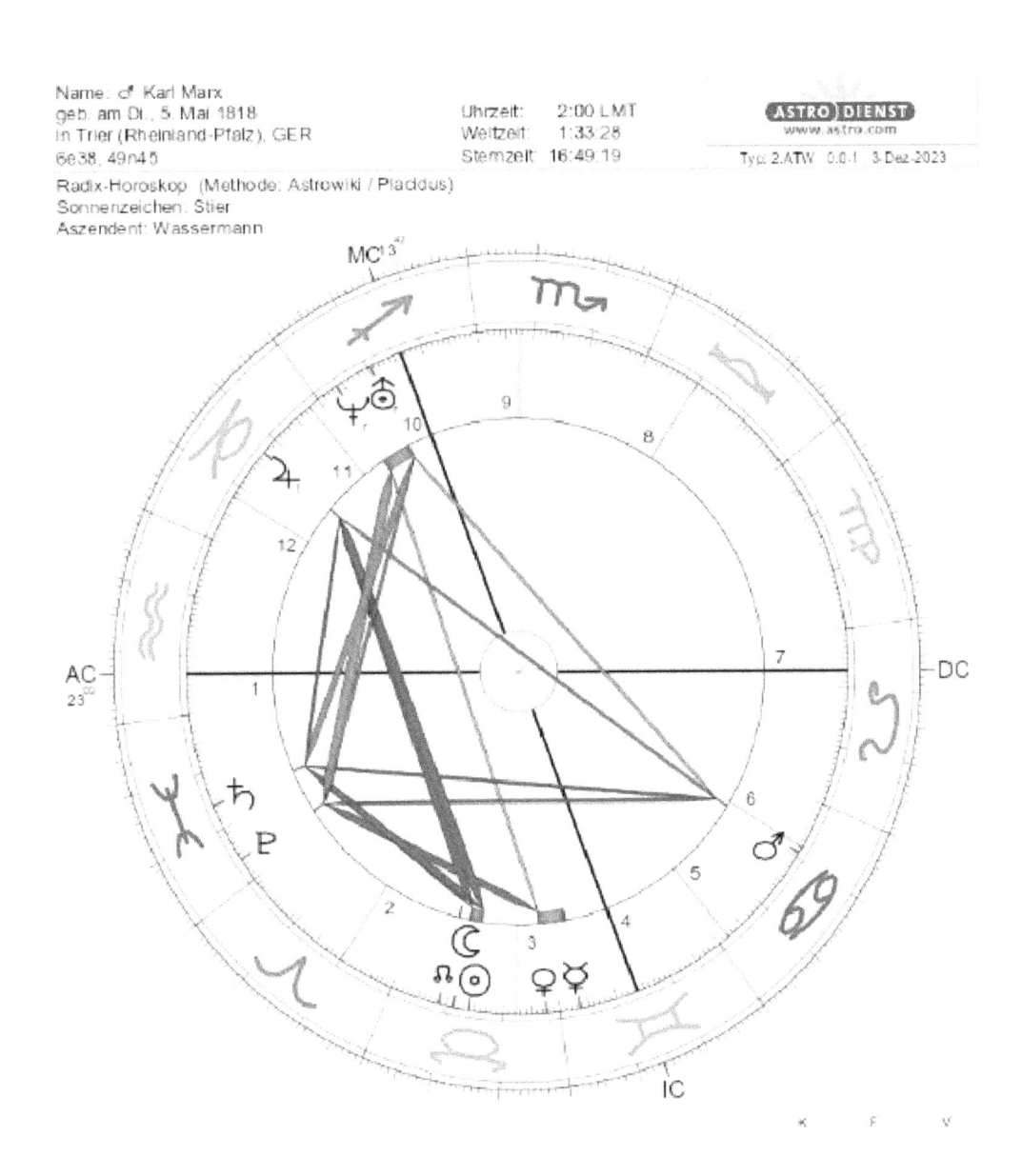

Karl Marx, author of the "Communist Manifesto," is also a Mars-3 archetype, perhaps the most notable, encouraging dissidence worlwide. The sexual revolution and sexual fredom movement has roots that come from Marxism's anti-religion stance. Abortion and the "my body my choice " moniker is a major characteristic derived from communist/libertarian ideas.

Here is an example of how the Mars 360 system would work for the Mars-4 demographic. Here is a sample of charts below, all of which would be classified as Mars-4. First notice the layout of the seals and apply that to the charts below.

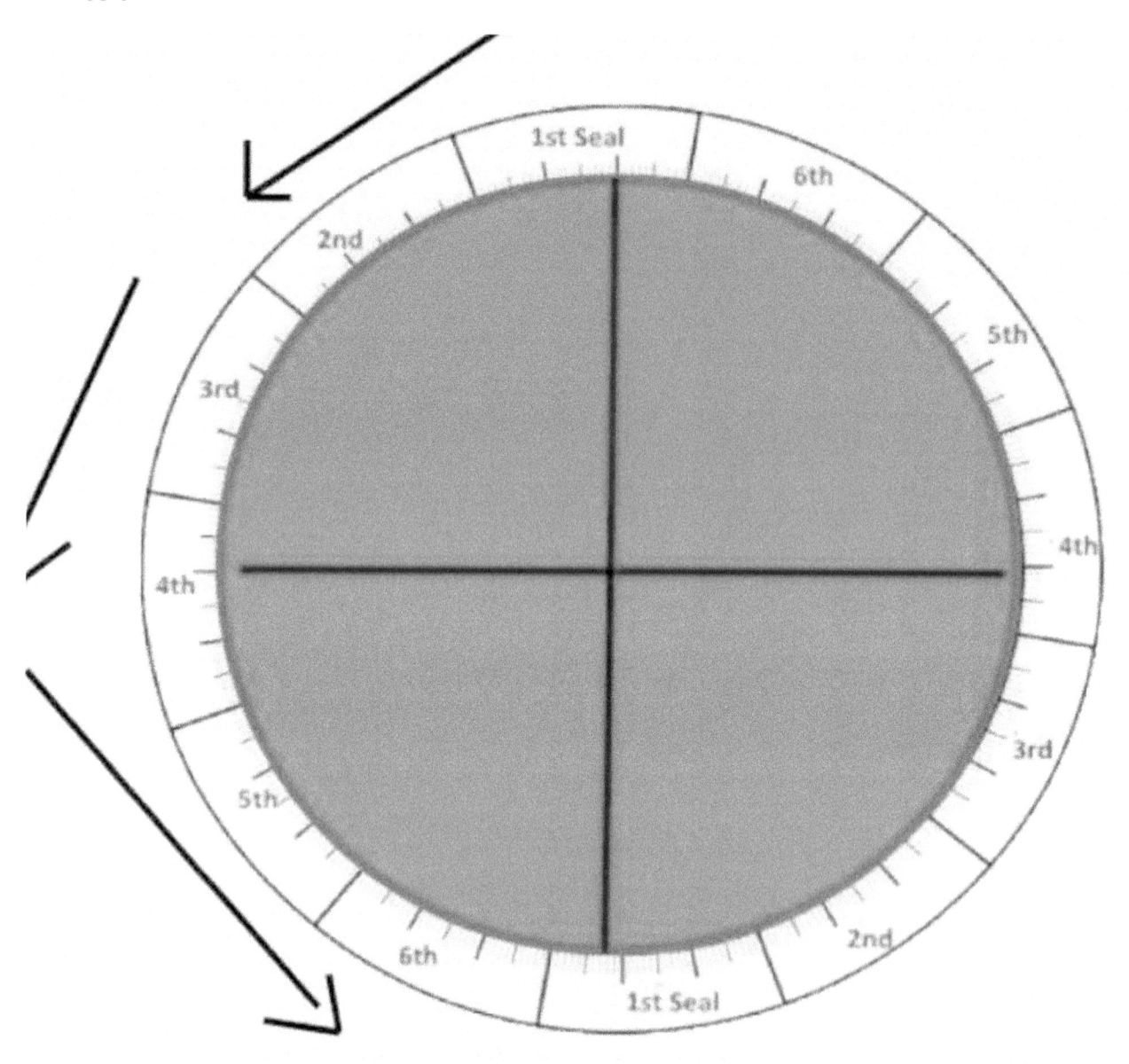

Notice where the 4th seal is located. The 4th seal is designated as causing a person to lack the energy to concern himself with the interests and values of other groups outside of his own demographic, whether it be regarding nationality, race, or religion These are nationalistic/rable rousing archetypes and every person in this sample has this same inclination as a result of Mars's position. Under Mars 360, for example, each person's behavior would reflect more on the Mars-4 demographic, and not so much on the racial or religious demographic that they belong to. For example, the burden of guilt regarding the atrocities of Hitler would have to be caried by the entire Mars-4 demographic, as opposed to just the German people.

4th seal ↙

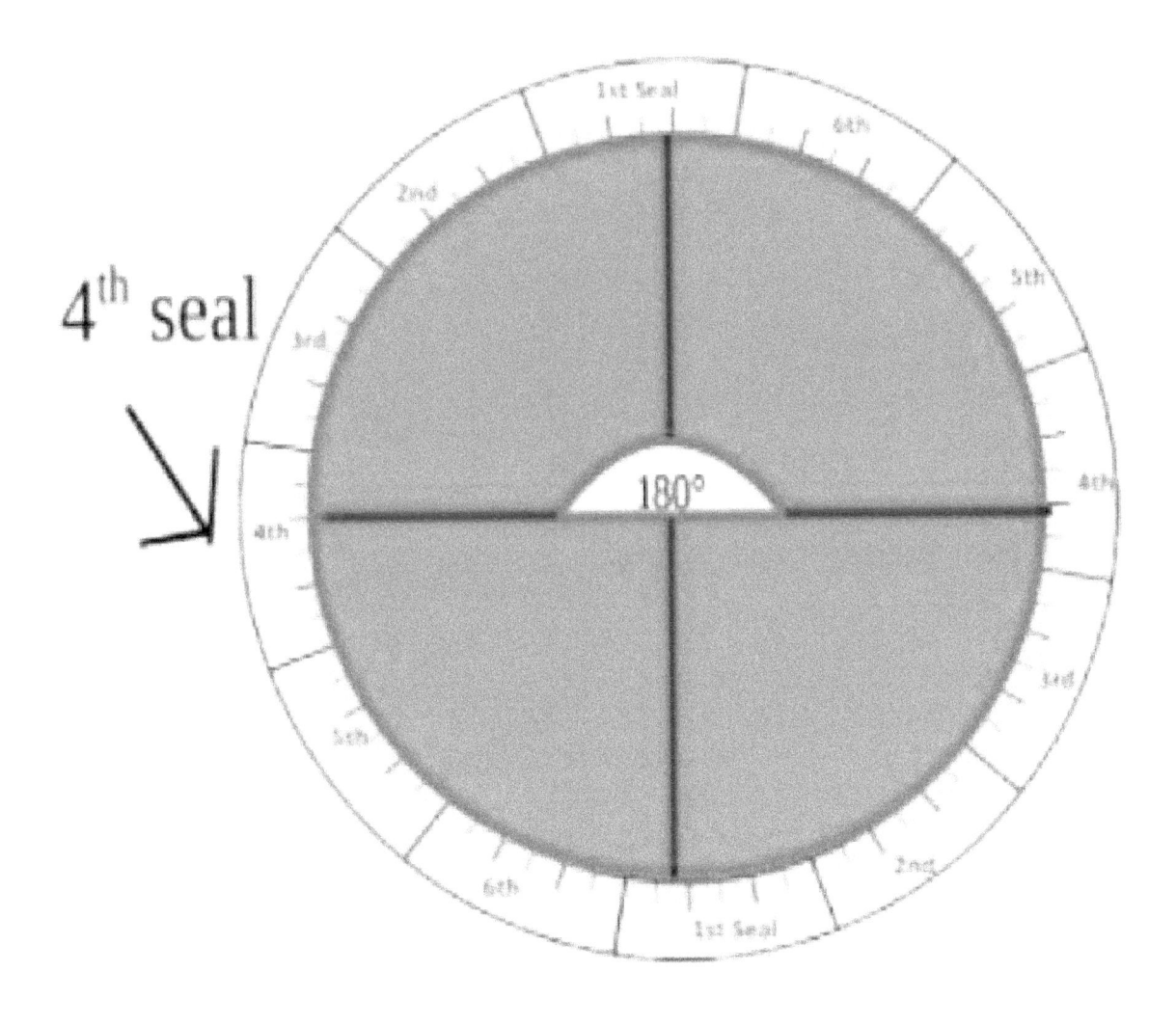

(diagram showing a circle divided into seals with 180° marked)

The worst expresion of this archetype is in the form of Adolf Hitler. This does not mean that everyone who is a Mars-4 wil become a Hitler, but it does consign every Mars-4 to a new demographic that Hitler is a part of. Mars in this position causes a person to lack the energy and concern for groups outside of one's own demographic. People with this placement tend to be somewhat relaxed when it comes to indirect speech regarding the status of other groups outside of one's own demographic. People like Malcolm X, Donald Trump, Ben Shapiro, David Duke, Jordan Peterson, Al Sharpton, and Adolf Hitler are now part of the same race under Mars 360 and thus share the burden of their similar frame of outlok.

So now, here are the charts

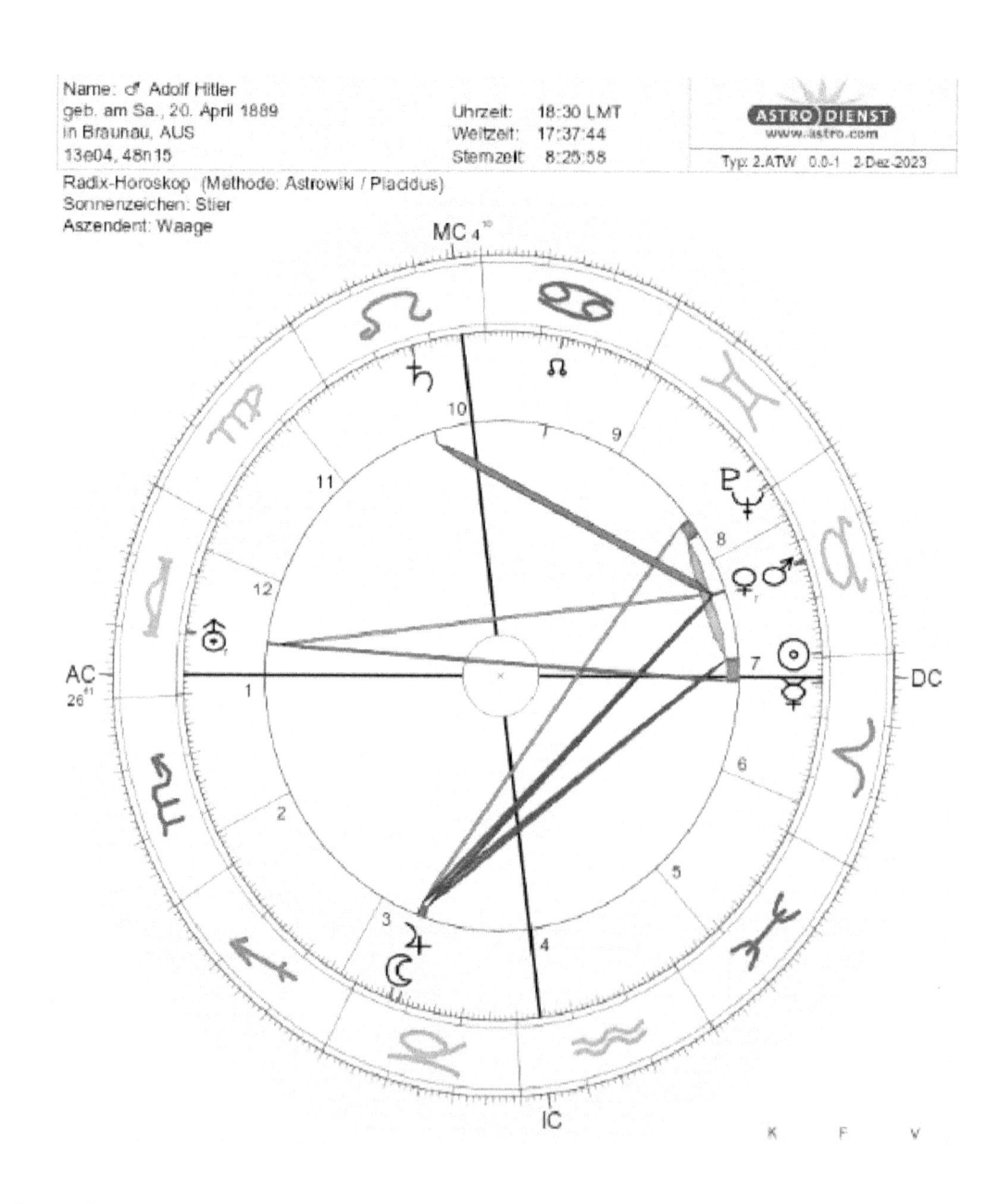

Adolf Hitler is the worst expression of this Mars-4 archetype.

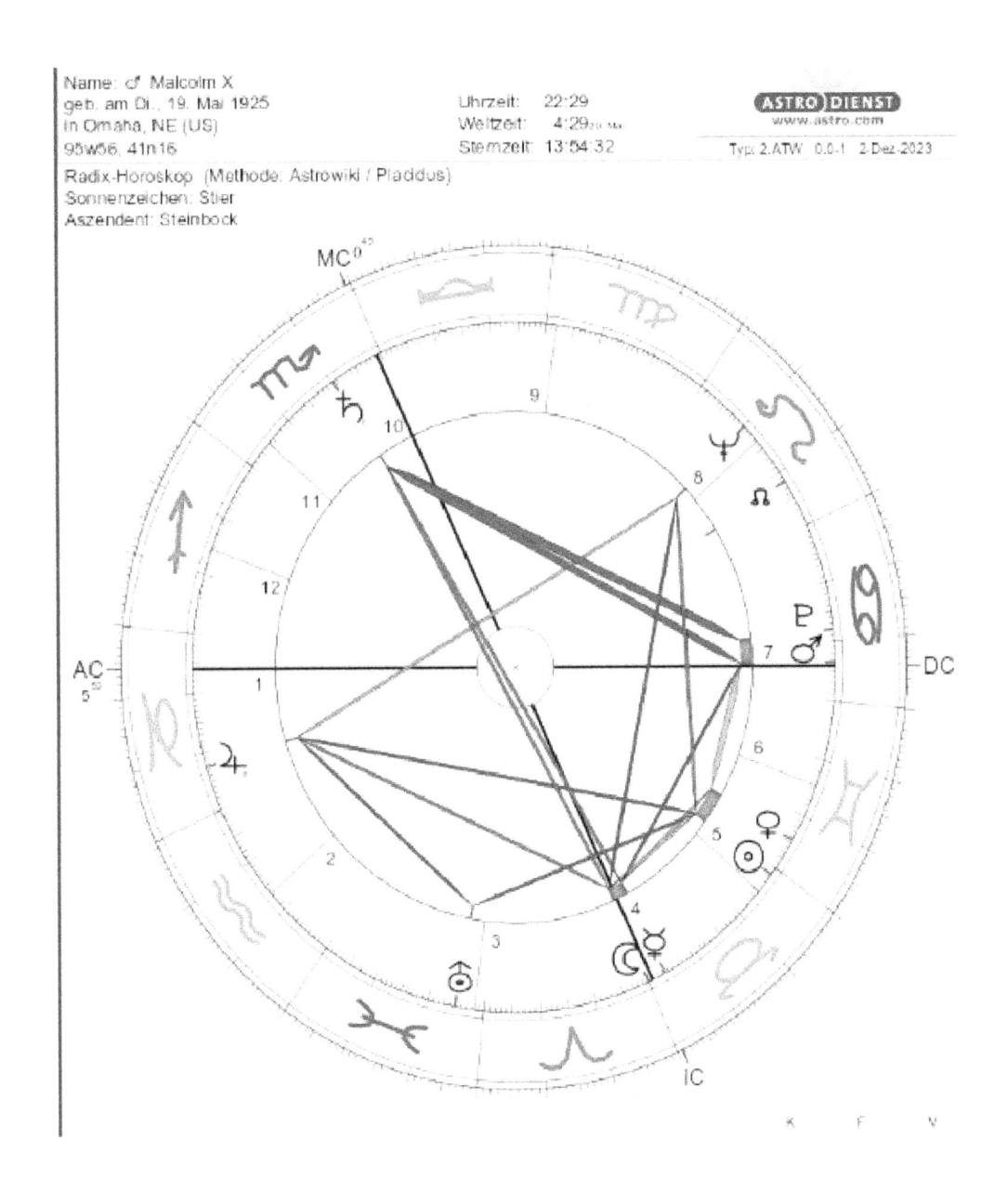

Another Mars-4 archetype is Malcolm X. Same rabble rousing tendencies as Adolf Hitler, but only as it pertained to his own demographic, which in the case of Malcolm X was the black demographic.

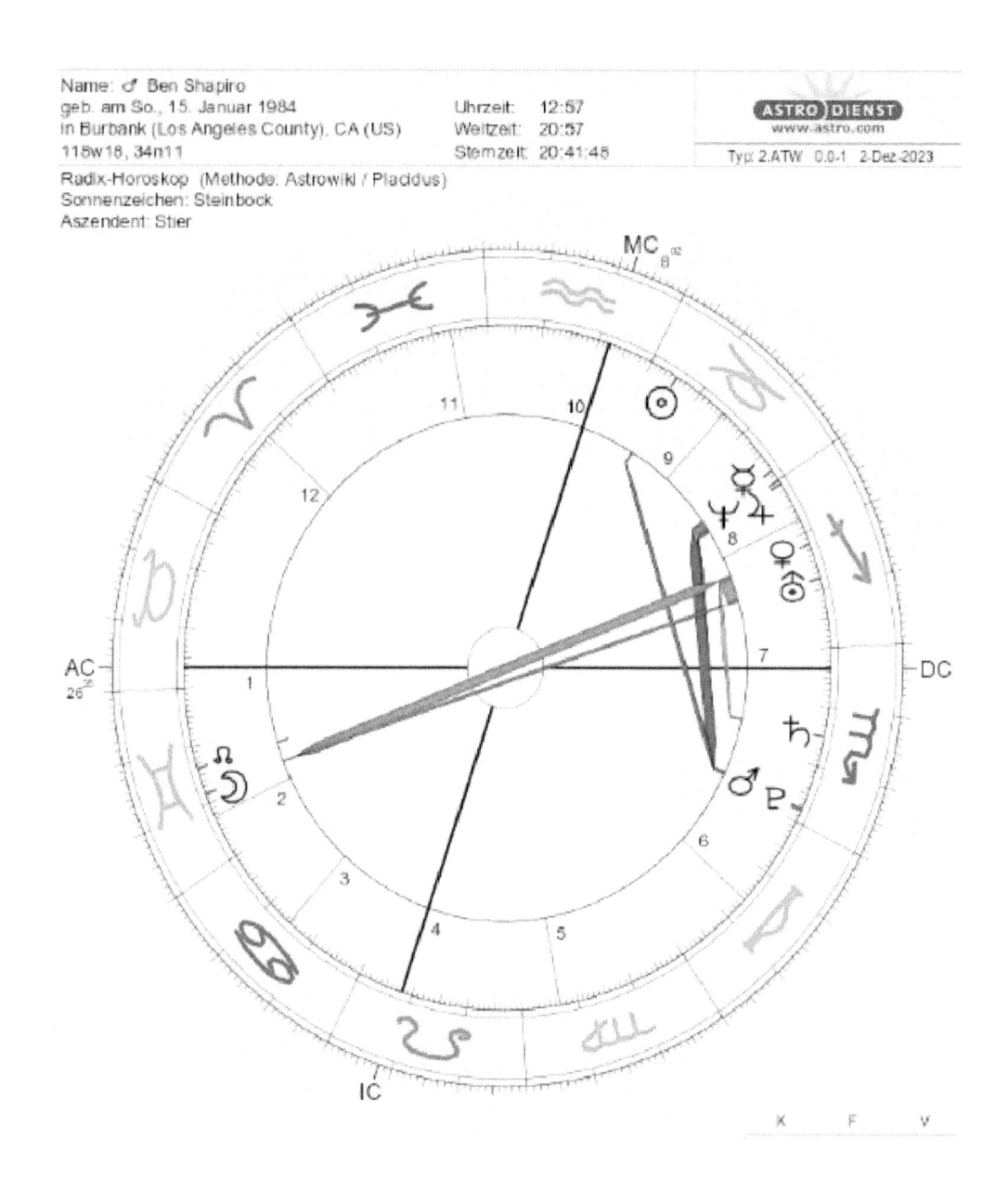

Name: ♂ Ben Shapiro
geb. am So., 15. Januar 1984
in Burbank (Los Angeles County), CA (US)
118w18, 34n11
Uhrzeit: 12:57
Weltzeit: 20:57
Sternzeit: 20:41:48

Radix-Horoskop (Methode: Astrowiki / Placidus)
Sonnenzeichen: Steinbock
Aszendent: Stier

Ben Shapiro is a political commentator, who is outspoken against the self-interest of other groups like the black nationalist group called Black Lives Matter. He is also a strong defender of his own Jewish/American cultural background

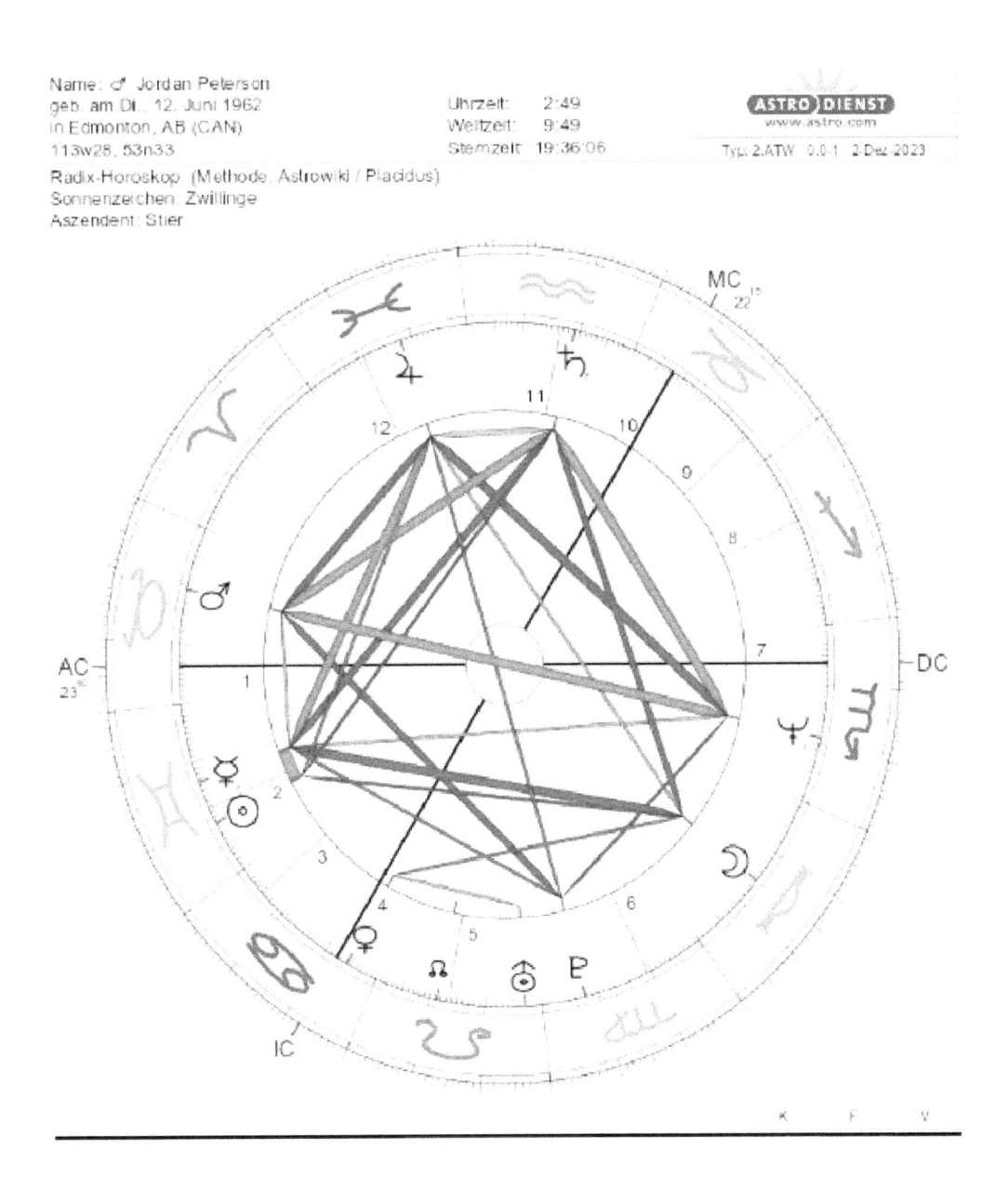

Jordan Peterson is a Mars-4 archetype and usually a very healthy expression of it. Strong supporter of western/Christian values and very suspicious of other outlooks outside of that paradigm.

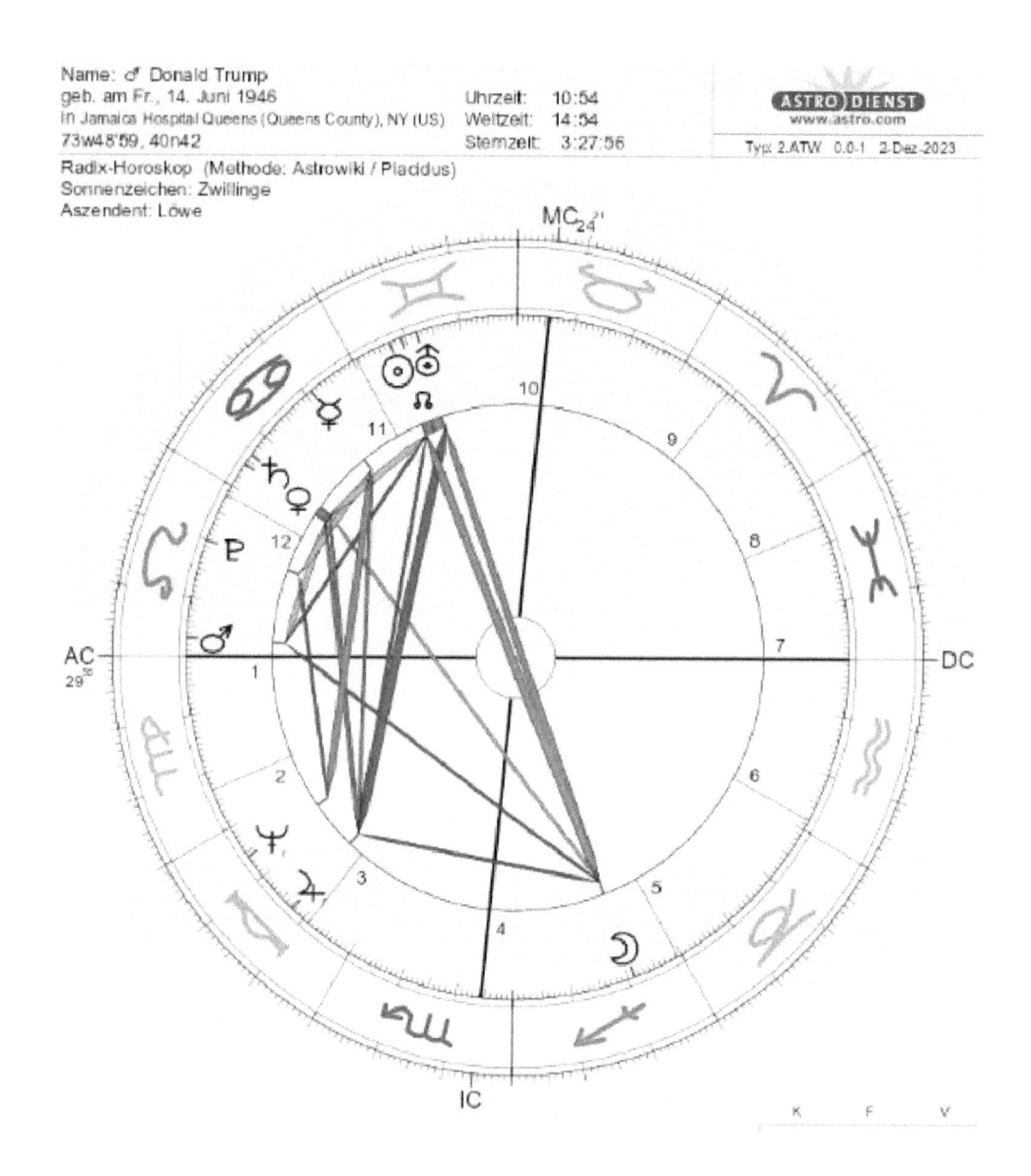

Donald Trump is the 45th president of the United States and was a major representation of the Mars-4 archetype, putting his own American nationality first, above all else, and boldly speaking against anything outside of it.

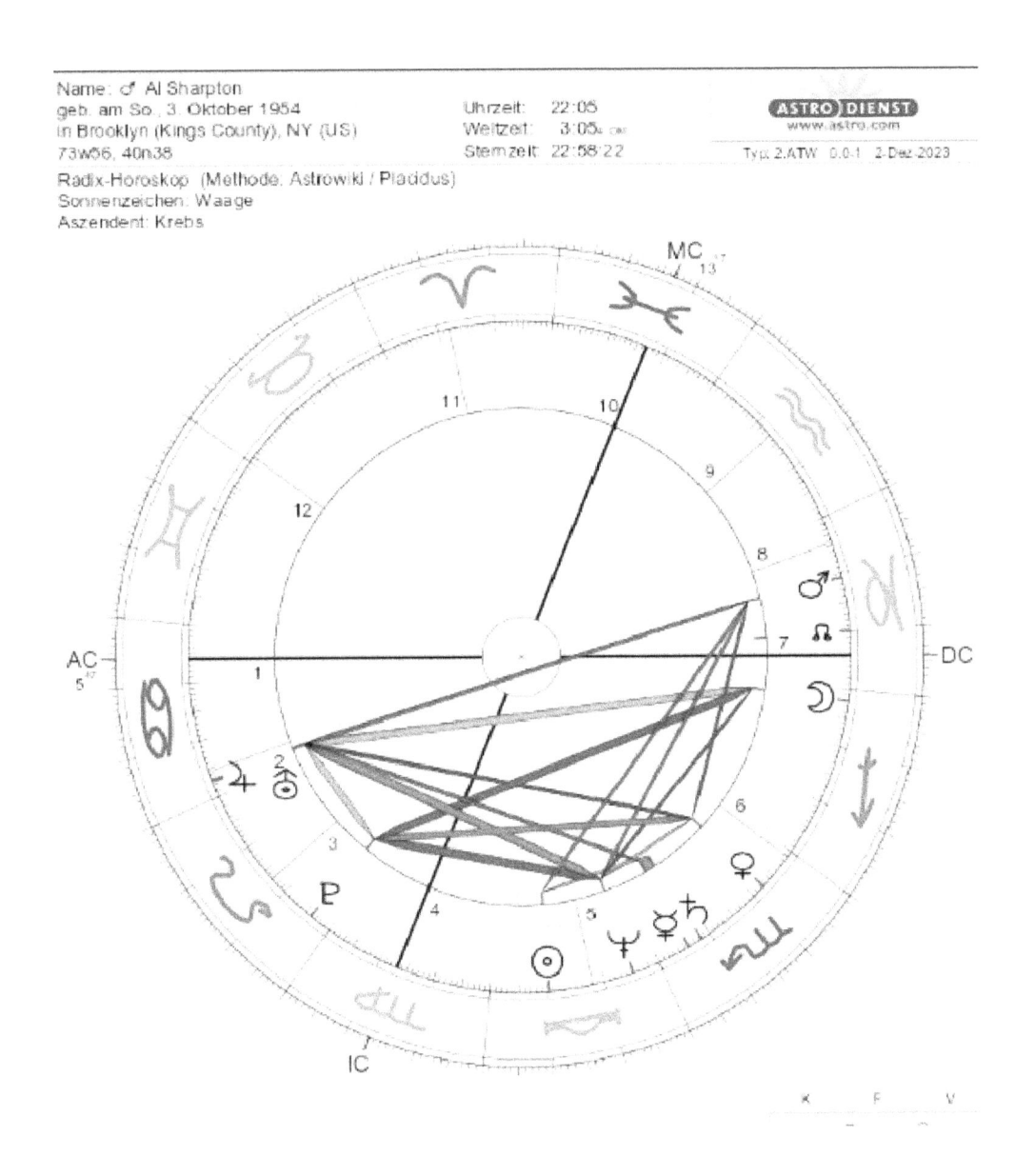

Al Sharpton is a rabble rousing, race-baiting, black nationalistic Mars-4 archetype and a very negative expression of the Mars-4. Under Mars 360, he would no longer represent black people. He would represent his Mars-4 archetype, which would include the likes of Hitler

David Duke is another Mars-4 archetype that loudly proclaims and prioritizes the interests of Europeans above all other interests.

Here is an example of how the Mars 360 system would work for the Mars-5 demographic. Here is a sample of charts below, all of which would be classified as Mars-5. First notice the layout of the seals and apply that to the charts below.

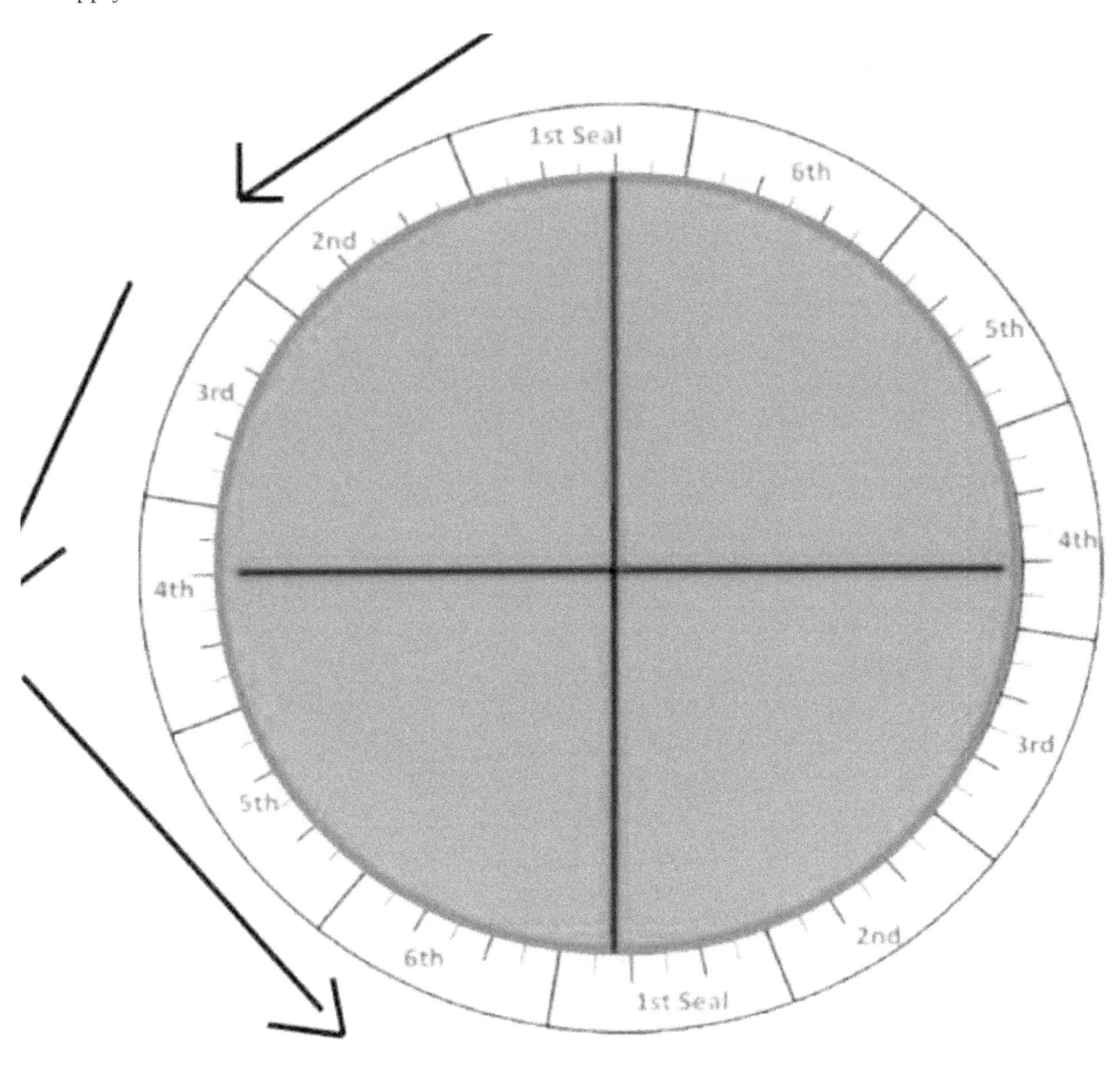

Notice where the 5th seal is located. The 5th seal is designated as causing a person to lack the energy to concern himself with the necessary reverence to authority, established authoritarian structures, regular work, obedience, and finance. At their worst, these are genuine threats to established authority, the economy, and public figures. Under Mars 360, these types would be granted the privilege of not having to work a day job. If they do work, the system would see to it that they are granted full autonomy, without having to answer to authority figures. These archetypes will be labeled potential lazy anarchists at birth with a Mars-5 designation. They would also be labeled communists and pacifist, but hostile to the authorities.

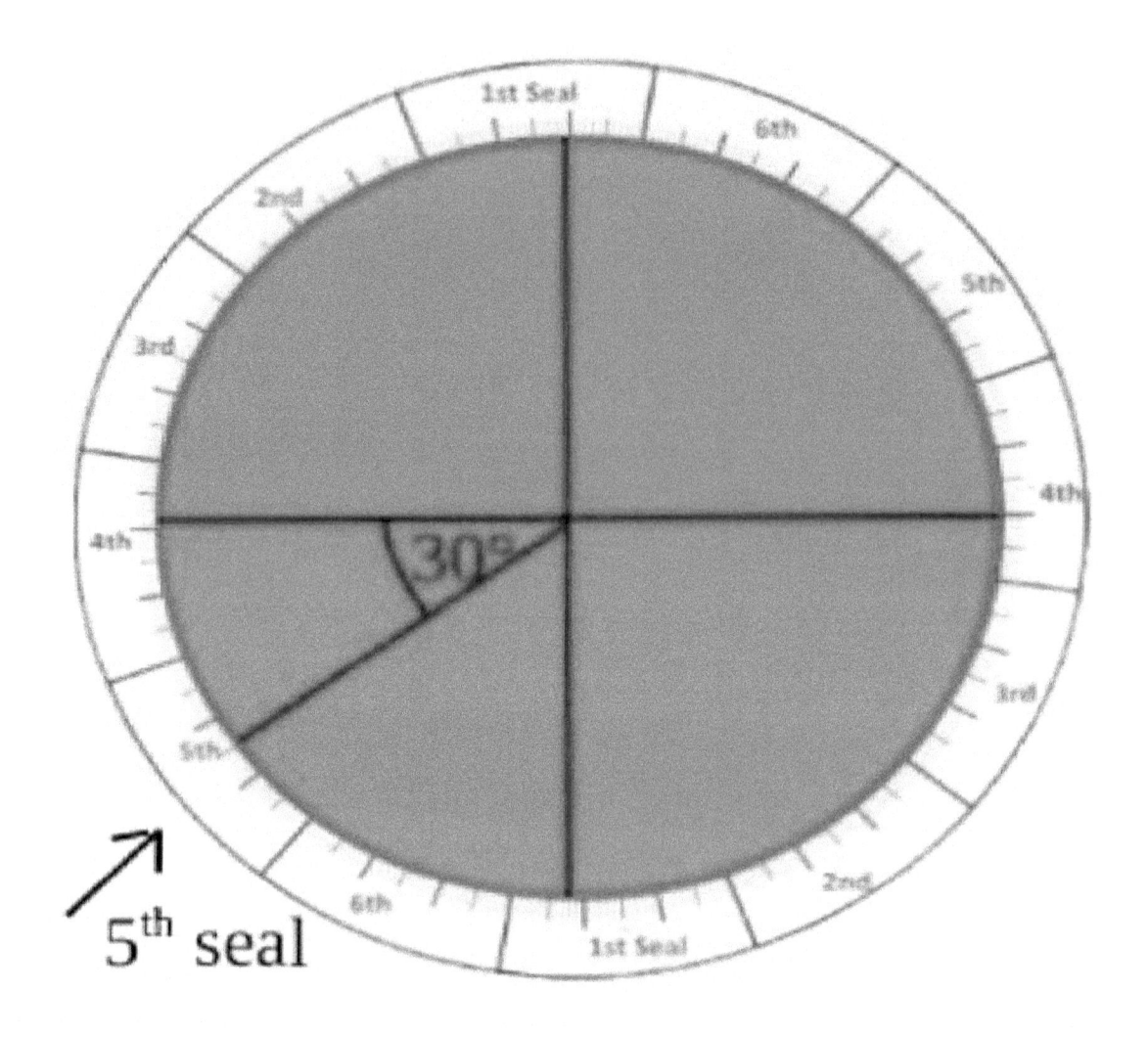

This archetype lacks the energy to concern himself with the basic work requirements of daily life. These are inherently unable to work a regular job and often develop pacifist anti-authority communist leanings regarding work and finance. As a result, the Mars 360 system will pander to them by having them live for free without having to work a regular day job. Notables here are Martin Luther King Jr?, Noam Chomsky, Jim Jones(cult leader), Lee Harvey Oswald, Mark David Chapman, Andrew Cunanan, and Barack Obama

So now, here are the charts

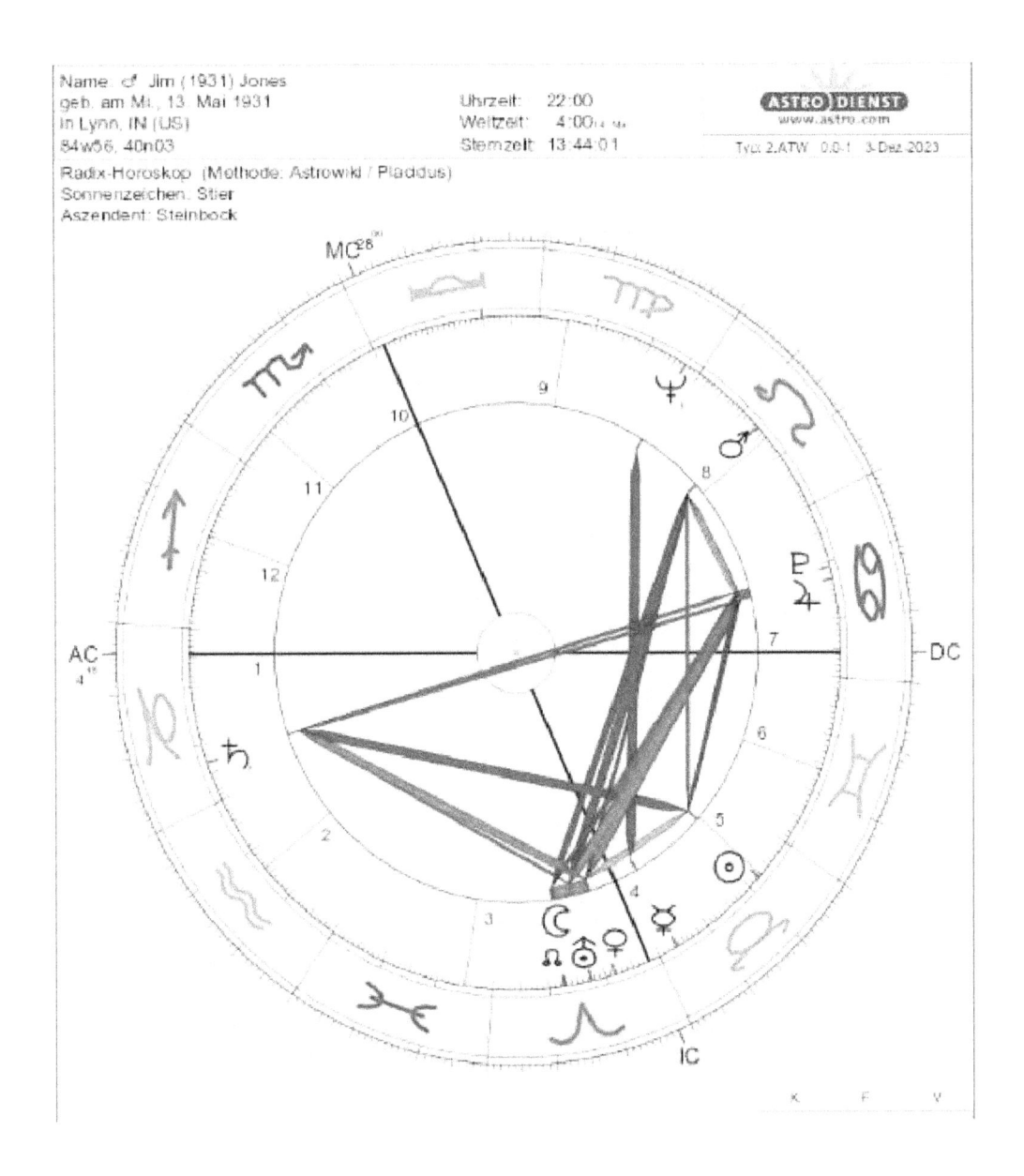

This is Jim Jones, communist, God-hating religious leader that led 900 people to commit suicide by poison. He was on the government's watchlist, as he expressed his desire for communism and his disdain for the authorities, including God. He would have been classified as a Mars-5 at birth and been given the subsidies that would have pandered to his lazy and comminist outlook

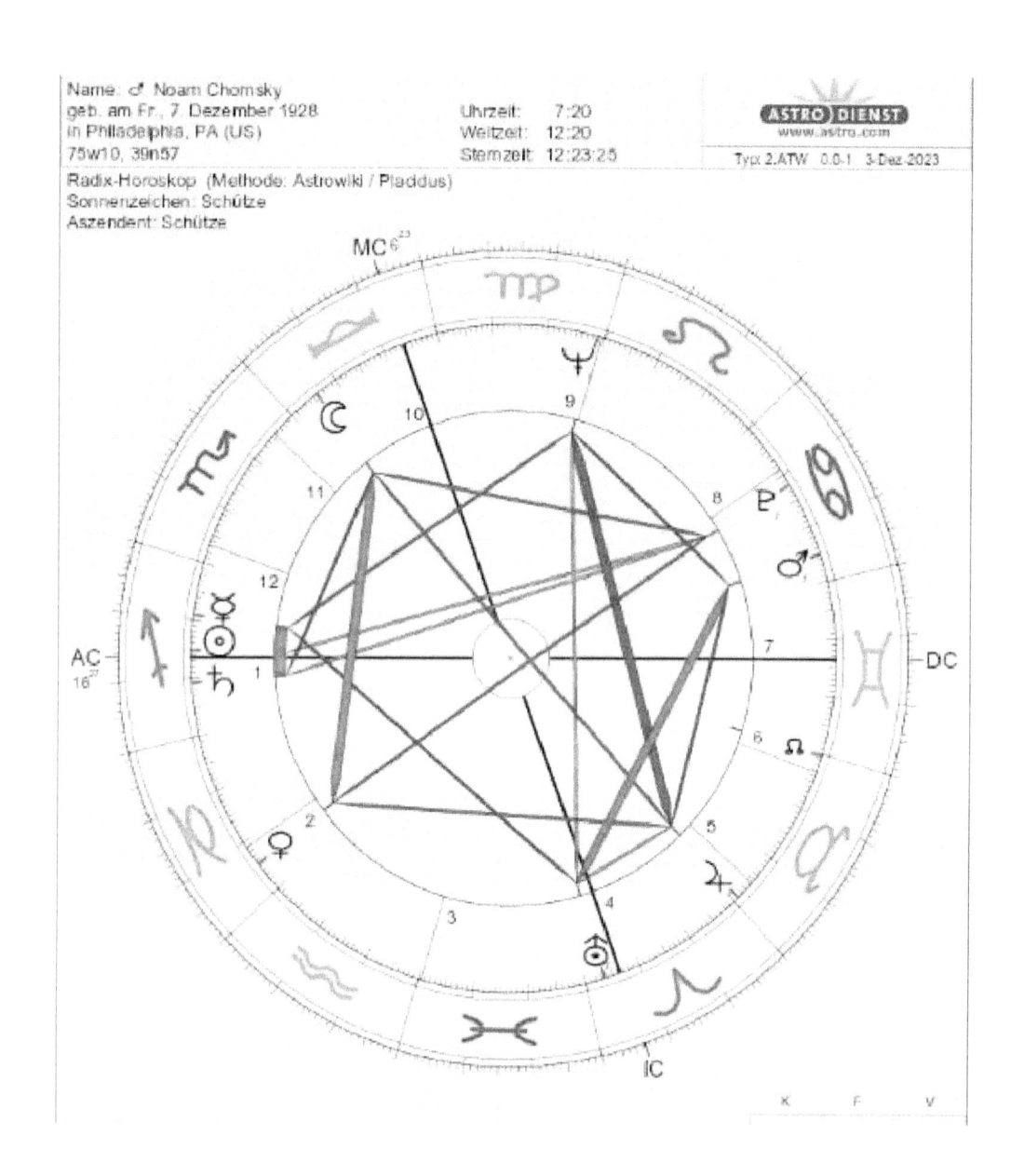

This is Noam Chomsky, the pacifist writer and linguist who was critical of the US military and their operations oversees. Noam Chomsky has expressed disdain for authority and authority strutures, including religion. He is considered an anarchist and a threat to the authority structure. He also spoke out against the need to have a job, saying in an interview

"When you have a job, you're under total control of the masters of the enterprise. They determine what you wear, when you go to the bathroom, what you do – the very idea of a wage contract is selling yourself into servitude. These are private governments. They're more totalitarian than governments are."

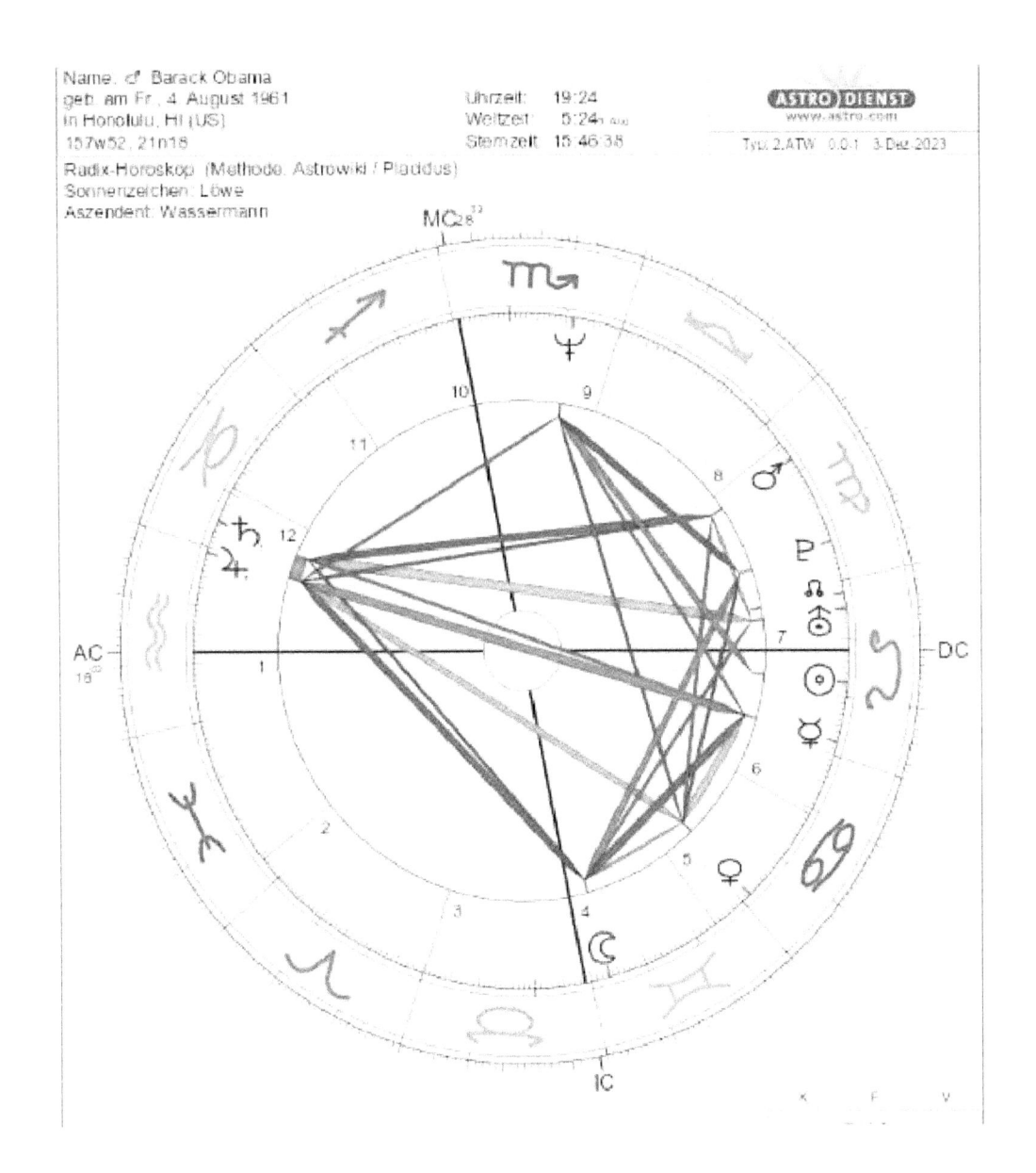

This is Barack Obama, the 44th President of the United States, who never worked a regular 9-5 job and admitted that his worst trait was laziness. GW Bush also had this placement. Any president with this Mars-5 placement is a threat in that their pacifism/laziness will lead them to delegate all work and responsibility.

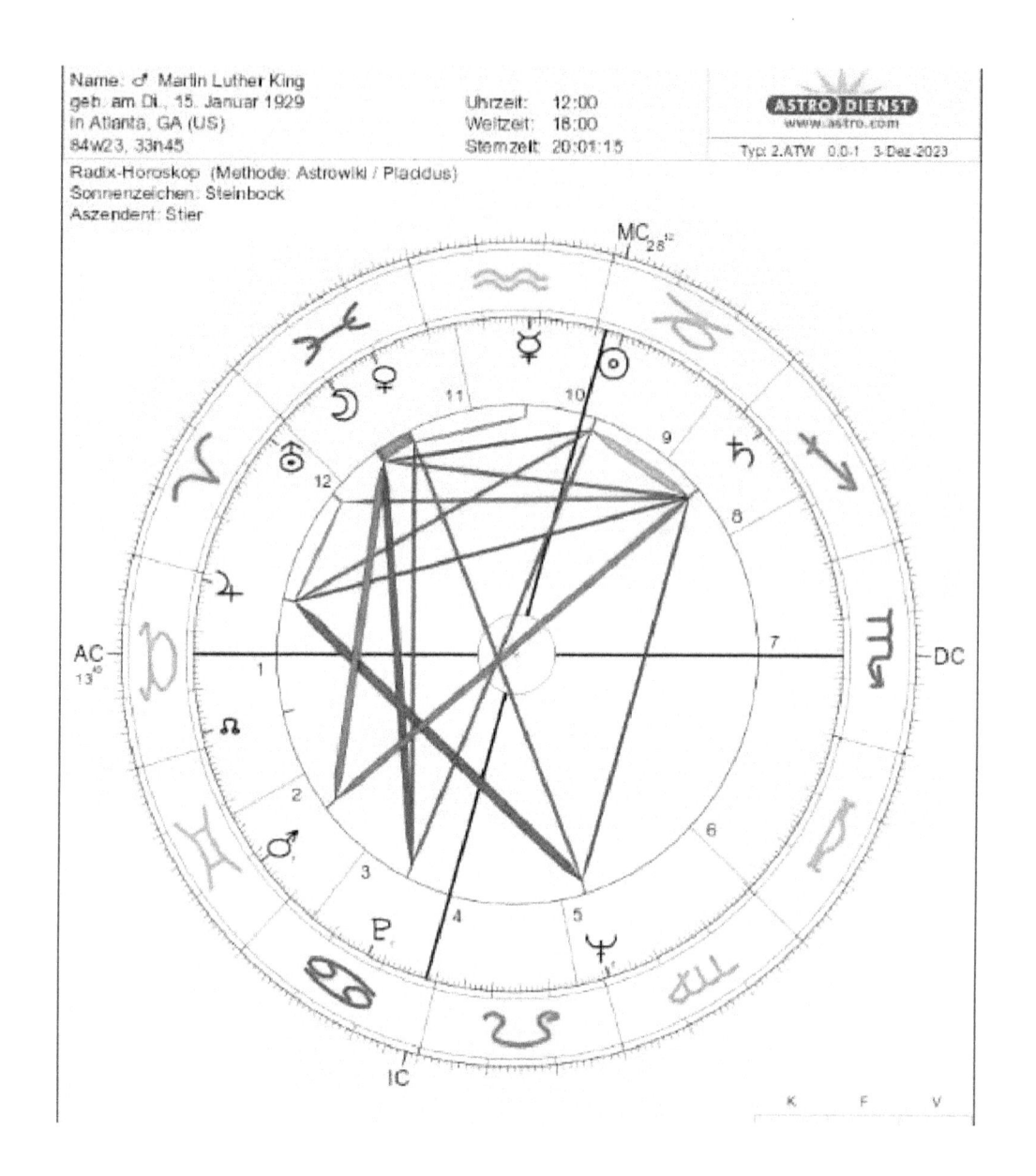

Martin Luther King is somewhere between a Mars-5 and Mars-6. Mars-5 is possible because of his pacifist, communist leanings, as well as the fact that he was considered a threat to the authorities. Hence why the FBI had him under intense surveillance. He was still nonetheless a champion of non-violence, albeit a threat to the established structure of segregation at that time.

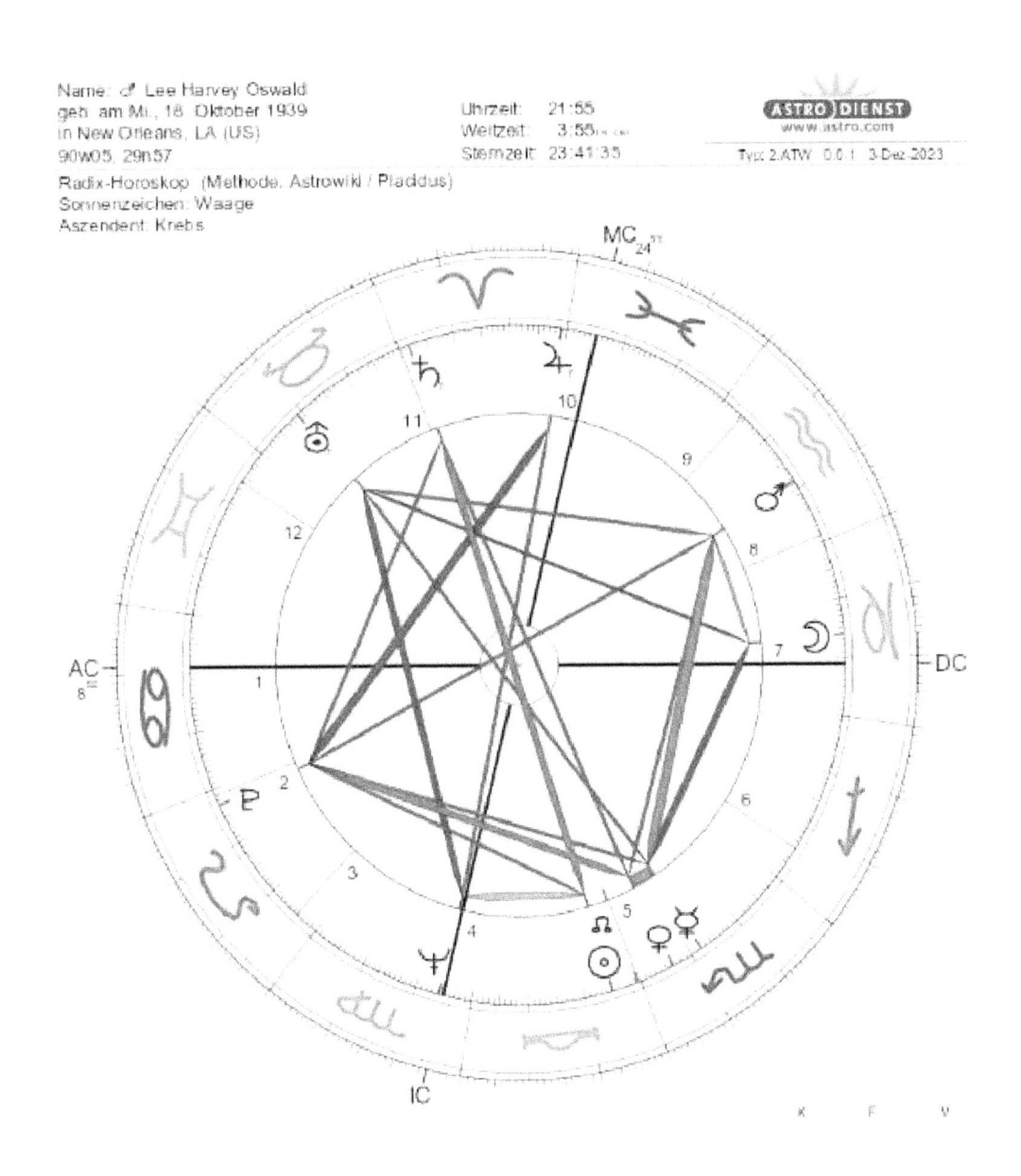

Lee Harvey Oswald, an assasin and communist, who shot and killed John F Kennedy. He wanted to defect to the Soviet Union because he felt the workers were slaves in the US capitalist society. Under Mars 360, he would have been marked as a Mars-5 at birth and given government subsidies so that he would not have to work.

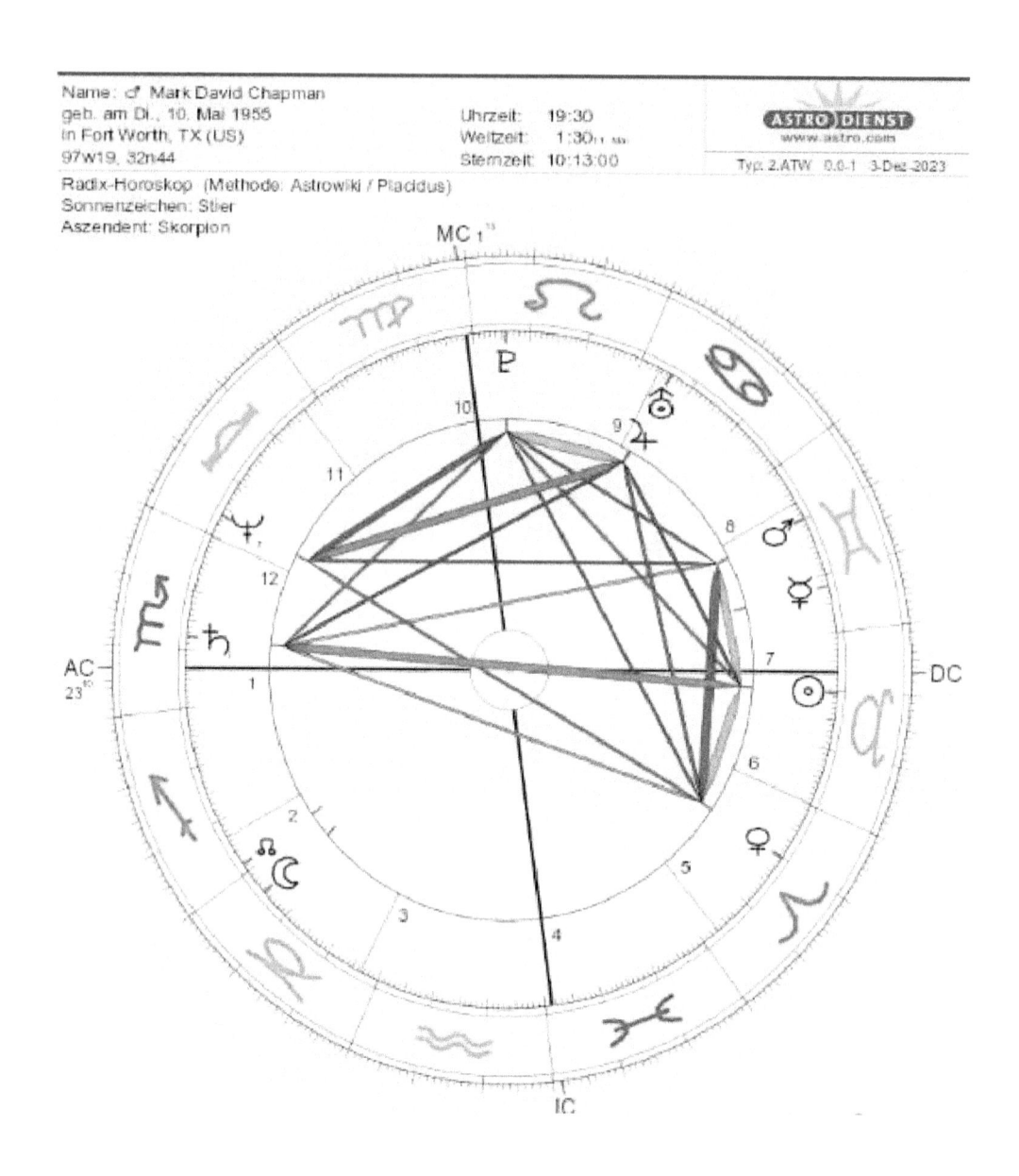

Mark David Chapman was a protoype loser, college dropout who could not hold a stead job. He targeted and killed status figure John Lennon. He would have been marked as a Mars-5 under Mars 360 and given subsidies so that he would not have to work.

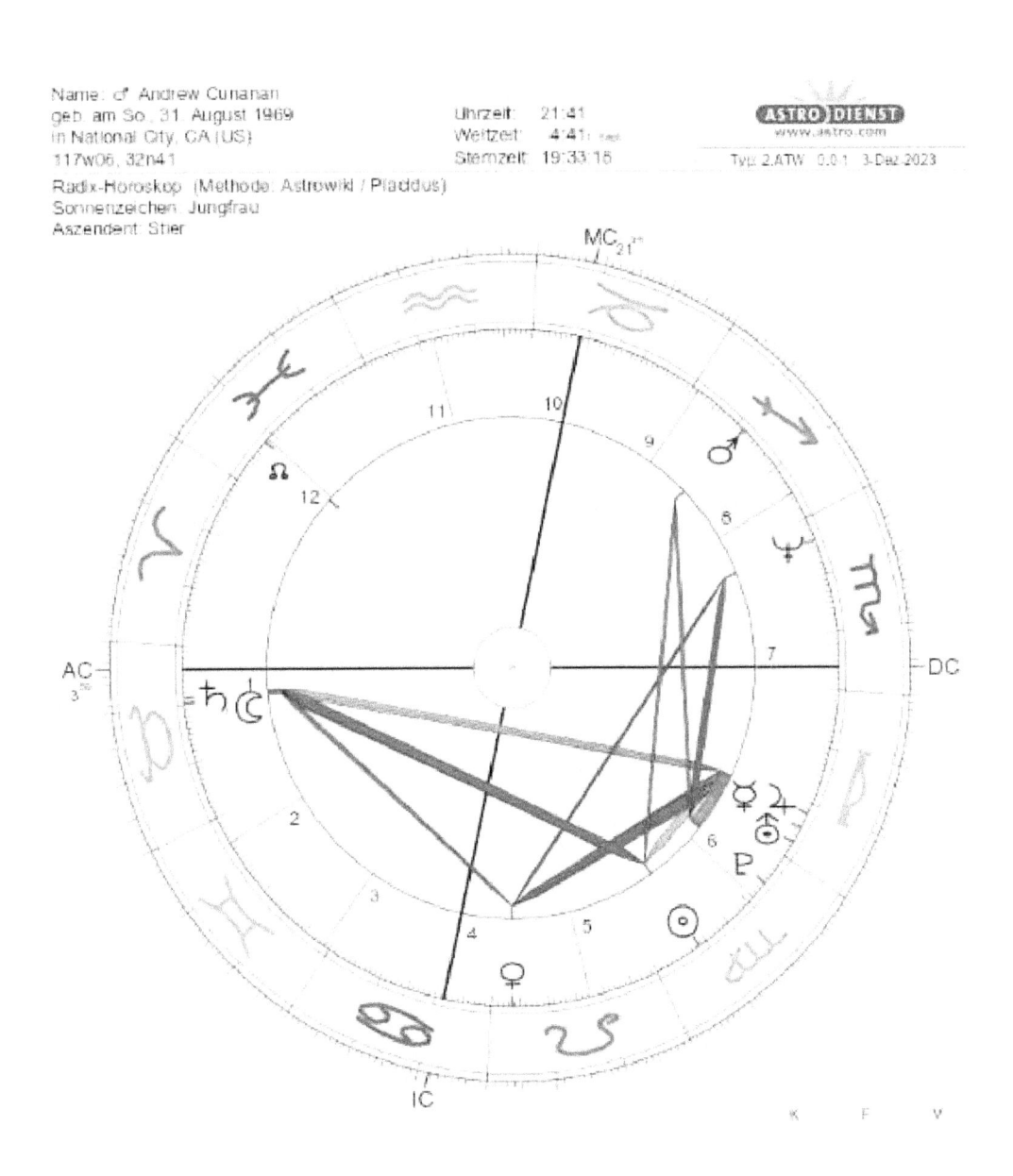

Andrew Cunnanan was another work shy person who could not work a regular job and had to seek the company of sugar daddies in order to sustain himself. He later shot and killed status figure Gianni Versace. He would have been marked as a Mars-5 at birth and given the means to live without having to work a regular job.

Here is an example of how the Mars 360 system would work for the Mars-6 demographic. Here is a sample of charts below, all of which would be classified as Mars-6. First notice the layout of the seals and apply that to the charts below.

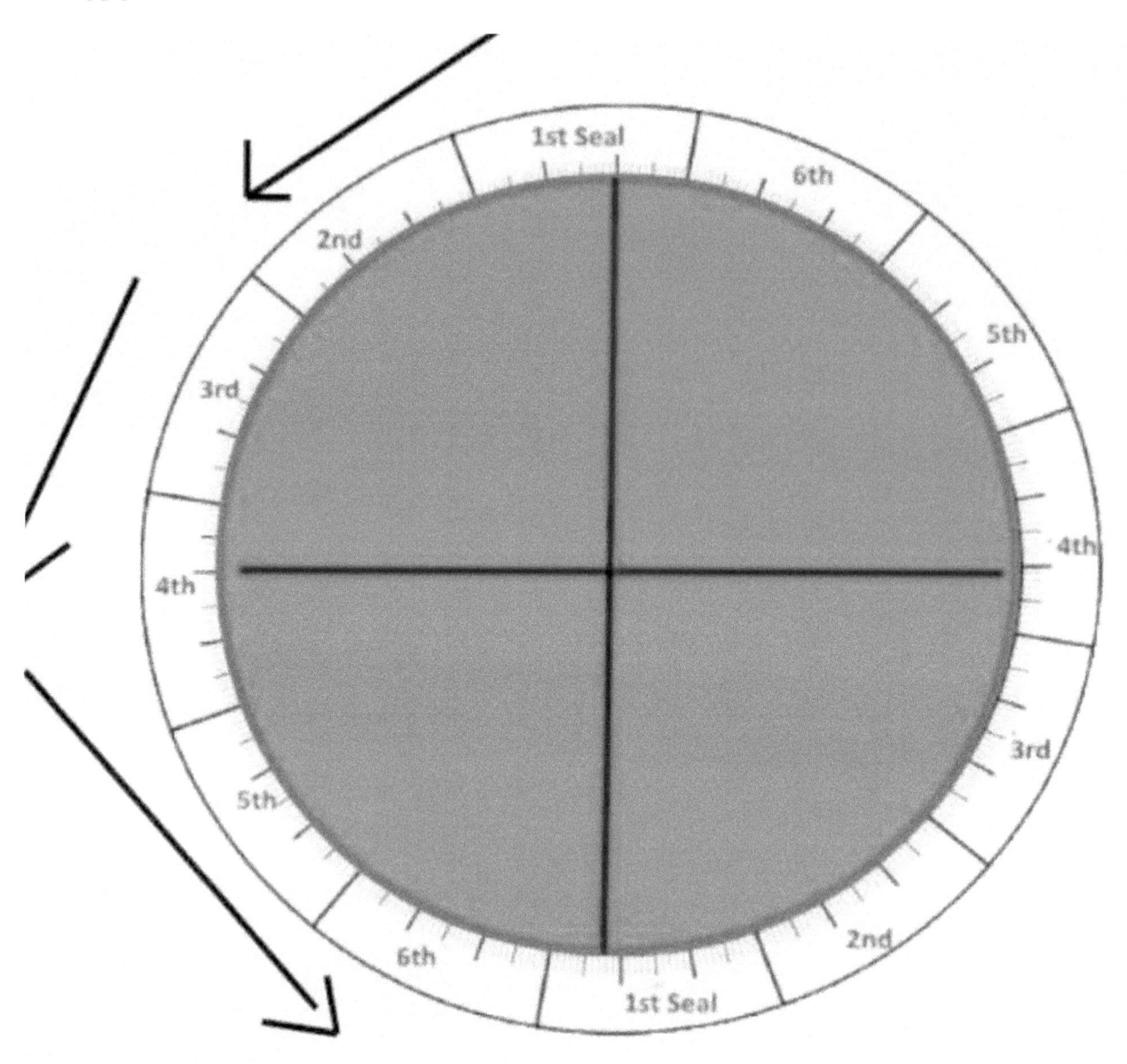

Notice where the 6th seal is located. The 6th seal is designated as causing a person to lack the energy to concern himself with appearance. These are liberal/pacifist archetypes and every person in this sample has this same inclination as a result of Mars's position. Under Mars 360, for example, each person's behavior would reflect more on the Mars-6 demographic, and not so much on the racial or religious demographic that they belong to.

6th seal

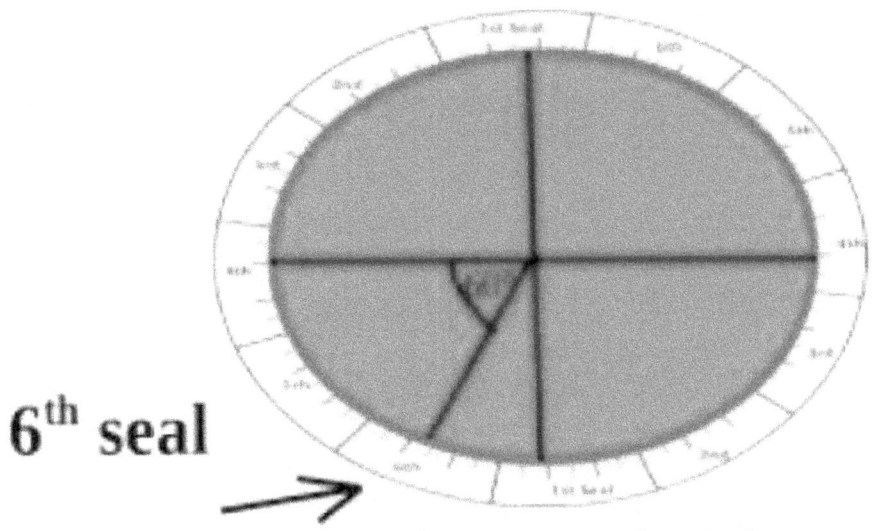

What the 6th seal is referring to is Mars exerting influence on humanity through bringing a sense of opposition to being seen properly, hence why the sun turning black metaphors the avoidance of a light which makes us visible. The 6th seal essentially refers to a desire to deny one's DNA makeup with regard to one's appearance and also disregard any reverence toward the eyes of others. It is related to one's hair, skin, nails, ethnicity, and facial expression. Modern Liberalism would be an example of this opposing effect towards one's identity. The moving of things out of their rightful place, as mentioned in the passage, symbolizes the rebellion of humanity to resist cultural norms related to how they are seen. The most negative culmination of this quality displays itself in exposing oneself foolishly through engaging in improper acts in plain view such as those who perform publicly in scantily clad attire or take their clothes off in front of a camera. Another negative culmination is a stage comedian in which the performer pays no attention to how he is being perceived by others. At the basic day to day level, it results in a lack of hygiene and proper rectitude along with a high degree of shyness and social awkwardness. The ability to hold a smile becomes limited, leading the person to display a "stern face" even when he is not aware of it. The failure to conform to cultural standards of dress and appearance can discourage meeting new people and getting involved socially, which often results in extreme introversion. This opposing attitude can extend beyond the individual and into anything or anyone that may resemble one's identity.

So now, here are the charts

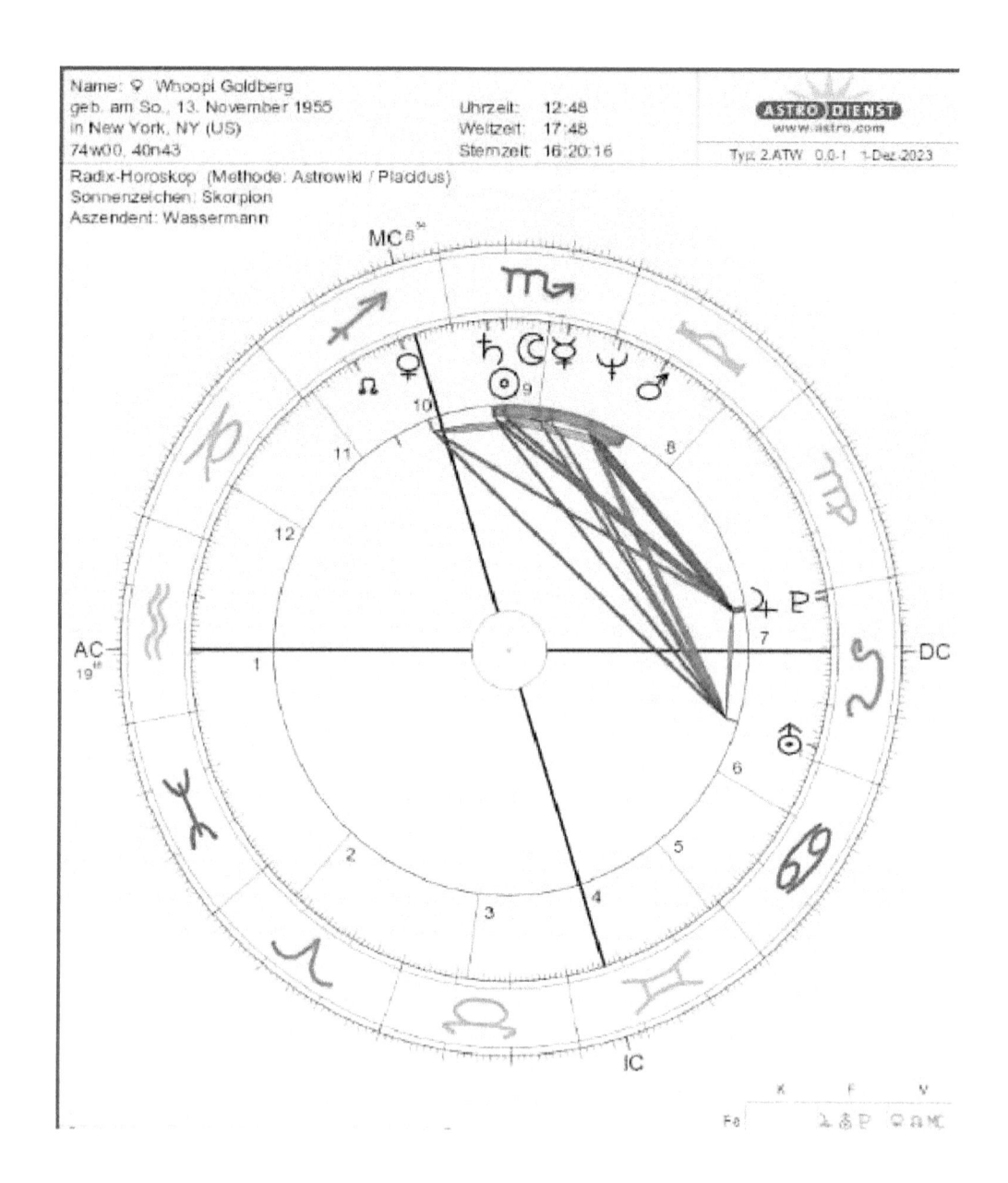

Whoopi Goldberg, a liberal, doesn't give importance to apearance and cultural expectations.

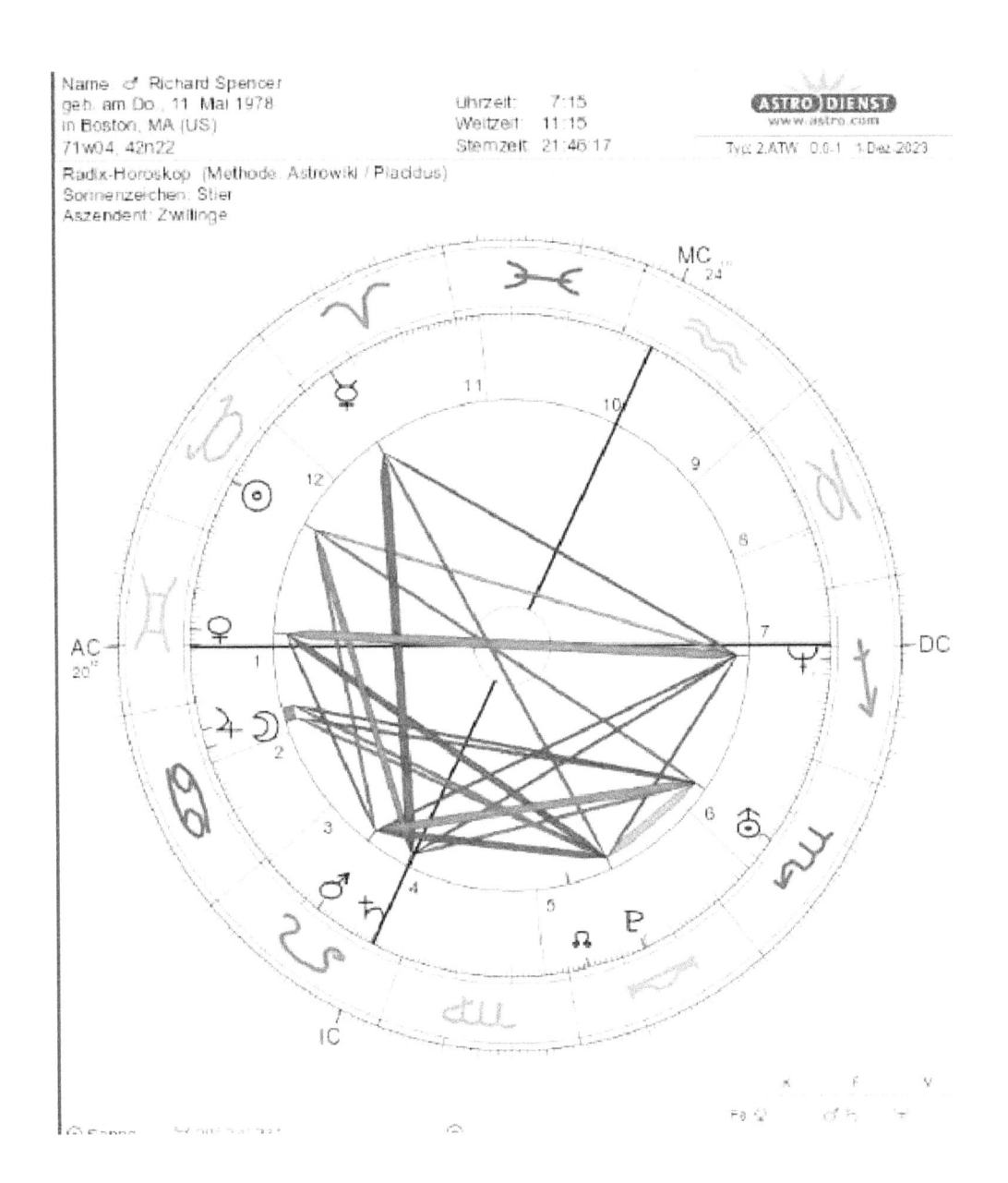

Another liberal is Richard Spencer, who has behaved wildly in public, playing the role of villain as neo-nazi, unconcerned about public perception. Under Mars 360, however, he couldn't fully identify as white. He would be classified as Mars-6, same as myself and Richard Pryor, and Whoopi Goldberg

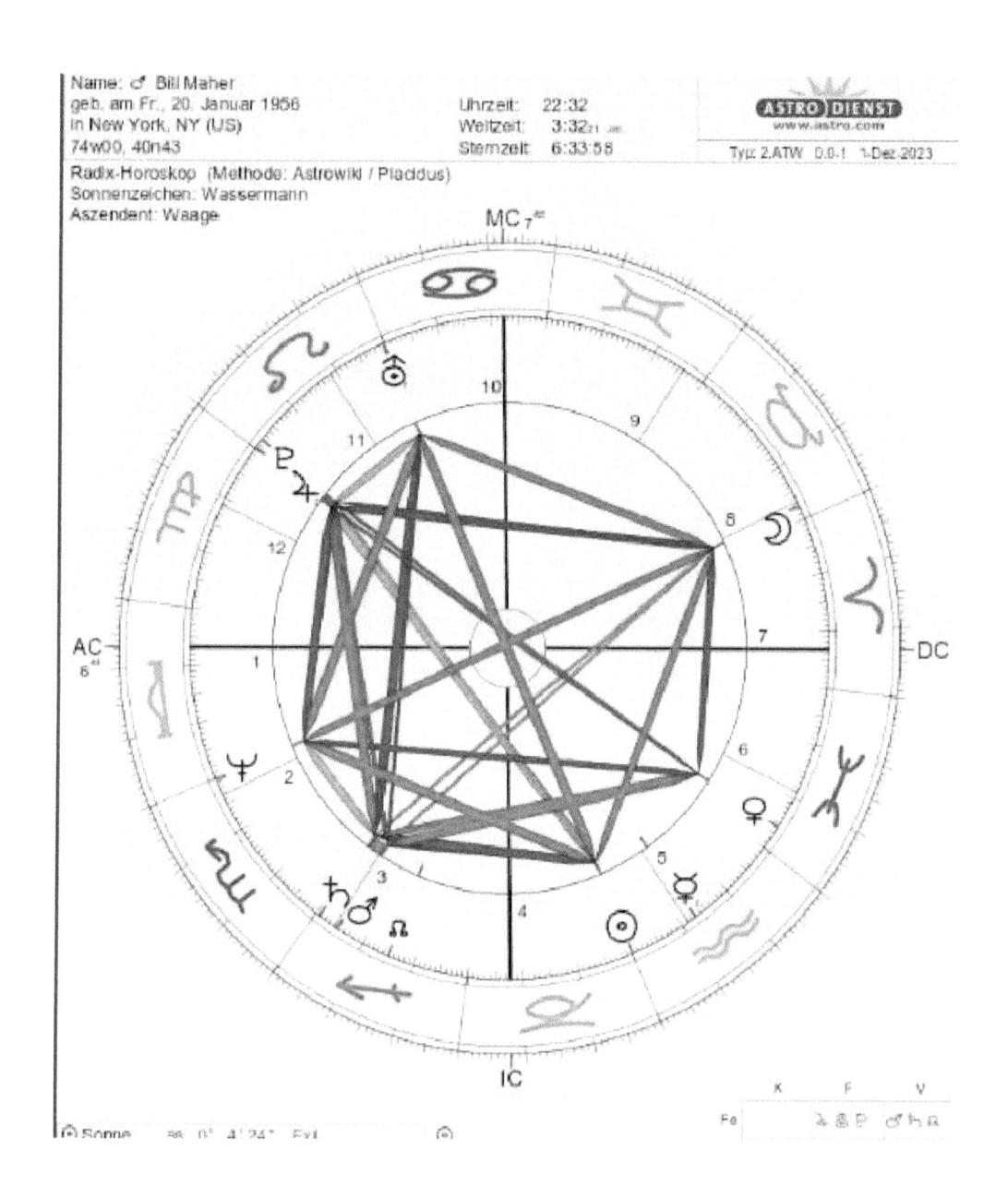

Bill Maher, a comedian, is clearly a liberal archetype and would be part of the Mars-6 tribe

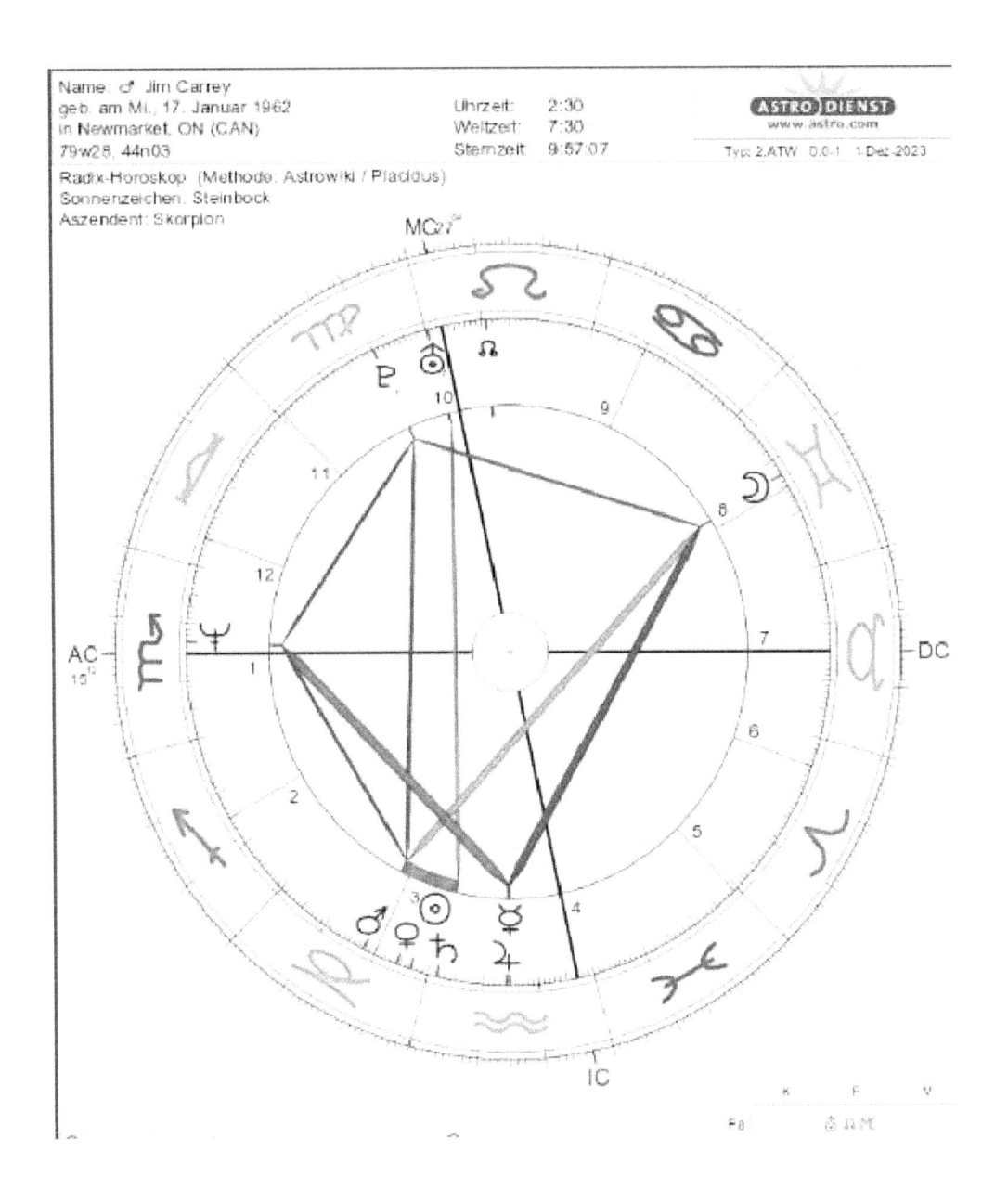

No explanation needed. Jim Carrey is a high priest of the Mars-6 archetype.

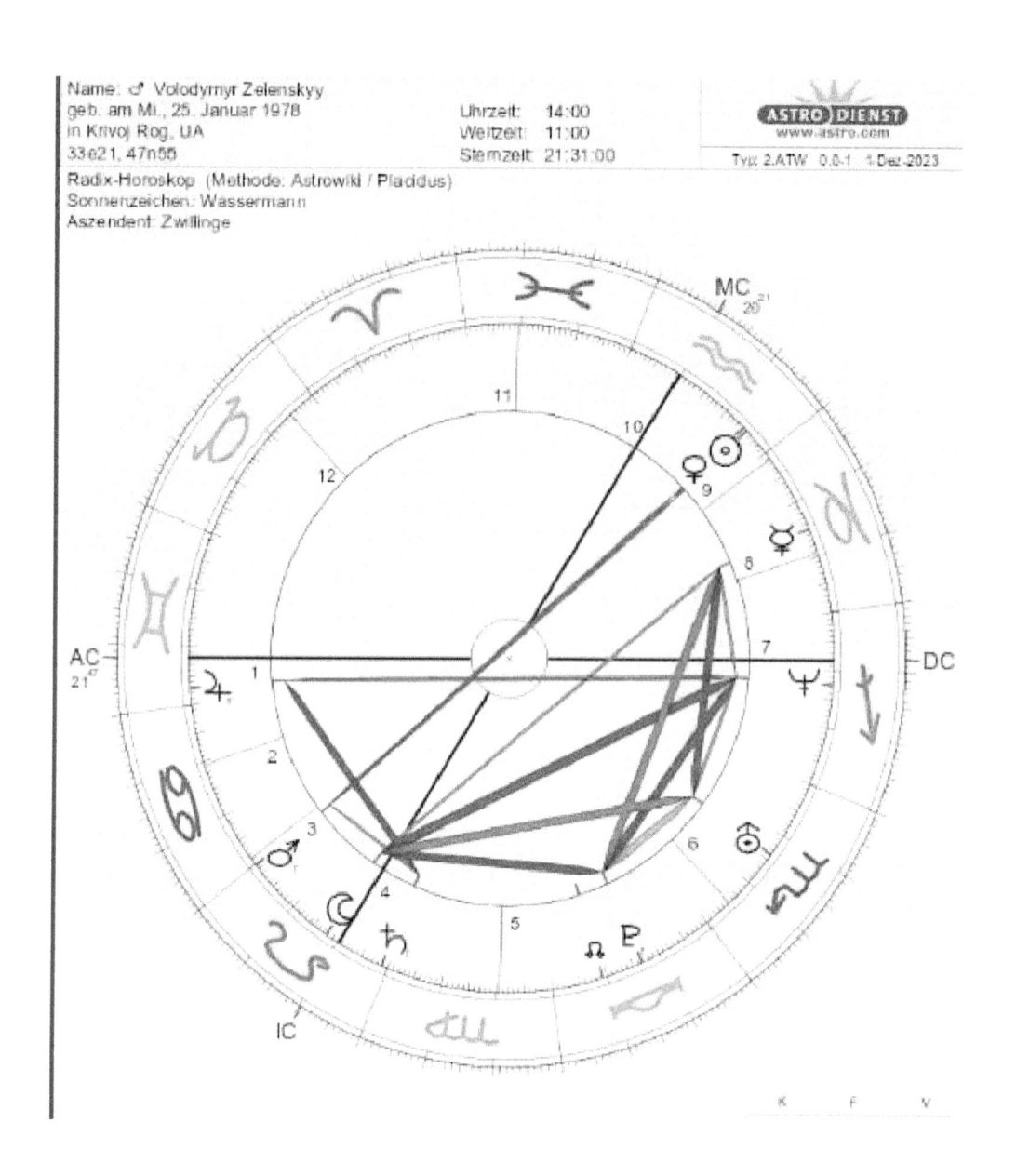

Zelenskyy is President of Ukraine, former comedian and very liberal. Public presure, however, led him to give into far right demands. But he is a classic liberal a Mars-6 archetype. Look at his appearance. Doesn't care for how other see him

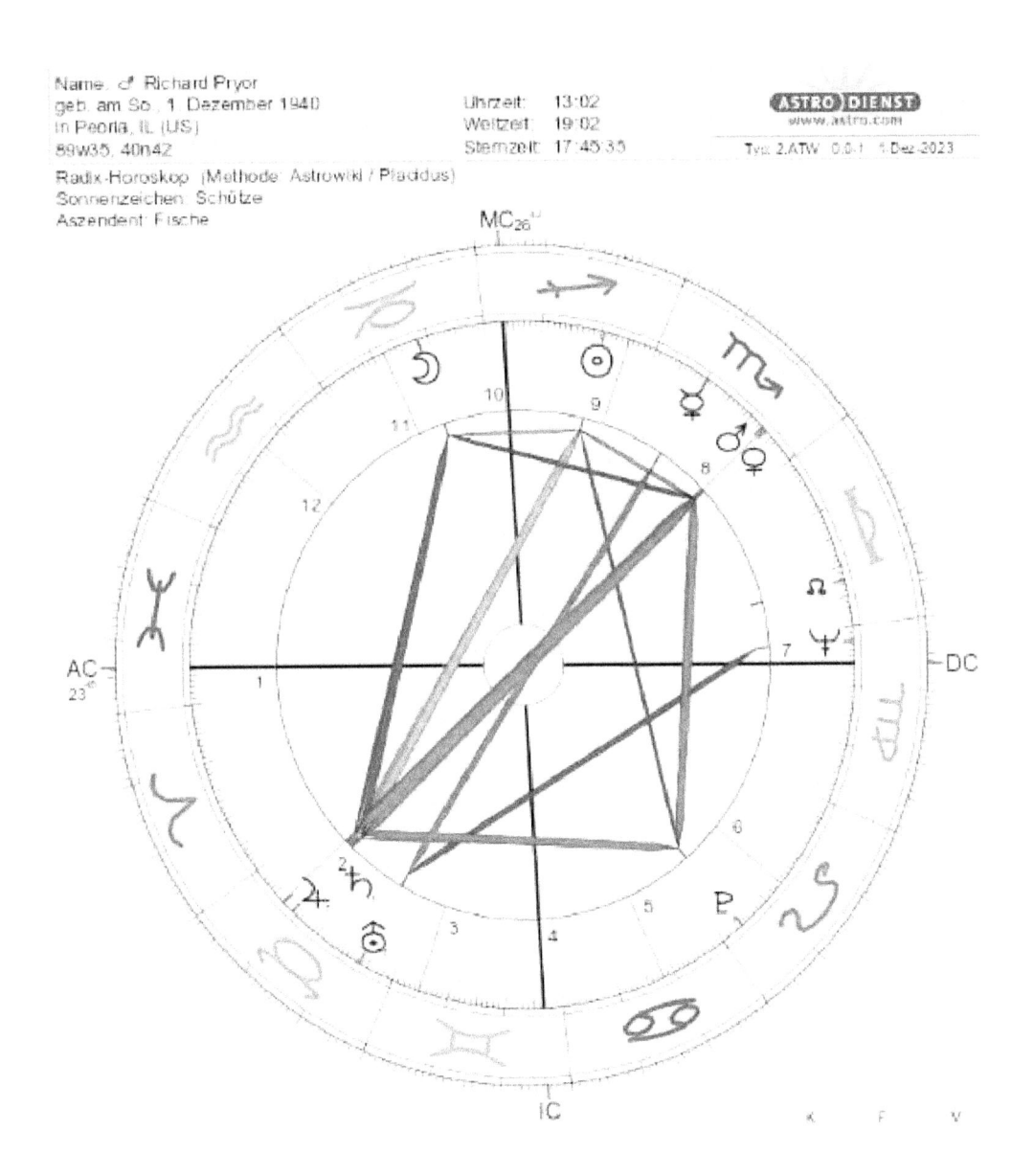

Richard pryor, a comedian, who downplayed his own race often throughout his career.

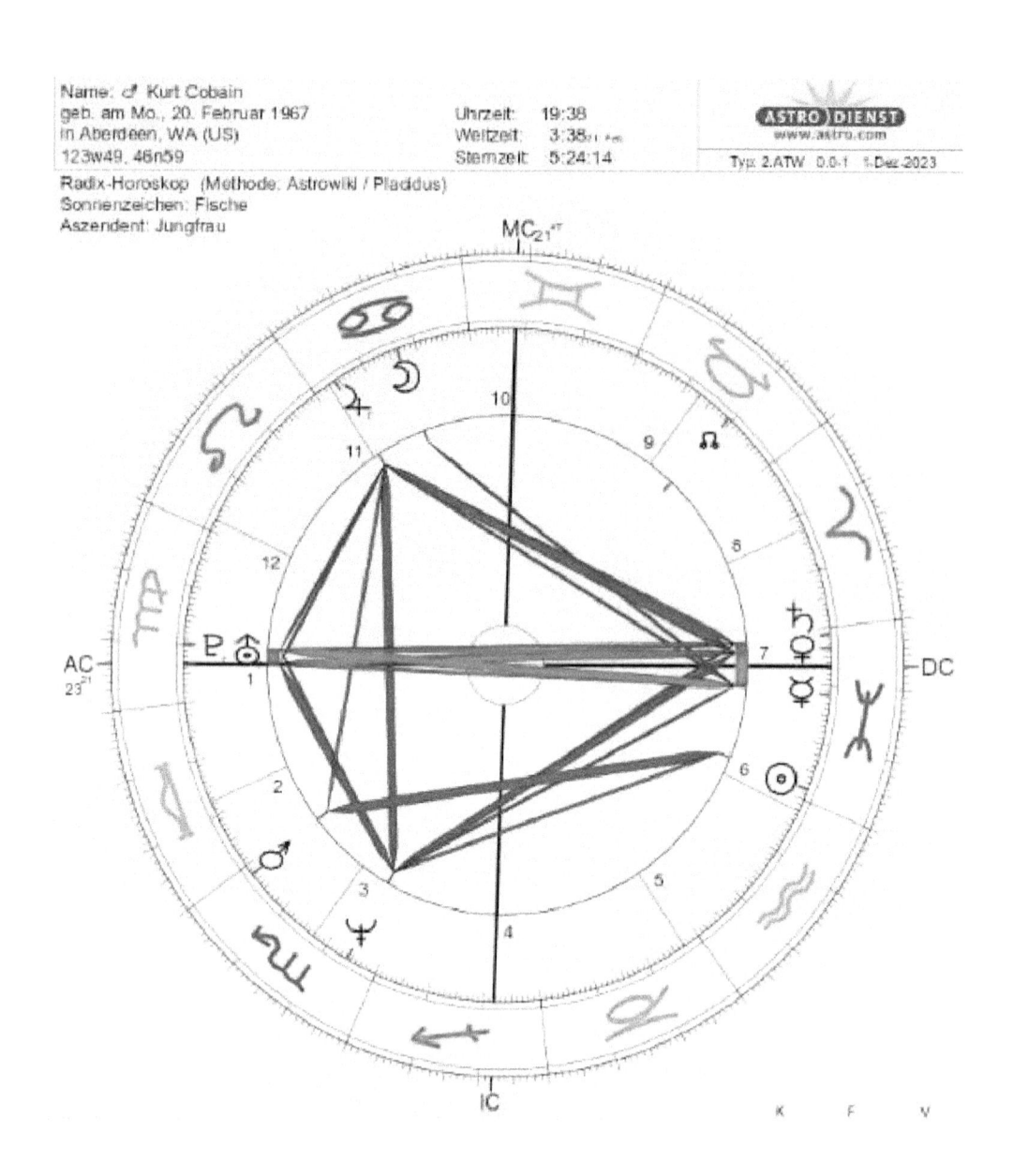

Kurt Cobain, a classic Mars-6, who rarely smiled and didn't care for appearance. Under Mars 360, Kurt Cobain would be consigned to the Mars-6 demographic.

Other swho could classify as a Mars 6 would be Martin Luther King jr, John Cusack, Will Ferrel, and Tom Brady, and Clarence Thomas

This is an example of how a new demographic created under the Mars 360 system transcends racial, cultural and even national boundaries. This one world system is explained in the book "The Mars 360 Religious and Social System"

Volume II - Evidence Justifying Faith in Mars Influence

Now with legal and economic system explained, we can look for evidence to justify our faith in Mars influence. The book "The Mars Hypothesis" by Anthony of Boston presents the idea that the Federal Reserve can set interest rates based on the movements of the planet Mars. In this book, data going back to 1896 shows that as of April 2020, percentage-wise, the Dow Jones rose 857%. When Mars was within 30 degrees of the lunar node since 1896, the Dow rose 136%. When Mars was not within 30 degrees of the lunar node, the Dow rose 721%. Mars retrograde phases during the time Mars was within 30 degrees of the lunar node was not counted in that data as Mars being within 30 degrees of the lunar node. The purpose of the book is to not only hypothesize that the Federal Reserve can set interest rates based on the movements of the planet Mars, but to also demonstrate exactly how and at the same time, formulate a system that would enable the Federal Reserve to carry out its application in real time. Using the observation of the planet Mars, the book contains a strategy for controlling inflation, interest rate setting recommendations and the predicted dates of future bear market time periods all the way thru the year 2098.

The overall hypothesis is that Mars influences human behavior in a very negative way, not just on investors, but people in general. I have been demonstrating how that same Mars/lunar node alignment also affects military conflict. Here is a look at some convincing correlations that will foster faith. Keep in mind that the ancient Romans believed that the planets were involved in the affairs of men.

Here is the chart for the October 29 stock market crash (notice where Mars is located in relation to the lunar node)

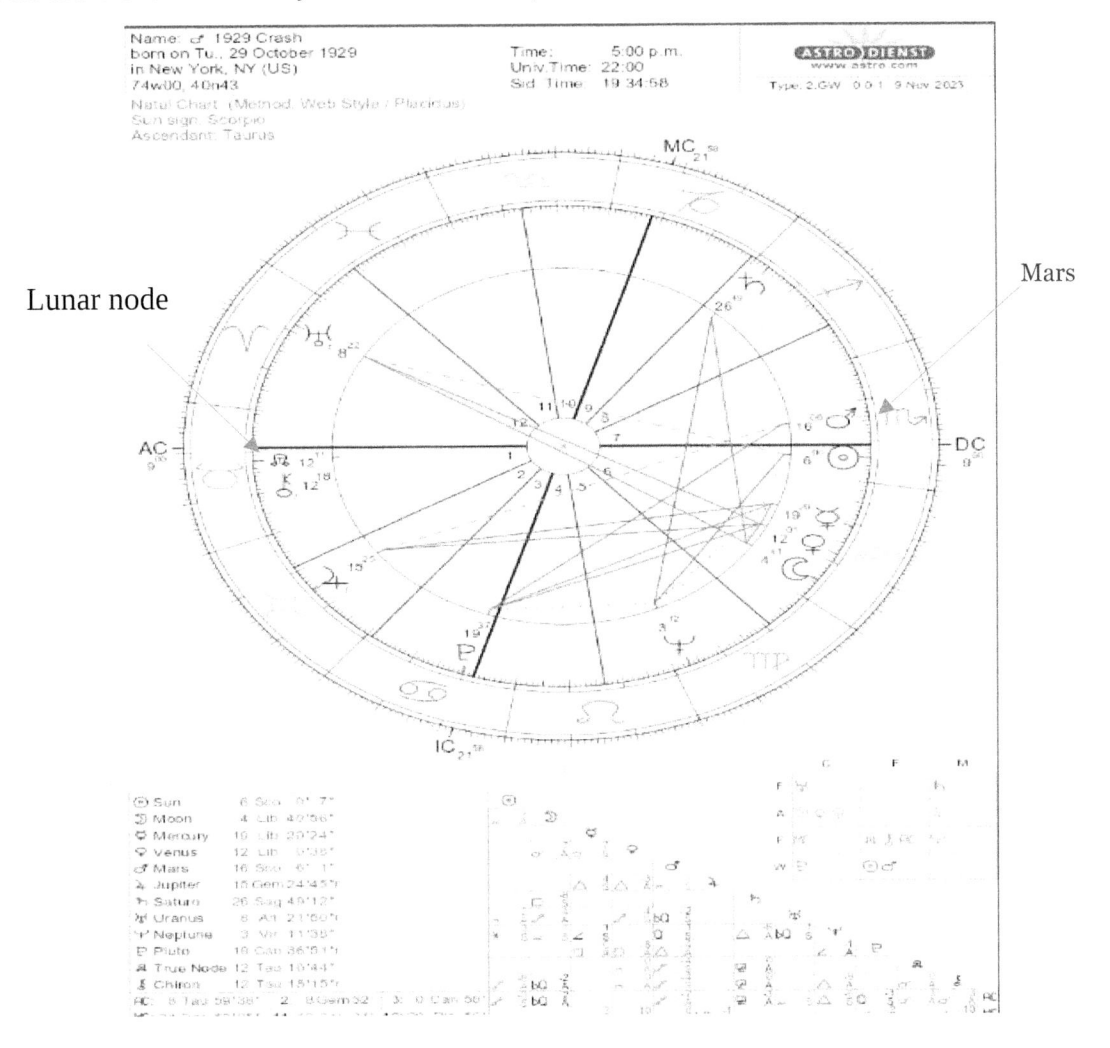

Mars is within 4 degrees of the lunar node in the chart.

Here is the chart for 9/11 (notice where Mars is located in relation to the lunar node)

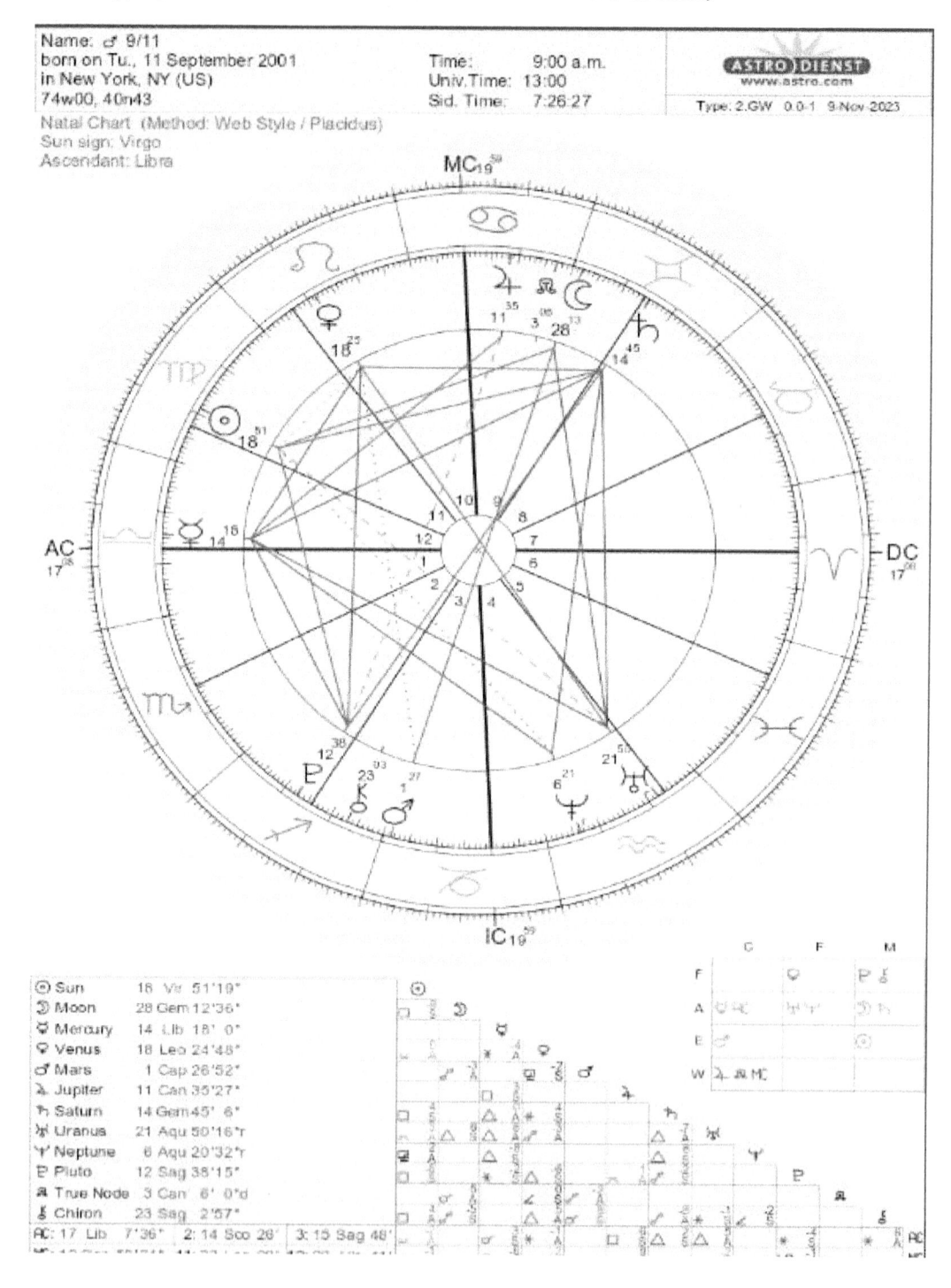

Notice in the chart for the wall stret crash in 1929 and the chart for the 9/11 terrorist atack, how Mars was within just 2 – 4 degrees of the lunar node. Both of these were earth shaking events. Other major stock market crashes such as the 1987 and the 2020 crash had the same alignment.

Here is the chart for the 1987 stock market crash. Notice Mars and the lunar node

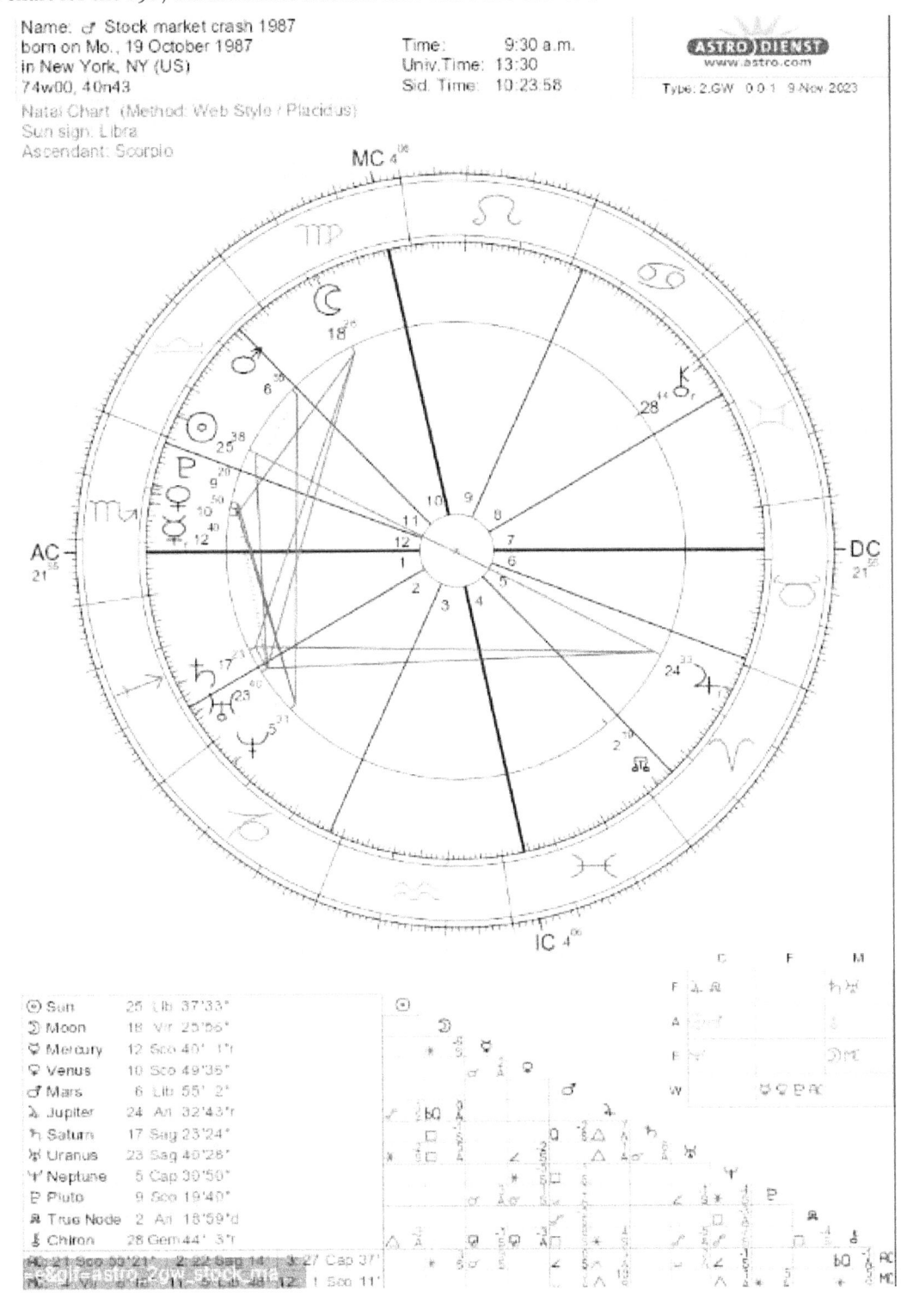

Notice how Mars is within 4 degrees of the lunar node, exactly like the October 29th 1929 crash.

Here is the chart for the 2020 Stock market crash

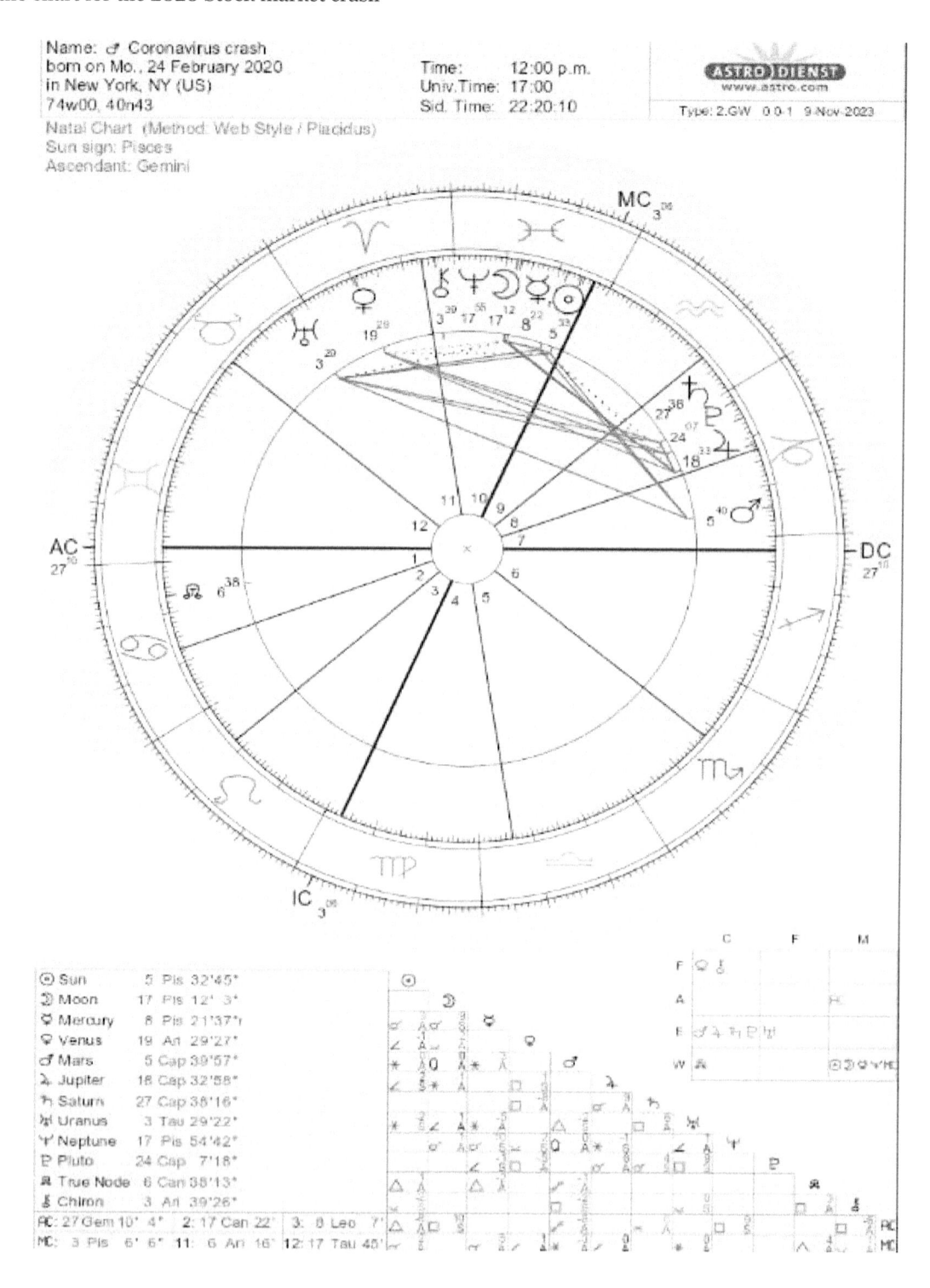

Notice how Mars is within 1 degree of the lunar node. Very close.
Now continue reading this document and see where Mars is in relation to the lunar node during Israel/Palestine rocket fire conflict escalation dates. Notice October 7th 2023

Evidence indicates that the start of escalation of rocket fire from Gaza can possibly be narowed down to the very day. Below are the exact start dates of the major esclation period during a given year. This data is taken from https://www.jewishvirtuallibrary.org/palestinian-rocket-and-mortar-attacks-against-israel

In 2023, Mars was within 30 degrees of the lunar node between August 24th and November 15th. Here is the recent escalation in 2023, which began on October 7th. The astrology chart for October 7, 2023 shows Mars at near the exact same degree of the lunar node. Just 1 degree past the lunar node.

2023

October 7-23	7,750+	In the early days of the war in Gaza started by the Hamas infiltration and attack on Israeli civilians, more than **6,000** rockets were fired from Gaza. The bombardment has continued.

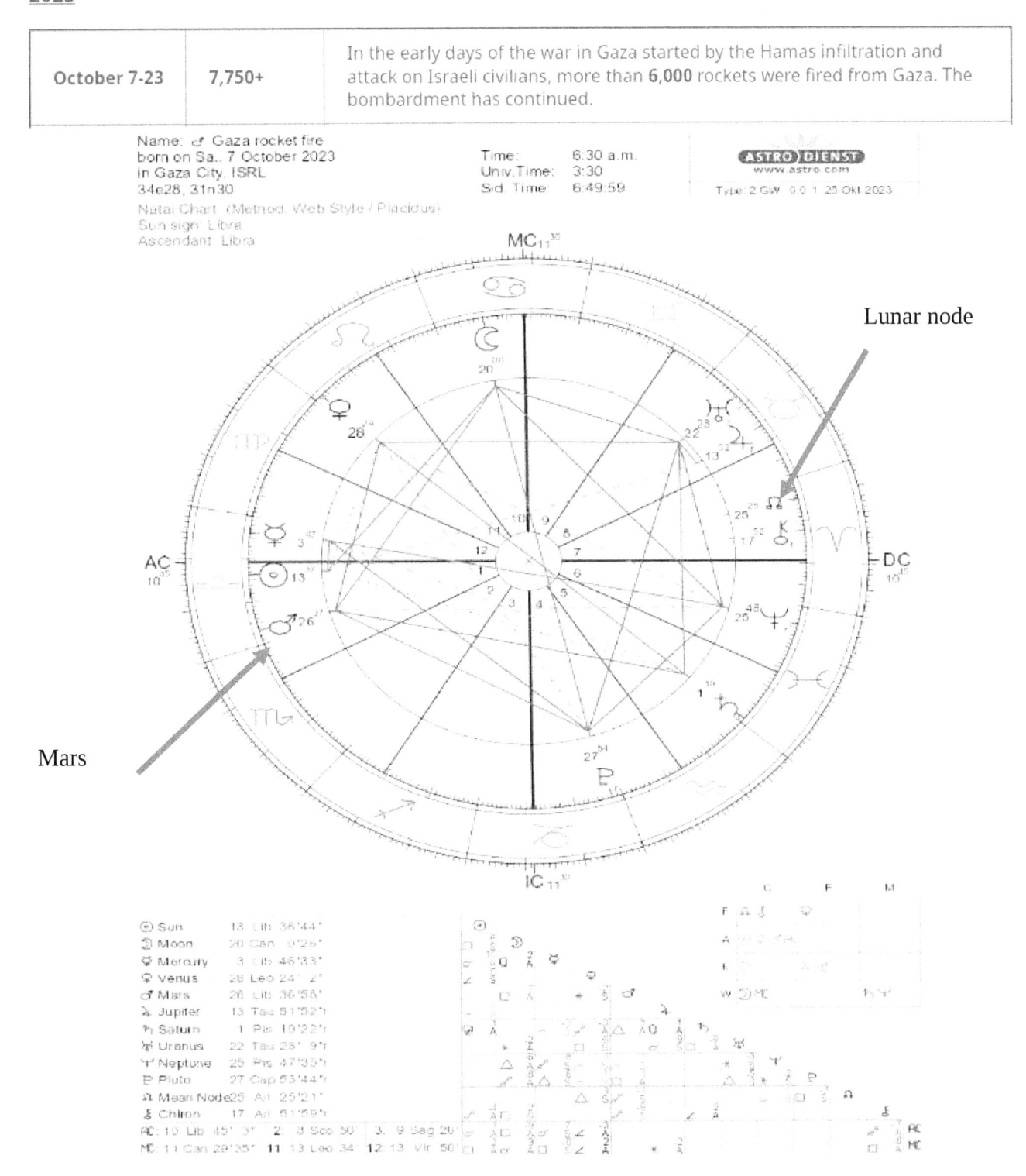

In 2022, Mars was within 30 degrees of the lunar node between June 22nd and September 19th.
Here is the escalation period in 2022, which began on August 5th, 2022. The astrology chart for August 5th, 2022 shows Mars at near the exact same degree of the lunar node. Just 2 degrees past the lunar node

2022

| August 5-8 | 1,100 Rockets | An estimated **1,100** rockets were launched from Gaza by Islamic Jihad. At least 200 malfunctioned and exploded within the Gaza Strip, and the Iron Dome intercepted 380. |

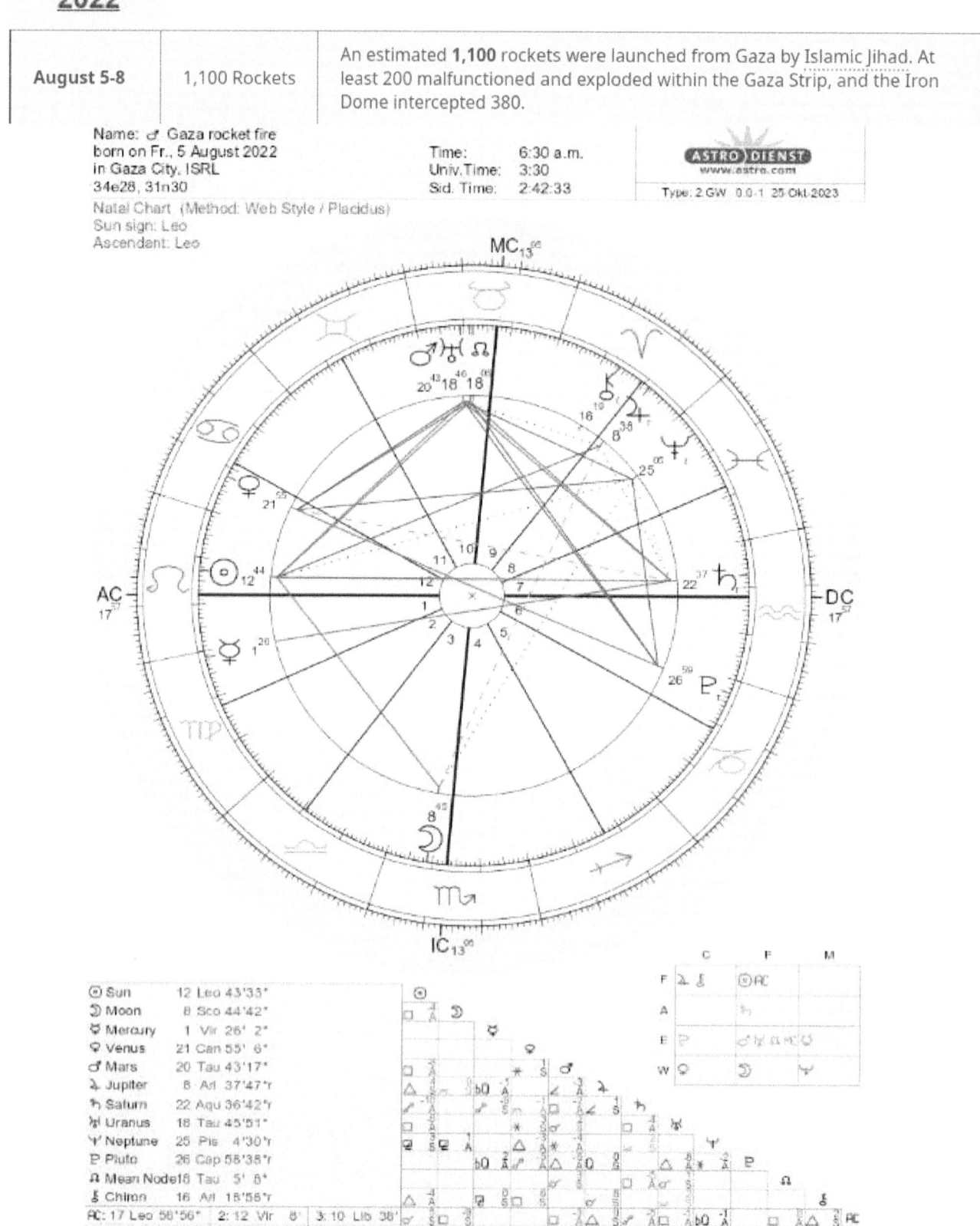

Name: ♂ Gaza rocket fire
born on Fr., 5 August 2022
in Gaza City, ISRL
34e28, 31n30
Natal Chart (Method: Web Style / Placidus)
Sun sign: Leo
Ascendent: Leo

Time: 6:30 a.m.
Univ.Time: 3:30
Sid. Time: 2:42:33

ASTRO)DIENST
www.astro.com
Type: 2.GW 0.0-1 25-Okt-2023

☉ Sun   12 Leo 43'35"
☽ Moon   8 Sco 44'42"
☿ Mercury   1 Vir 26' 2"
♀ Venus   21 Can 55' 6"
♂ Mars   20 Tau 43'17"
♃ Jupiter   8 Ari 37'47"r
♄ Saturn   22 Aqu 36'42"r
♅ Uranus   18 Tau 45'51"
♆ Neptune   25 Pis 4'30"r
♇ Pluto   26 Cap 58'38"r
☊ Mean Node 18 Tau 5' 8"
⚷ Chiron   16 Ari 16'58"r
AC: 17 Leo 56'56' 2: 12 Vir 8' 3: 10 Lib 38'

In 2021, Mars was within 30 degrees of the lunar node between February 9th and May 13th.
Here is the escalation period in 2021, which began on May 10th 2021. The astrology chart for May 10th, 2021 shows Mars 28 degrees past the lunar node, towards the end of the phase.

2021

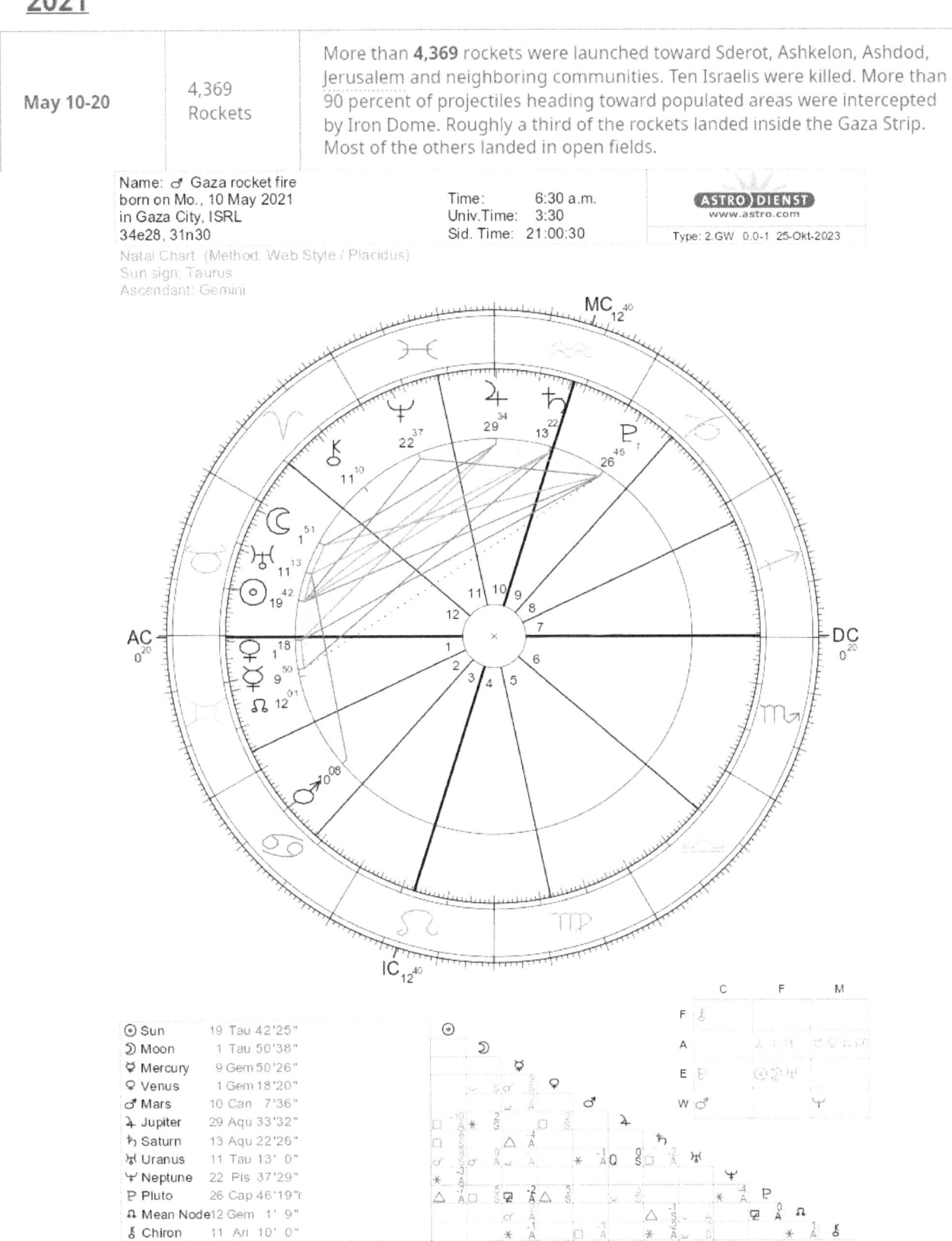

| May 10-20 | 4,369 Rockets | More than **4,369** rockets were launched toward Sderot, Ashkelon, Ashdod, Jerusalem and neighboring communities. Ten Israelis were killed. More than 90 percent of projectiles heading toward populated areas were intercepted by Iron Dome. Roughly a third of the rockets landed inside the Gaza Strip. Most of the others landed in open fields. |

Name: ♂ Gaza rocket fire
born on Mo., 10 May 2021
in Gaza City, ISRL
34e28, 31n30
Time: 6:30 a.m.
Univ.Time: 3:30
Sid. Time: 21:00:30

Natal Chart (Method: Web Style / Placidus)
Sun sign: Taurus
Ascendant: Gemini

☉ Sun   19 Tau 42'25"
☽ Moon   1 Tau 50'38"
☿ Mercury   9 Gem 50'26"
♀ Venus   1 Gem 18'20"
♂ Mars   10 Can 7'36"
♃ Jupiter   29 Aqu 33'32"
♄ Saturn   13 Aqu 22'26"
♅ Uranus   11 Tau 13' 0"
♆ Neptune   22 Pis 37'29"
♇ Pluto   26 Cap 46'19"r
☊ Mean Node 12 Gem 1' 9"
⚷ Chiron   11 Ari 10' 0"

AC: 0 Gem 20' 3"   2: 25 Gem 44'   3: 18 Can 25'
MC: 12 Aqu 39'32"   11: 12 Pis 19'   12: 19 Ari 50'

In 2020, Mars was within 30 degrees of the lunar node between January 15th and April 3rd
Here is the escalation period in 2020, which began on February 23rd, 2020. The astrology chart for February 23rd, 2020 shows Mars within 1 degree of the lunar node

2020

| Feb 23-24 | 90 Rockets | Over the course of Sunday and Monday, some **90 rockets** were fired at Israel from the Gaza Strip — most of them by the Palestinian Islamic Jihad terror group — and approximately 90 percent of those heading toward populated areas were intercepted by the Iron Dome system. |

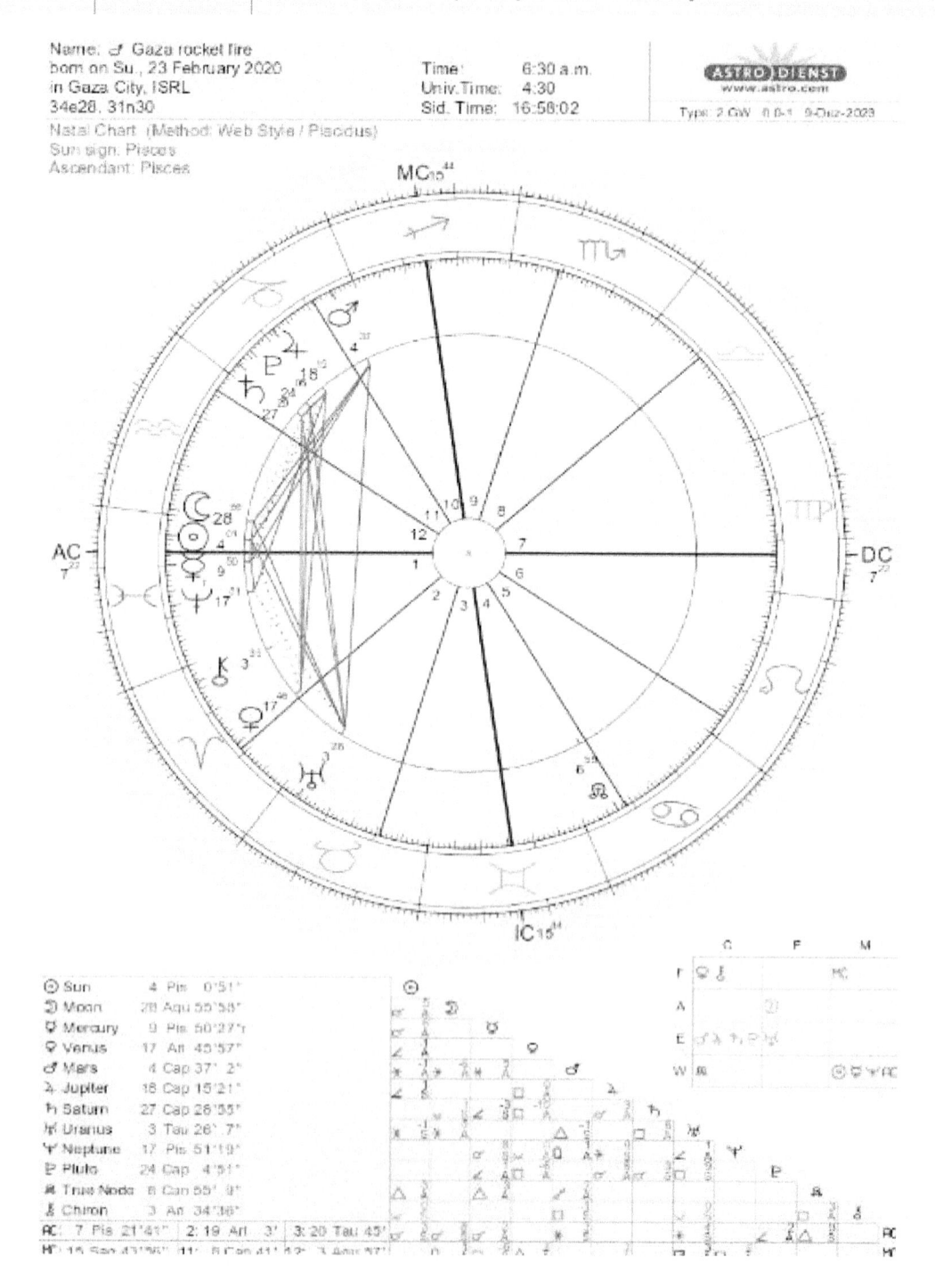

86

In 2019, Mars was within 30 degrees of the lunar node between May 1st and July 29th.
Here is the escalation period in 2019, which began on May 4th, 2019. The astrology chart for May 4th 2019 shows Mars within 30 degrees of the lunar node

2019

May 5	200 Rockets	A barrage of **200 rockets** was fired at Israel from Gaza. Two people were killed when rockets hit a factory in Ashkelon.
May 4	250 Rockets	A barrage of **250 rockets** was fired at Israel from Gaza, killing an Israeli man in Ashkelon.

Name: ♂ Gaza rocket fire
born on Sa., 4 May 2019
in Gaza City, ISRL
34e28, 31n30

Time: 6:30 a.m.
Univ.Time: 3:30
Sid. Time: 20:34:48

ASTRO DIENST
www.astro.com
Type: 2.GW 0.0-1 25-Okt-2023

Natal Chart (Method: Web Style / Placidus)
Sun sign: Taurus
Ascendant: Taurus

☉ Sun   13 Tau 24' 9"
☽ Moon   3 Tau 49'45"
☿ Mercury   25 Ari 17' 5"
♀ Venus   16 Ari 19'46"
♂ Mars   22 Gem 13'50"
♃ Jupiter   23 Sag 30'31" r
♄ Saturn   20 Cap 30'18" r
♅ Uranus   3 Tau 10' 4"
♆ Neptune   18 Pis 6'12"
♇ Pluto   23 Cap 7'49" r
☊ Mean Node   21 Can 2'46"
⚷ Chiron   4 Ari 12' 3"
AC: 22 Tau 55'58"   2: 19 Gem 41'   3: 12 Can 36'
MC: 6 Aqu 19' 9" 11: 4 Pis 51' 12: 11 Ari 29'

87

In 2018, Mars was within 30 degrees of the lunar node between April 8th and November 14th.
Here is the escalation period in 2018, which began on July 14, 2018. The astrology chart for July 14th 2018 shows Mars within 1 degree of the lunar node

2018

July 14	174 Rockets/Mortars	A barrage of **174 rockets and mortars** was fired from Gaza toward Israel on July 14, 2018. The Israeli Iron Dome Missile Defense system only intercepted forty of the projectiles. Three Israelis were wounded after a rocket struck their house in Sderot. The Israelis carried out airstrikes on over forty Hamas military installations in retaliation.

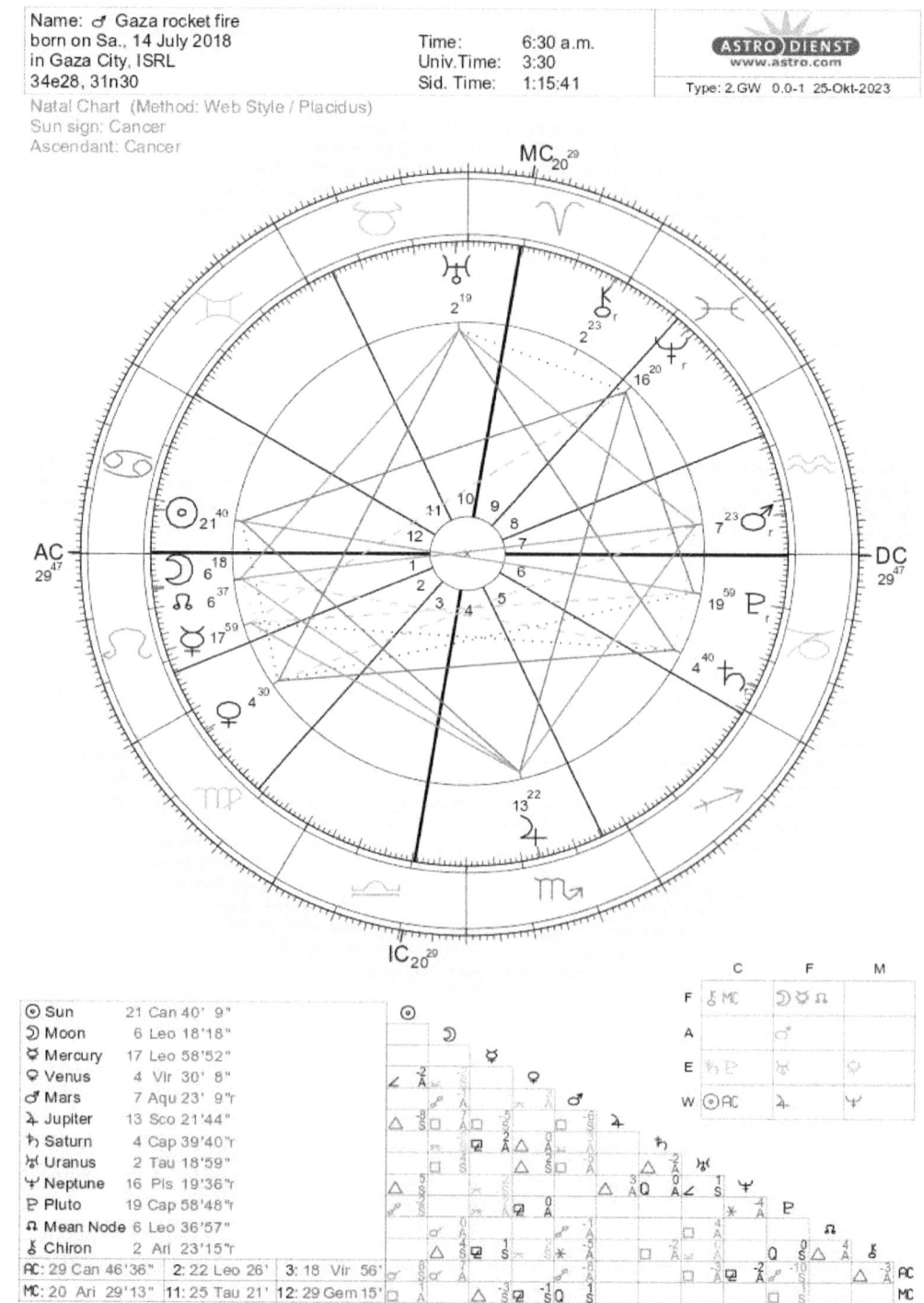

Name: ♂ Gaza rocket fire
born on Sa., 14 July 2018
in Gaza City, ISRL
34e28, 31n30
Time: 6:30 a.m.
Univ.Time: 3:30
Sid. Time: 1:15:41

ASTRO DIENST
www.astro.com
Type: 2.GW 0.0-1 25-Okt-2023

Natal Chart (Method: Web Style / Placidus)
Sun sign: Cancer
Ascendant: Cancer

☉ Sun   21 Can 40' 9"
☽ Moon   6 Leo 18'18"
☿ Mercury   17 Leo 58'52"
♀ Venus   4 Vir 30' 8"
♂ Mars   7 Aqu 23' 9"r
♃ Jupiter   13 Sco 21'44"
♄ Saturn   4 Cap 39'40"r
♅ Uranus   2 Tau 18'59"
♆ Neptune   16 Pis 19'36"r
♇ Pluto   19 Cap 58'48"r
☊ Mean Node 6 Leo 36'57"
⚷ Chiron   2 Ari 23'15"r
AC: 29 Can 46'36" 2: 22 Leo 26' 3: 18 Vir 56'
MC: 20 Ari 29'13" 11: 25 Tau 21' 12: 29 Gem 15'

88

In 2014, Mars was within 30 degrees of the lunar node between December 19th 2013 and August 28, 2014. Here is the escalation period in 2014, which began on July 16, 2014. The astrology chart for July 16h 2014 shows Mars within 1 degree of the lunar node

2014

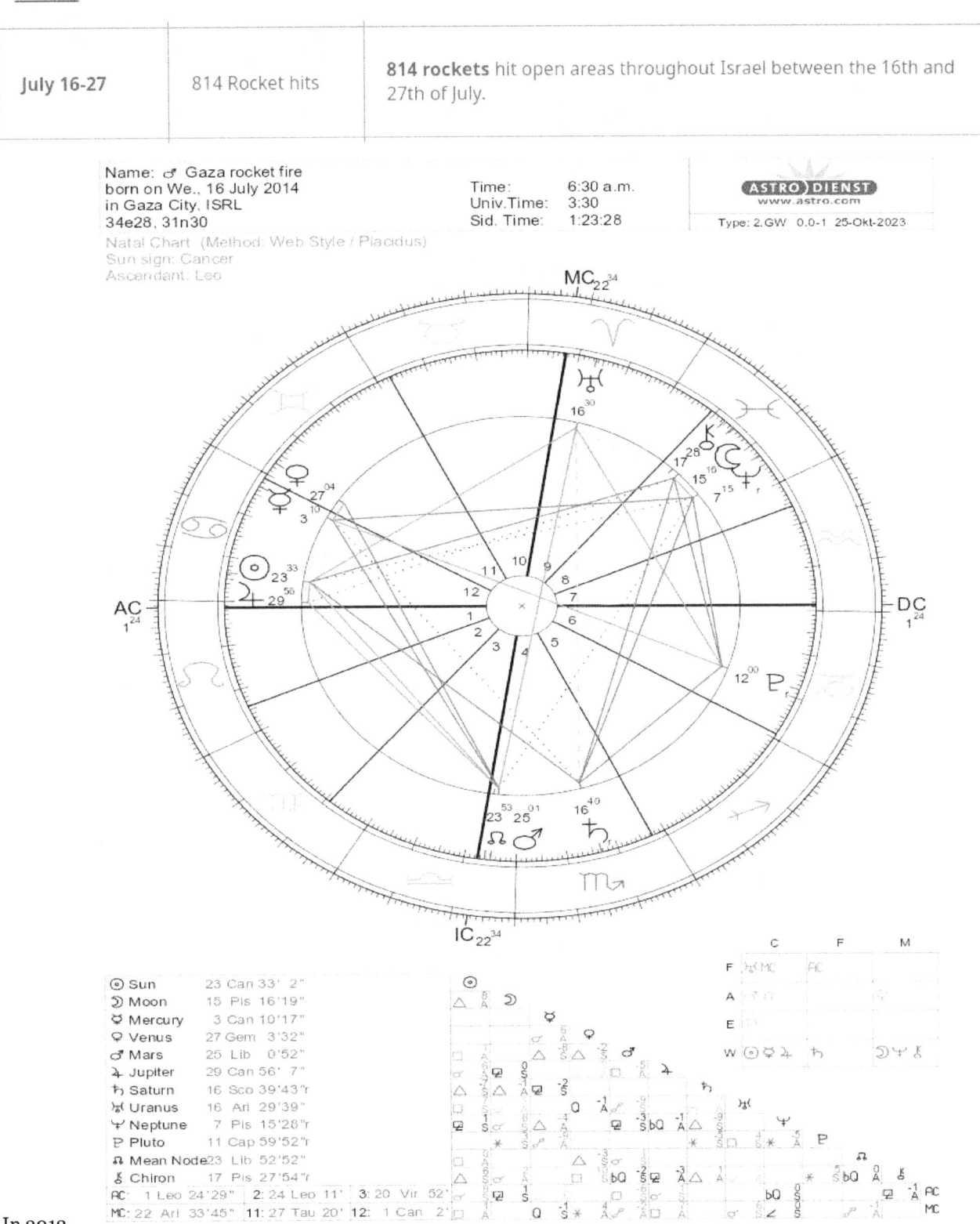

| July 16-27 | 814 Rocket hits | **814 rockets** hit open areas throughout Israel between the 16th and 27th of July. |

Name: ♂ Gaza rocket fire
born on We., 16 July 2014
in Gaza City, ISRL
34e28, 31n30
Natal Chart (Method: Web Style / Placidus)
Sun sign: Cancer
Ascendant: Leo

Time: 6:30 a.m.
Univ.Time: 3:30
Sid. Time: 1:23:28

ASTRO)DIENST
www.astro.com
Type: 2.GW 0.0-1 25-Okt-2023

☉ Sun	23 Can 33' 2"
☽ Moon	15 Pis 16'19"
☿ Mercury	3 Can 10'17"
♀ Venus	27 Gem 3'32"
♂ Mars	25 Lib 0'52"
♃ Jupiter	29 Can 56' 7"
♄ Saturn	16 Sco 39'43"r
♅ Uranus	16 Ari 29'39"
♆ Neptune	7 Pis 15'28"r
♇ Pluto	11 Cap 59'52"r
☊ Mean Node	23 Lib 52'52"
⚷ Chiron	17 Pis 27'54"r
AC: 1 Leo 24'29"	2: 24 Leo 11'	3: 20 Vir 52'
MC: 22 Ari 33'45"	11: 27 Tau 20'	12: 1 Can 2'

In 2012,
Mars was within 30 degrees of the lunar node between August 24th and November 12th.

Here is the escalation period in 2012, which began on November 10, 2012. The astrology chart for November 10, 2012 shows Mars 30 degrees of the lunar node near the end of the phase

2012

November 14-21	933 rockets	**Operation Pillar of Defense:** On the morning of November 15, **three Israeli civilians were killed** when a rocket directly struck their apartment building in the city of Kiryat Malachi. **Three children, among them two young babies, were also wounded** in the strike. **Three IDF soldiers were wounded** in a separate attack when mortar shells exploded inside their base near the Gaza border. On November 16, a rocket fired from Gaza landed outside Jerusalem. On November 20, an **IDF soldier-Cpl. Yosef Fartuk-and a civilian- Alayaan Salem al-Nabari -were killed** when a mortar fired from Gaza exploded in the Eshkol regional council. **Five IDF soldiers were wounded** when a rocket landed inside their holding area on the Gaza border. Also on November 20, a GRAD rocket scored a direct hit on a residential apartment building in the city of Rishon L'Tzion, **wounding one person moderately and sending nearly ten others to the hospital with shock.** In total, terrorists in Gaza fired more than 1,500 rockets at Israel during this period-933 struck inside Israel, 421 were intercepted by the Iron Dome Missile Shield, and 152 rockets landed inside the Gaza Strip.
November 10-13	One hundred twenty-one (121) rocket hits	In distinct escalation, Palestinian terrorists in Gaza launched more than 150 rockets at Israel; at least 121 rocket hits were identified in Israeli territory. A total of 64 rockets hits were identified on November 11. A number of mortar shells were also fired. A number of Israeli civilians were wounded by the rocket fire, although not seriously; several were treated for shock and there was extensive property damage.

Name: ♂ Gaza rocket fire
born on Sa., 10 November 2012
in Gaza City, ISRL
34e28, 31n30

Time: 6:30 a.m.
Univ.Time: 4:30
Sid. Time: 10:06:50

Type: 2.GW 0.0-1 25-Okt-2023

Natal Chart (Method: Web Style / Placidus)
Sun sign: Scorpio
Ascendant: Scorpio

☉ Sun	18 Sco 11' 1"
☽ Moon	27 Vir 1'34"
☿ Mercury	3 Sag 29'48"r
♀ Venus	15 Lib 23'38"
♂ Mars	24 Sag 47'53"
♃ Jupiter	14 Gem 13'21"r
♄ Saturn	4 Sco 14'27"
♅ Uranus	5 Ari 4' 5"r
♆ Neptune	0 Pis 21'32"r
♇ Pluto	7 Cap 39'28"
☊ Mean Node	26 Sco 20'27"
⚷ Chiron	4 Pis 59'26"r
AC: 22 Sco 22'50"	2: 22 Sag 14'	3: 25 Cap 12'
MC: 29 Leo 36' 6"	11: 1 Lib 43'	12: 29 Lib 8'

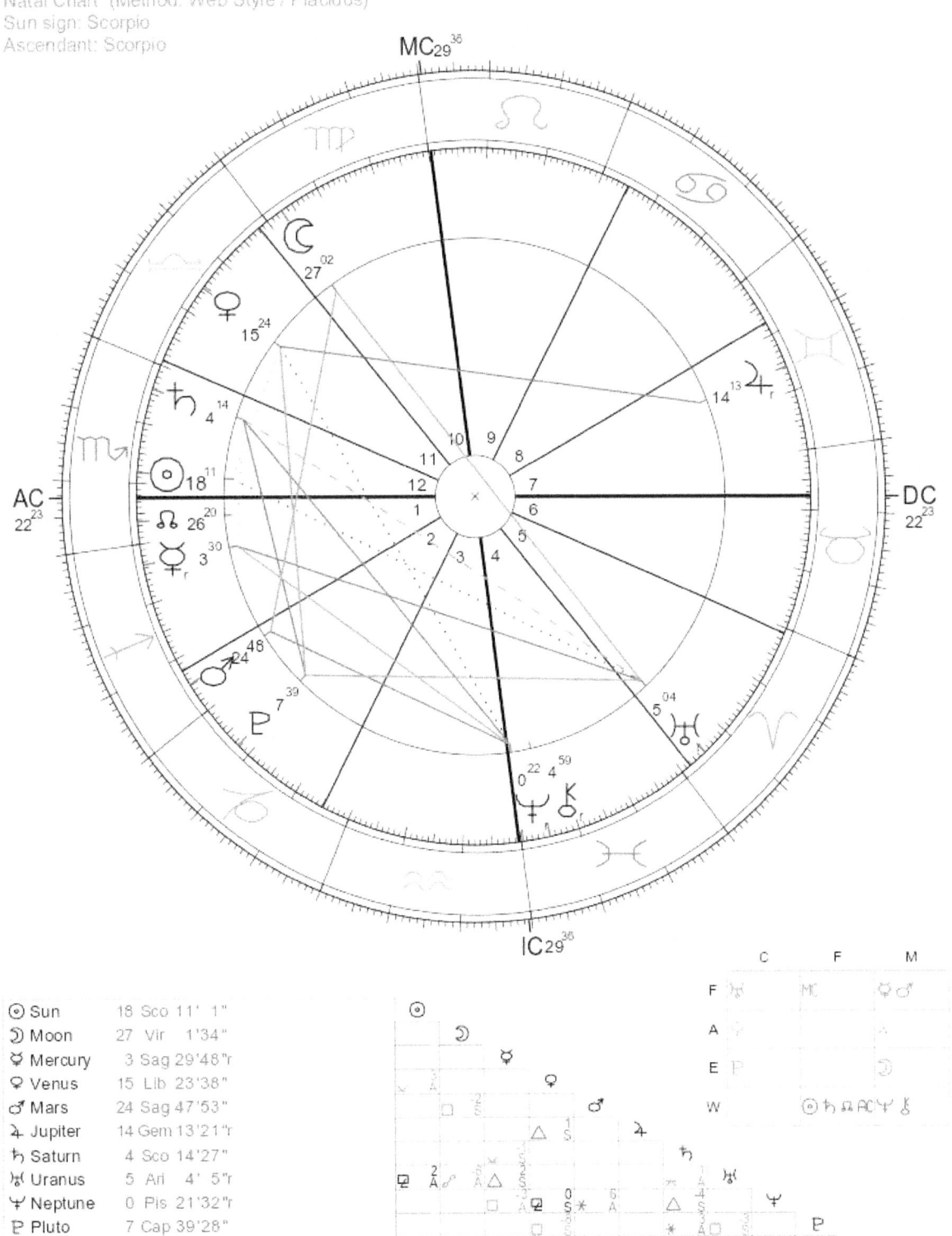

The key extrapolation we can take away from the most significant escalation periods over the past 10 years in Israel is that Gaza militants tend to launch attacks either at the exact beginning, the exact middle, or the exact end of the Mars-within-30-degrees-of-the-lunar-node phase. In these examples, the highest escalation of rocket fire for the years 2014, 2018, 2020, 2022, and 2023 all commenced when Mars was in the exact middle of the Mars-within-30-degrees-of-the-lunar-node phase, give or take 1 or 2 degrees. In the years 2012 and 2021, the highest escalation for the year commenced at the very end of the Mars-within-30-degrees-of-the-lunar-node phase, give or take 1 or 2 degrees. In 2019, the highest escalation for the year commenced at the very beginning of the Mars-within-30-degrees-of-the-lunar-node phase.

These three books can further induce faith in Mars influence and thus confer value to the Mars Redback currency system

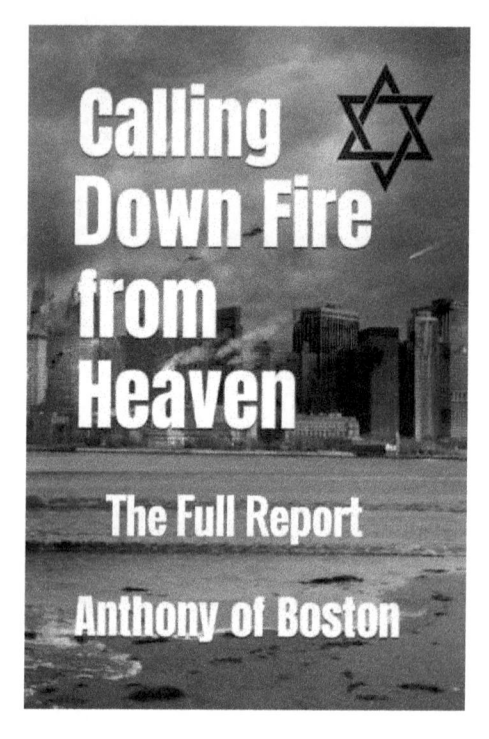

Volume III - Confirming Faith in Mars Influence

Now that we have our legal and economic system, as well as evidence justifying our faith in Mars influence. Let see how a real-time demonstration of prophecy will confirm the Mars 360 religion and a revival of the Roman empire and Mars

Here is the framework by which I have been able to accurately predict escalation of rocket fire from Gaza into Israel since 2019. There is a pattern in which the time frame of Mars's position within 30 degrees of the lunar node correlates with the highest concentration of rocket fire from Gaza into Israel in relation to the rest of the year. This has been demonstrated historically and in real time. The data is integral to inducing the faith needed to foster a religious, social, and economic system. After reading the data and demonstration, the reader should be able to contemplate the existence of another prominent force in the world and how such a force can be used to aid mankind. Following the demonstration, instructions on how to make use of this Mars force is laid out. Here are the charts of all the rocket attacks against Israel since 2007. Notice the times when there has been a spike in rocket fire relative to the year it happened. These statistics are taken from wikipedia

https://en.wikipedia.org/wiki/Palestinian_rocket_attacks_on_Israel.

Figure H - Gaza Rocket attacks on Israel

* = Largest amount of Rocket fire for the year

	2007	2008	2009	2010	2011	2012
Jan	28	241	566*	13	17	9
Feb	43	257	52	5	6	36
Mar	31	196	34	35*	38	173
Apr	25	145	5	5	87	10
May	257*	149	1	14	1	3
Jun	63	87	2	14	4	83
Jul	61	4	1	13	20	18
Aug	81	8	1	14	145*	21
Sept	70	1	~10	16	8	17
Oct	53	1	1	3	52	116
Nov	65	125	4	5	11	1734*
Dec	113	361*	4	15	30	1

Rocket attacks for 2013 – 2019 continued on the next page

cont'd
Figure H - Gaza Rocket attacks on Israel
* = Largest amount of Rocket fire for the year

	2013	2014	2015	2016	2017	2018	2019
Jan	0	22	0	6*	0	6	0
Feb	1	9	0	0	7	4	0
Mar	4	65	0	5	2	0	3
Apr	17*	19	1	0	1	0	0
May	1	4	1	2	1	70	600*
Jun	5	62	3	0	1	64	3
Jul	5	2,874*	1	2	2	174*	0
Aug	4	950	3	1	1	8	0
Sept	8	0	4	0	0	0	1
Oct	3	1	5*	0	1	0	0
Nov	0	0	3	0	0	17	455
Dec	4	1	4	0	28	0	4

Note: in 2019, the heaviest rocket fire from Gaza took place in May. 600 rockets were fired from Gaza on Israel

If we observe the number of rocket attacks from Gaza starting back around 2007 in "Figure H", you'll notice an asterisk next to some of the numbers. This indicates the month where the largest barrage of rocket attacks from Gaza were concentrated that year. We will reference "Figure H" when we pull up the astrocharts to see how the location of Mars correlates. In my research of how the position of the Planet Mars correlates to rocket attacks from Gaza, I found that Mars's location near the lunar node on both sides of the chart shows up around the time of escalating rocket fire. Here is what I mean:

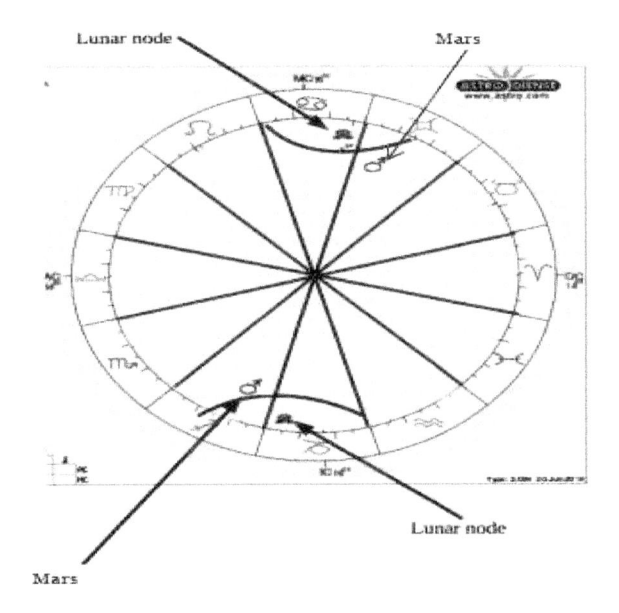

Mars is falling somewhere within a 30 degree vicinity of the lunar nodes on either side of the astrochart during the time to rocket fire escalation from Gaza. If we go back to "Figure H" and look at the rocket attacks for 2007, we can see that most

of the rocket fire for that year took place in May. There were 257 rockets fired from Gaza during that month. If we look at the astrochart for May 2007, we can see that Mars is close to the lunar node.

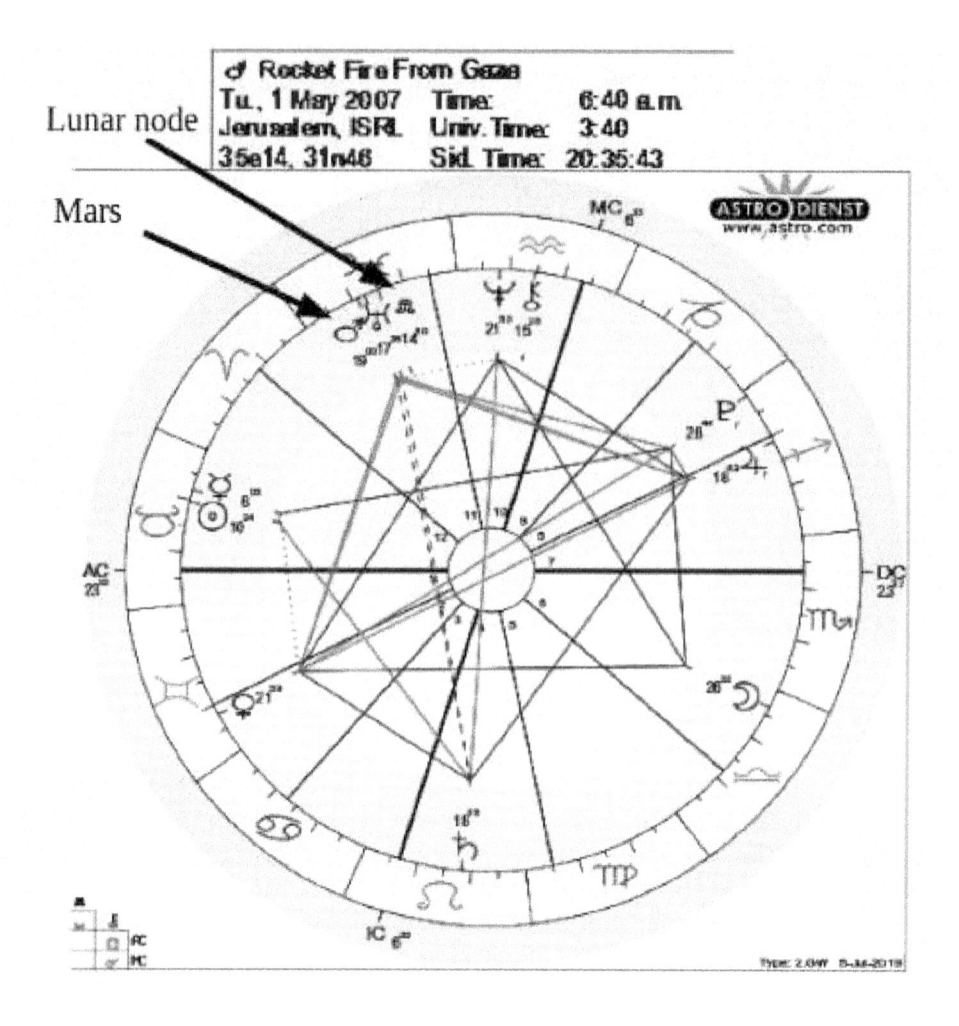

We can see Mars within close range of the lunar node in this Chart calculated for May 2007. If we go back to "Figure H" and look at late 2008/early 2009 when the Gaza War(also knows as Operation Cast Lead) took place, we'll find that once again Mars is in the vicinity of the lunar node. It gets to within 30 degrees of it in early January. See next page

♂ Rocket Fire From Gaza
Th., 8 January 2009   Time: 12:40 p.m.
Jerusalem, ISRL   Univ. Time: 10:40
35e14, 31n46   Sid. Time: 20:13:24

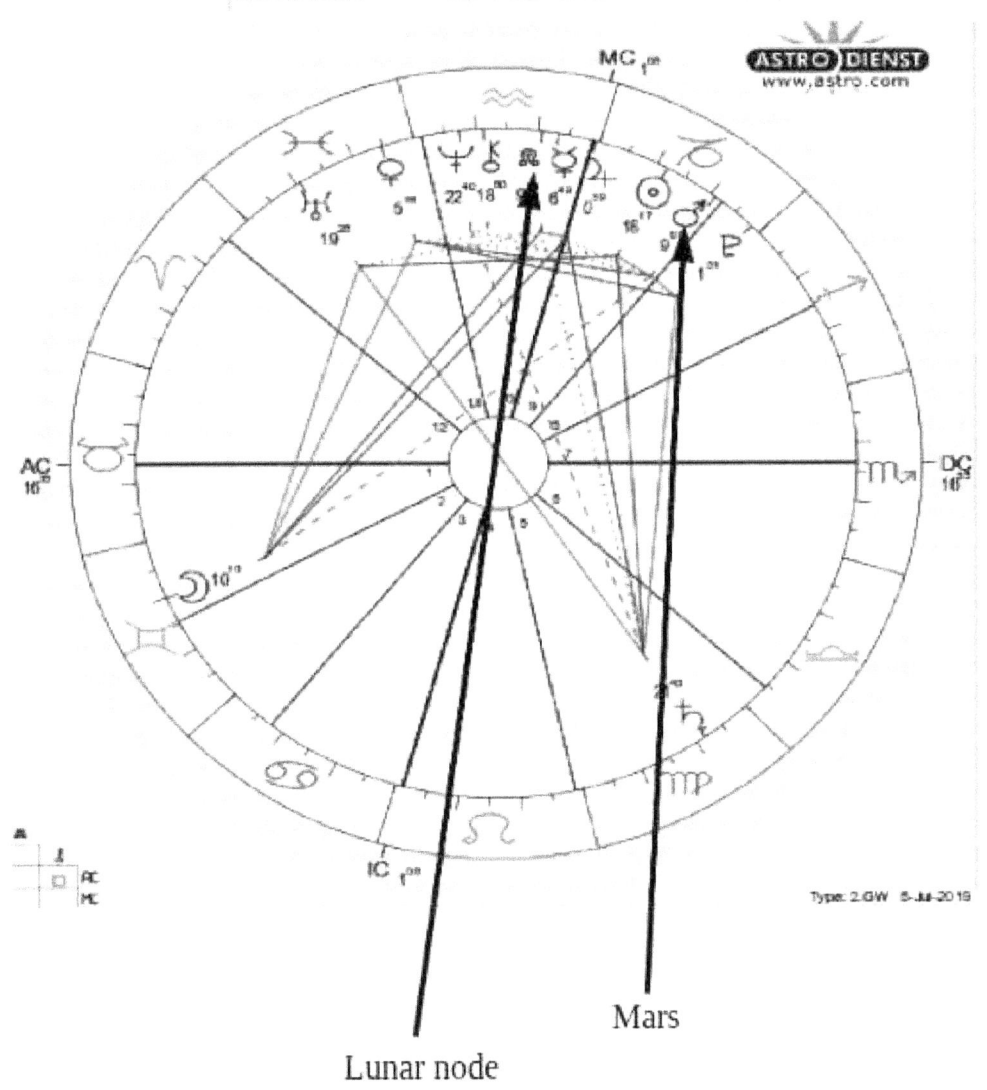

Lunar node   Mars

Here, on January 8th, 2009, Mars gets within 30 degrees of the lunar node. We can see in Figure H that the rocket fire doesn't really settle down until March 2009. Between January 8th and January 17th, Gaza militants fired over 100 rockets into Israel. Mars finished within 30 degrees of the lunar node on March 24, 2009. This would align with Mars producing an effect while being near the lunar node during that timeframe. If we go back to Figure H and look at the year 2010, we notice that the highest concentration of rocket fire took place during the month of March. During that time, 35 rocket attacks took place. Here is the astrochart for March 2010.

♂ Rocket Fire From Gaza
Mo., 1 March 2010   Time: 12:40 p.m.
Jerusalem, ISRL   Univ.Time: 10:40
35e14, 31n46   Sid. Time: 23:37:28

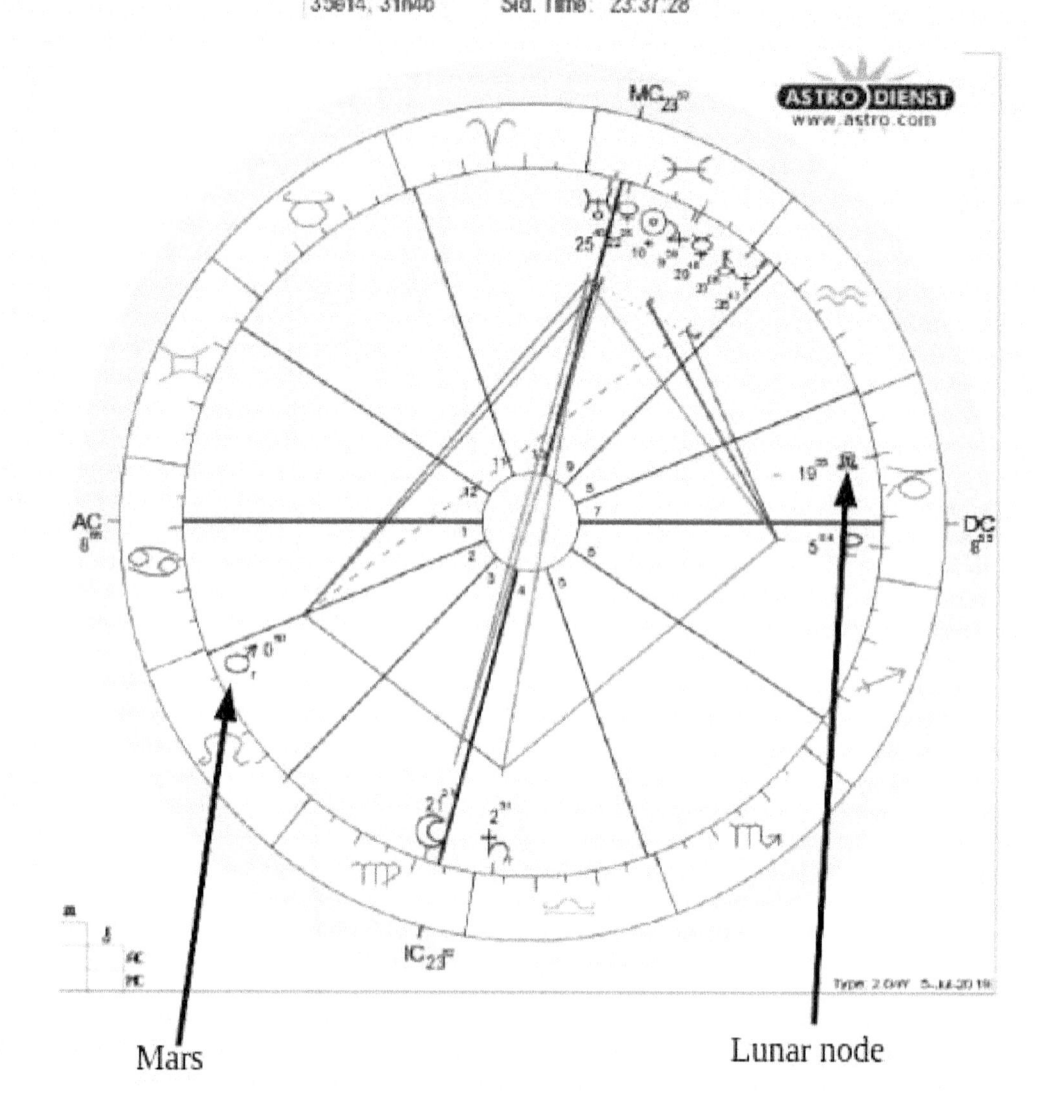

Mars   Lunar node

Once again, same thing, but this time Mars in on the opposite side of the lunar node, but within 30 degrees. This still aligns with Mars on either side(near conjunction or near opposition) of the lunar node being a factor in rocket attacks from Gaza. If we go back to Figure H and look at the year 2011, we find that most of the rocket attacks that year took place in August. There were 145 rockets fired from Gaza into Israel territory. Lets look at the astrochart for August of 2011 and see if Mars falls within 30 degrees of the lunar node.

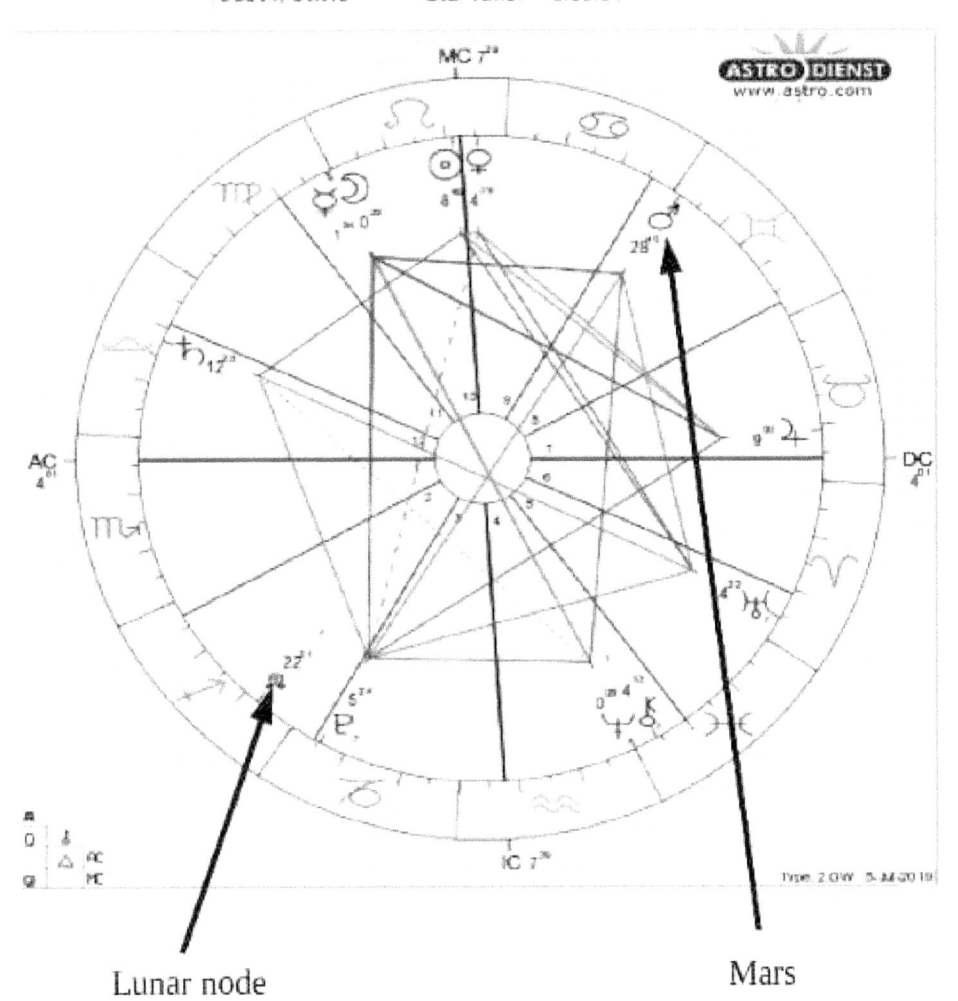

Once again Mars falls within 30 degrees of the lunar node during a month where the highest level of rocket fire for the year was concentrated. If we go back to Figure H and look at the next year, which would be 2012, we find that the highest level of rocket fire took place in the month of November, in which there was 1734 rockets fired from Gaza into Israel. That's a significant spike in rocket fire. If we pull up the astrochart for November of 2012(see next page), we can see Mars is once again within a 30 degree vicinity of the lunar node.

♂ Rocket Fire From Gaza
Th., 1 November 2012 Time: 12:40 p.m.
Jerusalem, ISRL Univ.Time: 10:40
35e14, 31n46 Sid. Time: 15:45:26

Mars Lunar node

Mars is clearly within 30 degrees of the lunar node during a significant rise in rocket attacks against Israel in November of 2012. If we go back to Figure H and look at 2013, we find that the highest concentration of rocket fire from Gaza that year took place in April, which is also the month that the Boston Marathon Bombing took place in the US. In April, there were 17 rockets fired from Gaza.

Here is the astrochart for April 2013.(next page)

![Astrological chart for Rocket Fire from Gaza, Th., 4 April 2013, 12:00 p.m., Jerusalem, ISRL, with arrows pointing to Mars and Lunar node]

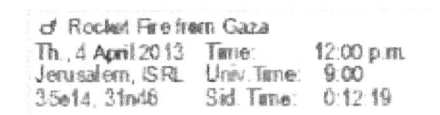

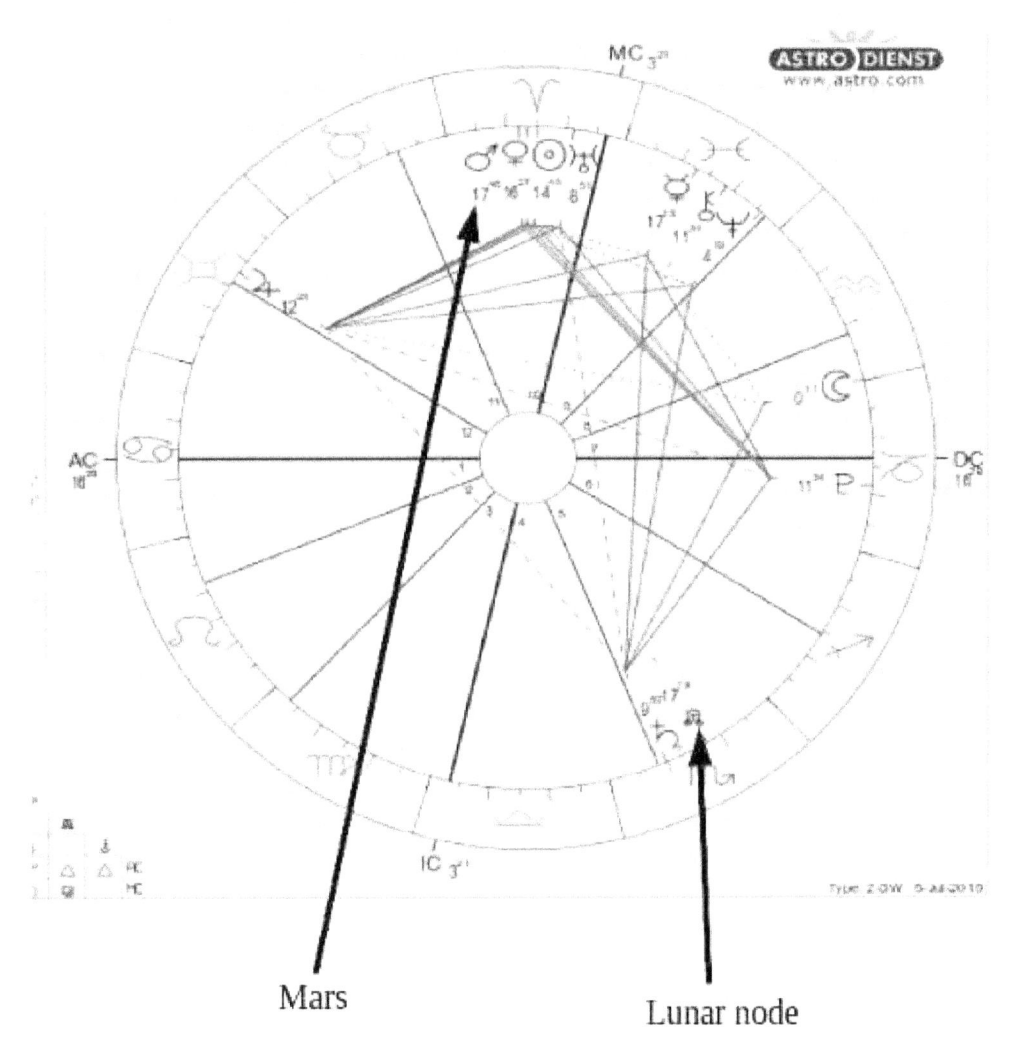

Mars Lunar node

Once again Mars makes it to within 30 degrees of the lunar node, on the exact opposite side. As stated before the both sides of the chart are the same. Now in going back to Figure H, we can have a look at 2014 and see which month had the highest concentration of rocket fire that year.

We can see in 2014, the month of July had an extreme spike in rocket fire with 2874 rockets being fired from Gaza into Israel. Here is the chart for July 2014 on the next page:

♂ Rocket Fire from Gaza
Tu., 1 July 2014   Time: 12:00 p.m.
Jerusalem, ISRL   Univ. Time: 9:00
35e14, 31n46   Sid. Time: 5:58:18

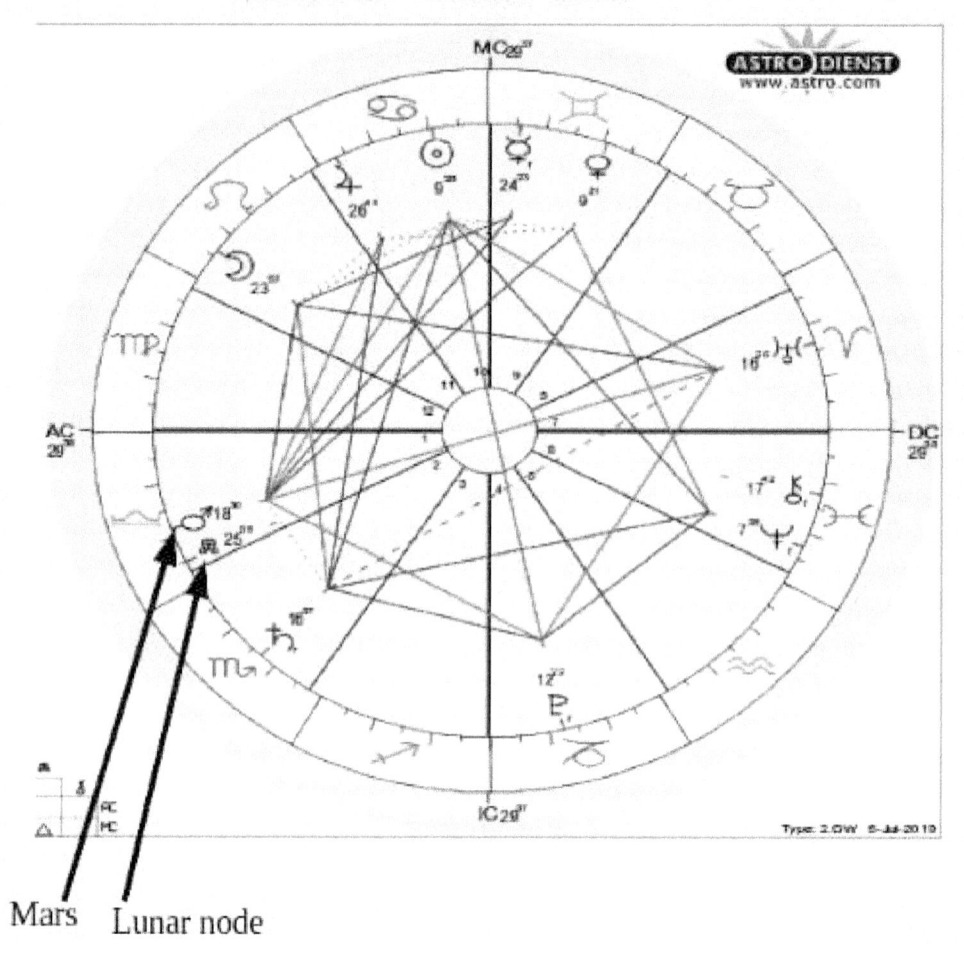

Mars   Lunar node

Once again, Mars is within 30 degrees of the lunar node, this time on the same side. Lets go back to Figure H and look at 2015 to see which month had the highest concentration of rocket fire from Gaza. 2015 doesn't seem to have much activity in terms of rocket attacks from Gaza. However, if we go ahead and observe anyway, we find that October turns out to be the month where the highest level of rocket attacks took place for 2015. Here is the chart for October 2015:

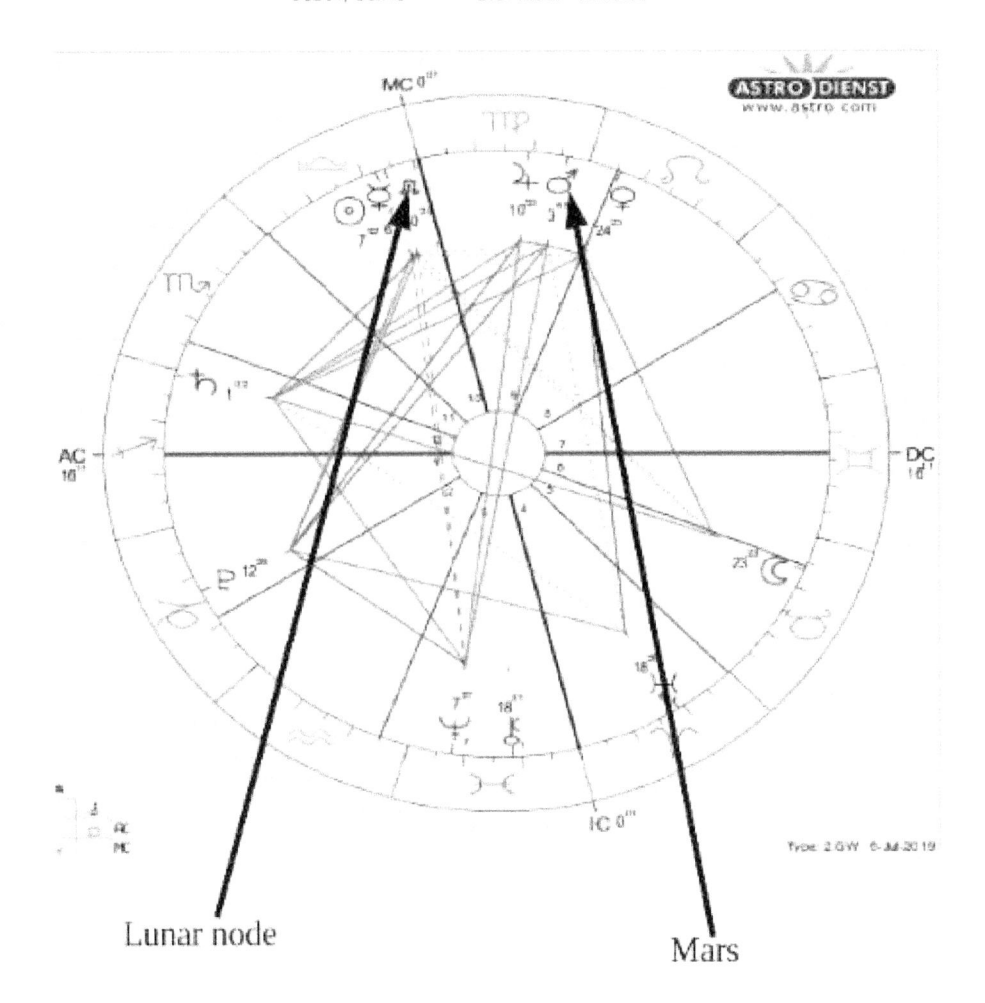

There it is again. Mars in within 30 degrees of the lunar node during a month of rocket fire escalation from Gaza. If we go back to Figure H to see which month had the highest concentration of rocket fire from Gaza in 2016, we find January to be the month where most of the activity took place. See the chart on the next page

Lunar node   Mars

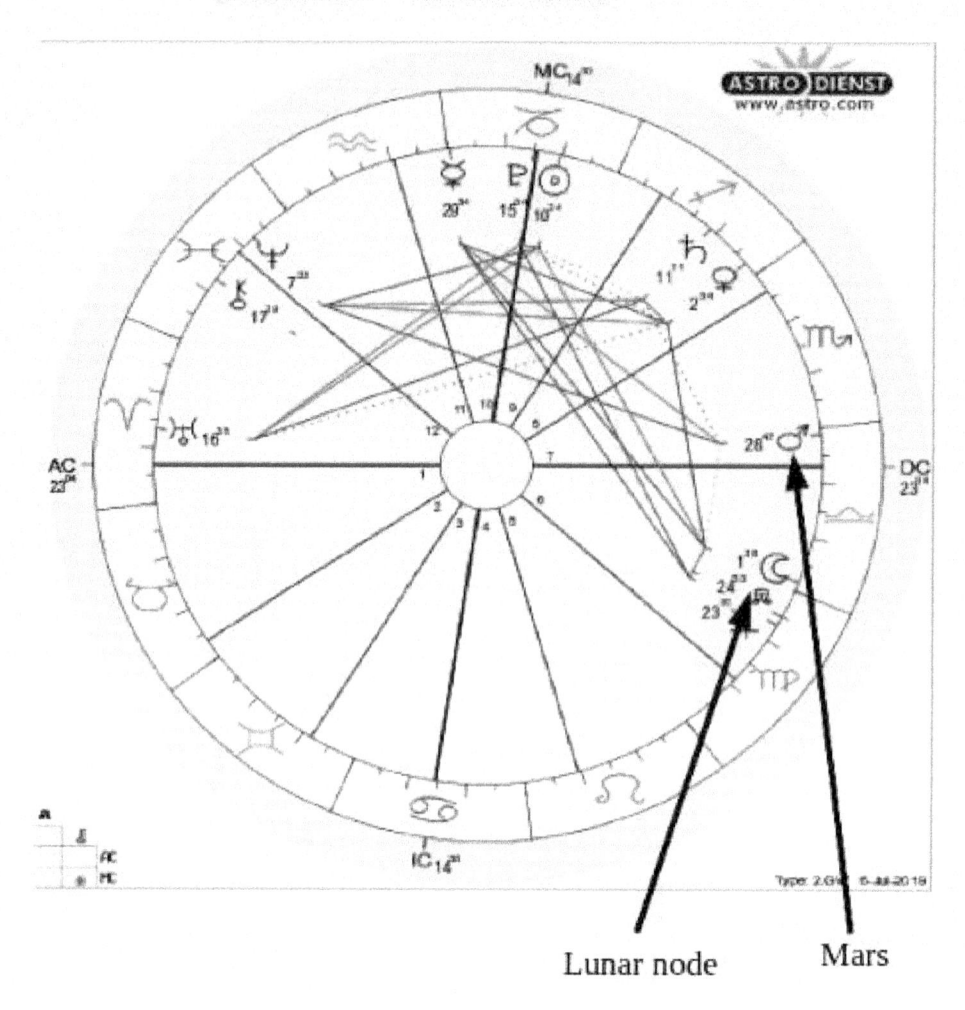

In January of 2016, Mars is just leaving from within 30 degrees of the lunar node. 2016, however, did not bear much significance in terms of violent conflict. In Figure H, the concentration of rocket fire in 2017 took place in December. 28 rocket were fired from Gaza during that month. See the chart on the next page.

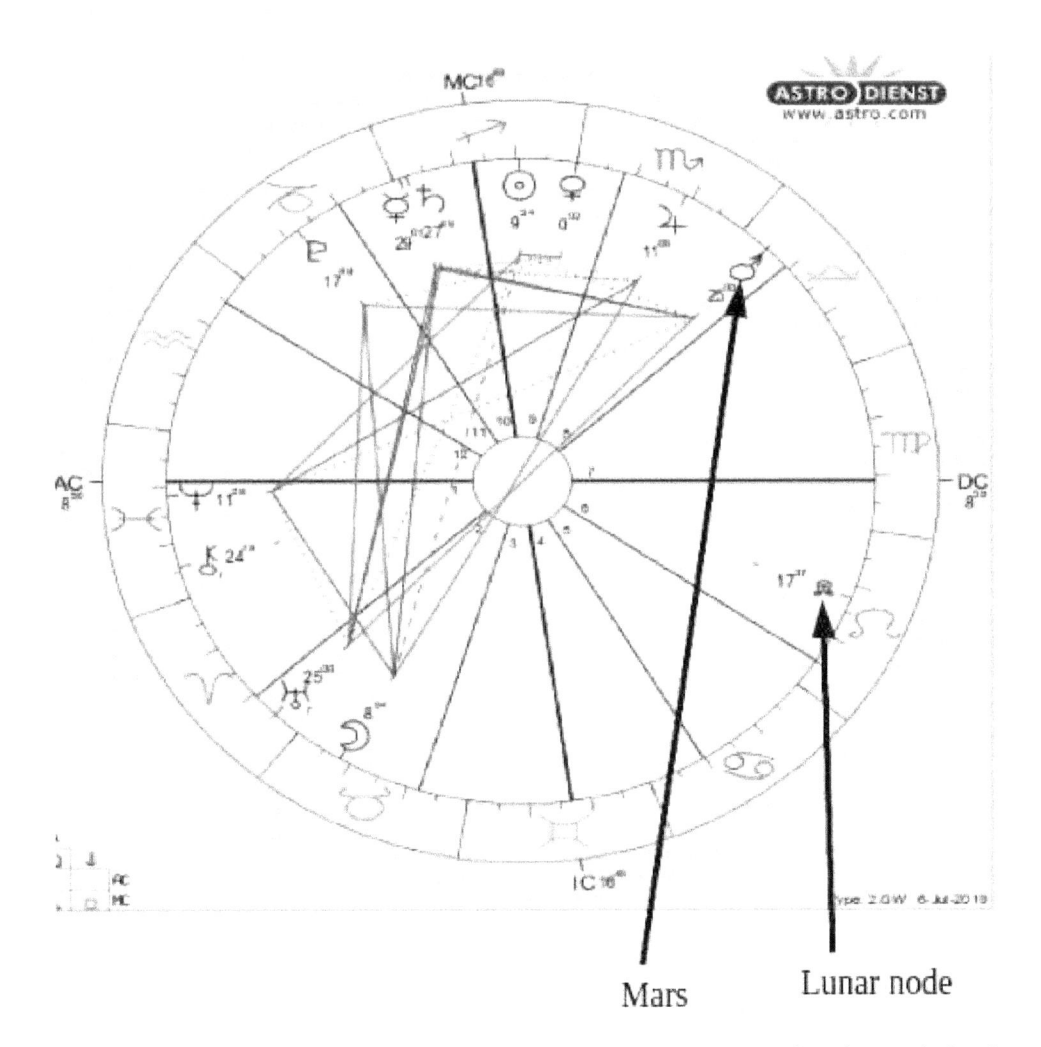

Mars is well out of range of being with 30 degrees of the lunar node, so one cannot say that the escalation in December of 2017 was related Mars. Mars would have last been within 30 degrees of the lunar node back in August of 2017, but there was only 1 rocket attack that month.

Lets go back to Figure H and have a look at 2018. We find that the month that had the greatest amount of rocket fire from Gaza that year was July. There were 174 rockets fired into Israel from Gaza during that time. See the astro chart on the next page

♂ Rocket Fire from Gaza
Su., 1 July 2018 Time: 12:00 p.m.
Jerusalem, ISRL Univ. Time: 9:00
35e14, 31n46 Sid. Time: 5:58:24

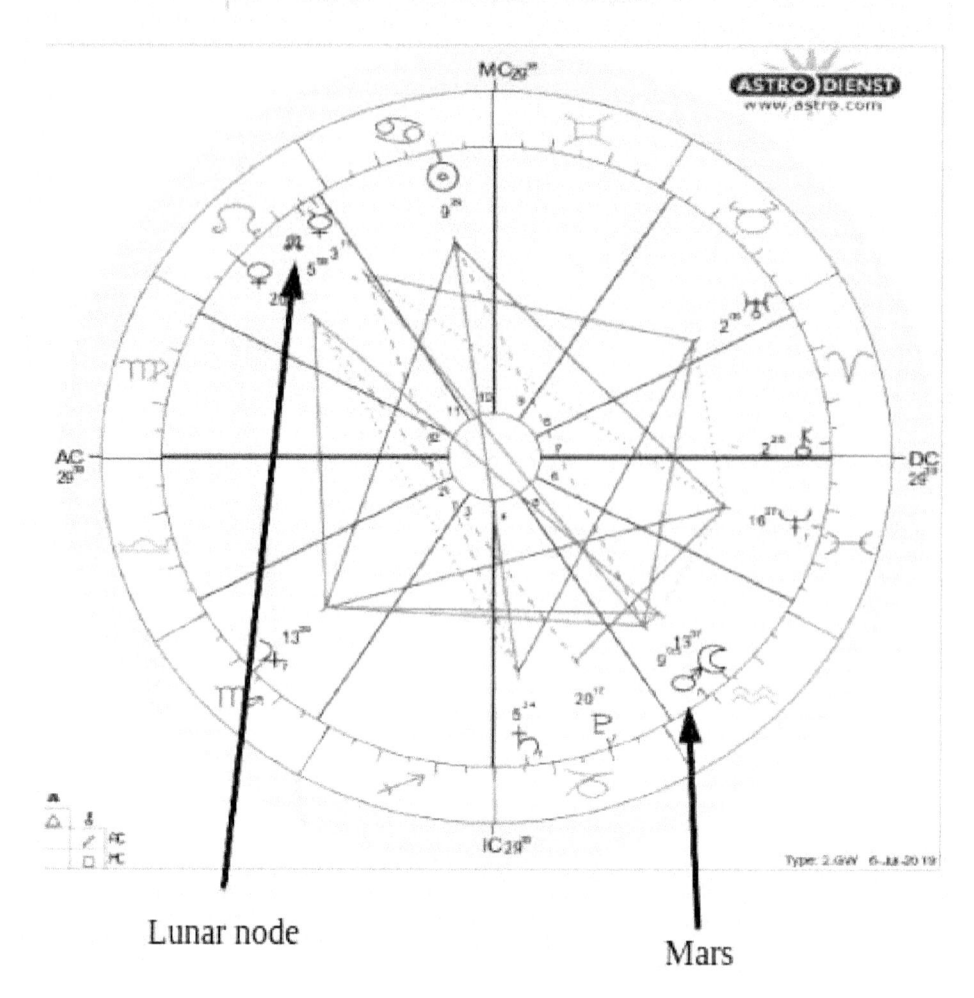

Lunar node   Mars

In this one, Mars is within 30 degrees of the lunar node, on the opposite side. So once again, that position of Mars has showed up during a month of escalation. In going back to Figure H for 2019, we see that May is the month with the highest concentration of Rocket Fire that year. There were 600 rockets fired from Gaza into Israel. Let see if the astro chart on the next page continues to show a correlation between Mars being within 30 degrees of the lunar node and escalating rocket fire from Gaza.

♂ Rocket Fire from Gaza
We., 1 May 2019 Time: 12:00 p.m.
Jerusalem, ISRL Univ Time: 9:00
35e14, 31n46   Sid. Time: 1:56:57

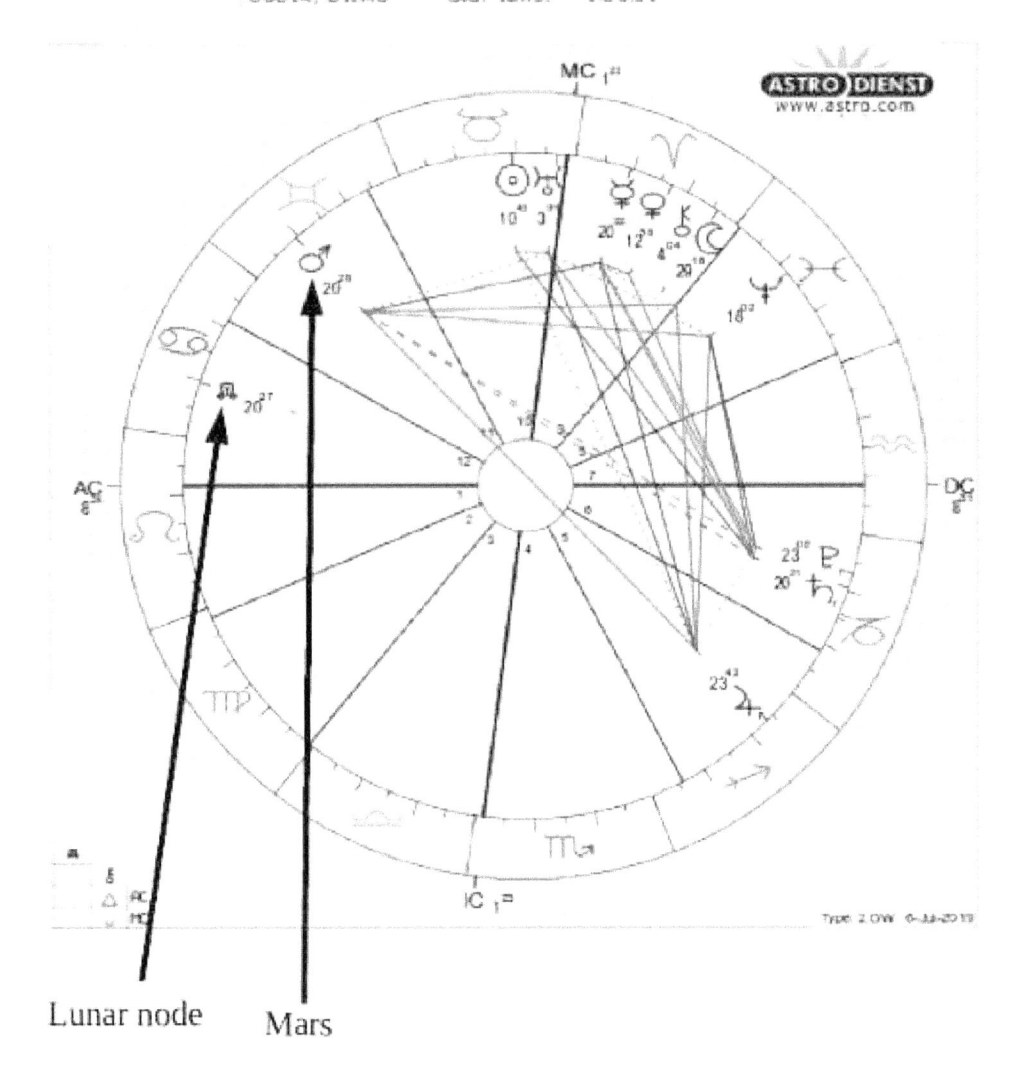

Lunar node   Mars

Once again, Mars is within 30 degrees of the lunar node during a month of escalating rocket fire. May 4, 2019 was the day that the rocket attacks were launched from Gaza. In this chart of May 1, we see Mars just entering within that 30 degrees from the lunar node.

One can say, after reviewing this, that there is a statistical significance regarding the correlation between escalating hostility from Gaza toward Israel and Mars being within 30 degrees of the lunar node.

Here are the remaining dates thru the year 2027 when Mars is within 30 degrees of the lunar node. Here you can review the past dates of Mars within 30 degrees of the lunar node and compare them to actual rocket fire statistics firsthand.

Chapter 24: Military Engineering Mandate

Figure H - Gaza Rocket attacks on Israel
* = Largest amount of Rocket fire for the year

	2007	2008	2009	2010	2011	2012
Jan	28	241	586*	13	17	0
Feb	43	257	52	5	6	36
Mar	31	196	34	35*	38	173
Apr	25	145	5	5	87	10
May	257*	149	1	14	1	3
Jun	53	87	2	14	4	83
Jul	61	4	1	13	20	18
Aug	81	8	1	14	149*	21
Sept	70	1	-10	16	8	17
Oct	53	1	1	3	52	118
Nov	85	125	4	5	11	1734*
Dec	113	361*	4	15	30	1

cont'd
Figure H - Gaza Rocket attacks on Israel
* = Largest amount of Rocket fire for the year

	2013	2014	2015	2016	2017	2018	2019
Jan	0	22	0	8*	0	6	0
Feb	1	3	0	0	7	4	0
Mar	4	65	0	5	2	0	3
Apr	17*	19	1	0	1	0	0
May	1	4	1	2	1	70	690*
Jun	5	62	3	0	1	84	3
Jul	5	2,874	1	2	2	174*	0
Aug	4	860	3	1	1	8	8
Sept	8	0	4	0	0	0	1
Oct	3	1	9*	0	1	0	0
Nov	0	0	3	0	0	17	455
Dec	4	1	4	0	26	0	4

Note: in 2019, the heaviest rocket fire from Gaza took place in May. 690 rockets were fired from Gaza on Israel.

cont'd
Gaza Rocket attacks on Israel
* = Largest amount of Rocket fire for the year

	2020	2021	2022	2023	2024	2025	2026
Jan	0						
Feb	104						
Mar	0						
Apr	0						
May	1						
Jun	3						
Jul	3						
Aug	15						
Sept	13						
Oct	3						
Nov	3						
Dec	2						

Dates of Mars-within-30-degrees-of-the-lunar node

March 19 2007 - May 30 2007	Apr 28 2008 - Jul 31 2008	Jan 08 2009 - Mar 24 2009	Aug 24 2009 - May 02 2010
Nov 02 2010 - Jan 18 2011	Jun 11 2011 - Sep 01 2011	Aug 24 2012 - Nov 12 2012	Apr 03 2013 - Jun 22 2013
Dec 19 2013 - Aug 28 2014	Jan 27 2015 - Apr 12 2015	Sep 27 2015 - Dec 26 2015	Nov 21 2016 - Feb 01 2017
Jul 11 2017 - Oct 10 2017	Apr 08 2018 - Nov 14 2018	May 01 2019 - Jul 29 2019	Jan 15, 2020 - Apr 3rd 2020

Below are future dates of Mars within 30 degrees of the lunar node

Feb 9, 2021 - May 13, 2021
Nov 4, 2021 - Jan 22, 2022
June 22, 2022 - Sept 19, 2022
Dec 26 2022 - Jan 24, 2023

Aug 24, 2023 - Nov 15, 2023
April 12, 2024 - June 25, 2024
June 5, 2025 - Sept 4, 2025
Feb 4, 2026 - April 19, 2026
Sept. 27, 2026 - June 12, 2027

For four consecutive years, following the info that I laid out on Gaza rocket fire, I further affirmed the thesis by predicting in real time the time-frame that an increased number of Gaza rockets would be fired into Israel relative to the rest of the year, all by observing the position of the planet Mars. Gaza militants are influenced by this planet, the ancient god of war. The same god of war that backed the Romans when they sacked the temple in AD 70.

Those future dates of Mars being within 30 degrees of the lunar node were set back in 2019 in Ares Le Mandat. Here is the earliest source. Go to the end of chapter 24 to see the list of dates for expected increased rocket fire relative to the rest of the year
https://archive.org/details/areslemandat_20191110/page/n349/mode/2up

Here is proof that the PDF is from November of 2019
https://archive.org/download/areslemandat_20191110

Not only did I show how historical data of rocket fire from Gaza into Israel going back to 2007 aligned with Mars and the lunar node, I also demonstrated this pattern in real time in 2020, 2021, 2022, and 2023 by making YouTube videos predicting escalated Gaza rocket fire relative to the rest of the year. Here is proof.

Here is the first demonstration of the thesis that says that the time-frame of when Mars is within 30 degrees of the lunar node is the time when rocket fire from Gaza into Israel will be highest compared to the rest of the year. This was the case in 2020, when I predicted that rocket fire between January 15, 2020 and April 3rd 2020 would exceed rocket fire during other months in 2020. This is confirmed. Gaza militants fired 104 rockets in February of 2020(highest relative to rest of the year) This video was made on November 18 2019(see transcript below)
https://www.youtube.com/watch?v=e5GxO4ZW2fc

Here is the transcript of the video

Hi this is Anthony. I want to do a follow up video. In the last video, I describe the lawless one as Mars 360 and i explained how I came to that conclusion. I used the English Sumerian gematria. So using that system, I was able to take the word Mars and add up the numerical value of each letter and get the number 306. I simply added 360 to 306 and that's how i got 666. So that's how I was able to link Mars 360 with 666. Mars 360 is the revolution of Mars around the sun and its influence on humanity. The difference between the way I describe it and the way contemporary astrology describes Mars has to do with energy. In contemporary astrology, the location of Mars at the time a person was born and what describes that location is the area of life where the person would infuse alot of energy and effort towards. The way I describe Mars, which is sort of opposite the way contemporary astrology describes it, has to do with the fact that Mars is actually the opposite. Mars is pulling energy away from the location of where it was at the time you were born and the description of that location or the area of life that describes that location. But for this video, i don't want to get into how Mars affects each human at the individual level. I want to talk about how Mars influences events and in chapter 24[of Ares le Mandat], you will notice I have information regarding the Israel/Palestinian issue in the middle east. In my research of rocket fire from Gaza into Israel, I noticed when looking at the statistics-in terms of month to month- the level of rocket fire from Gaza into Israel seems to correlate with the position of the planet Mars in relation to the lunar node. I noticed that the month where rocket fire from Gaza was highest compared to the rest of the year, that's the month where Mars was within 30 degrees of the lunar node and the statistics in chapter 24 go back to 2007 and the correlation is pretty significant. I think there might have been one year that finding didn't apply, but overall the results seem pretty significant and I want to use this video to extrapolate from that information when rocket fire may escalate again in Israel and rocket fire from Gaza towards Israel. So if we take the data from chapter 24[of Ares le Mandat and apply it to the future, Mars is within 30 degrees of the lunar node January 15 2020 all the way until April 3rd 2020. So during that time-frame, we can expect serious escalation of rocket fire from Gaza into Israel and the concentration of rocket fire during that time will exceed the amount of rocket fire at any other time during that year. So I just wanted to bring attention to that chapter. Its chapter 24. Its called Military Engineering Mandate and the statistics of rocket fire was taken from the internet, mostly from Wikipedia and the information there is very, its very interesting and I think if you take a look at it, you will find it quite profound that the correlation was this significant and I think its....I don't want to say that its fitting that it would apply to whats happening in the middle east, but I have concluded that Mars 360 is not only the Christian Antichrist, its also the Islamic Antichrist. the Antichrist equivalent in Islamic eschatology is called the Dajjal and Mars 360 applies to descriptions of Antichrist in Christian theology but it also can apply to description of the Dajjal in Islamic eschatology. so that's the information I wanted to put forth for this video. Thank you. .....end

Here is proof that the prediction was accurate. Here are the Gaza rocket stats. See 2020

Figure H - Gaza Rocket attacks on Israel
* = Largest amount of Rocket fire for the year

	2007	2008	2009	2010	2011	2012
Jan	28	241	566*	13	17	9
Feb	43	257	52	5	6	36
Mar	31	196	34	35*	38	173
Apr	25	145	5	5	87	10
May	257*	149	1	14	1	3
Jun	63	87	2	14	4	83
Jul	61	4	1	13	20	18
Aug	81	8	1	14	145*	21
Sept	70	1	~10	16	8	17
Oct	53	1	1	3	52	116
Nov	65	125	4	5	11	1734*
Dec	113	361*	4	15	30	1

cont'd
Figure H - Gaza Rocket attacks on Israel
* = Largest amount of Rocket fire for the year

	2013	2014	2015	2016	2017	2018	2019
Jan	0	22	0	6*	0	6	0
Feb	1	9	0	0	7	4	0
Mar	4	65	0	5	2	0	3
Apr	17*	19	1	0	1	0	0
May	1	4	1	2	1	70	600*
Jun	5	62	3	0	1	64	3
Jul	5	2,874*	1	2	2	174*	0
Aug	4	950	3	1	1	8	0
Sept	8	0	4	0	0	0	1
Oct	3	1	5*	0	1	0	0
Nov	0	0	3	0	0	17	455
Dec	4	1	4	0	28	0	2

Note: in 2019, the heaviest rocket fire from Gaza took place in May. 600 rockets were fired from Gaza on Israel

cont'd
Gaza Rocket attacks on Israel
* = Largest amount of Rocket fire for the year

	2020	2021	2022	2023	2024	2025	2026
Jan	6	3	0	1			
Feb	104	0	0	8			
Mar	0	0	0	0			
Apr	0	45	5	66			
May	1	4375	0	1470			
Jun	3	0	1	0			
Jul	3	0	4	6			
Aug	15	1	1100	0			
Sept	13	2	0	0			
Oct	3	0	0	5000+			
Nov	3	0	4				
Dec	2	0	1				

Dates of Mars-within-30-degrees-of-the-lunar node

March 19 2007 - May 30 2007 Apr 28 2008 - Jul 31 2008 Jan 08 2009 - Mar 24 2009 Aug 24 2009 - May 02 2010
Nov 02 2010 - Jan 18 2011 Jun 11 2011-Sep 01 2011 Aug 24 2012 - Nov 12 2012 Apr 03 2013 - Jun 22 2013
Dec 19 2013 - Aug 28 2014 Jan 27 2015 - Apr 12 2015 Sep 27 2015 - Dec 26 2015 Nov 21 2016 - Feb 01 2017
Jul 11 2017- Oct 10 2017 Apr 08 2018 - Nov 14 2018 May 01 2019-Jul 29 2019 Jan 15, 2020 - Apr 3rd 2020

Below are future dates of Mars within 30 degrees of the lunar node

Feb 9, 2021 - May 13, 2021
Nov 4, 2021 - Jan 22, 2022
June 22, 2022 - Sept 19, 2022
Dec 26 2022 - Jan 24, 2023

Aug 24, 2023 - Nov 15, 2023
April 12, 2024 - June 25, 2024
June 5, 2025 - Sept 4, 2025
Feb 4, 2026 - April 19, 2026
Sept 27, 2026 - June 12, 2027

It also happened again in 2021 when on record on video, I predicted that rocket fire from Gaza into Israel between February 9, 2021 to May 13, 2021 would exceed rocket fire in the other months in 2021. Once again confirmed. Gaza militants fired 4000 rockets beginning on May 10th(highest relative to other months) This video and real time prediction was actually made on May 7th 2020 https://www.youtube.com/watch?v=v1sA-ZS73Lw&t

Here is the transcript

I want to give the remaining dates from now until the year 2027, 'when Mars will be within 30 degrees of the lunar node—and subsequently when there would be an increase in the tensions between Israel and Gaza, resulting in an escalated rocket fire from Gaza into Israel. So here are the dates from now until 2027. We just finished the previous phase in which I predicted that there would be an escalation of rocket fire from Gaza into Israel due to the influence of Mars being within 30 degrees of the lunar node. Mars was within 30 degrees of the lunar node between January 15th 2020 to April 3rd 2020. It will go within 30 degrees of the lunar node again on February 9th 2021 and last until May 13th 2021. After that the next phase of Mars being within 30 degrees of lunar node will be from November 4th 2021 to January 22nd 2022. After that will be June 22 2022 to September 19th 2022. Then December 26 2022 to January 24th 2023. August 24th 2023 to November 15 2023. April 12 2024 to June 25th 2024. June 5th 2025 through September 4th 2025. February 4th 2026 to April 19th 2026. lastly September 27 2026 to June 12th 2027 So after having completed this first phase in which I was able to predict by simply observing the position of Mars in relation to the node and having now having demonstrated an ability to forecast this year the escalation that took place between January 15th and April 3rd, I think it would be prudent for us to try and understand what this Mars phenomenon means in a religious sense. Now, this isn't done to draw discord between the Israelis and the Palestinians. The reason all of this is being presented is to try and present a new perspective right now. The perspective is that God or Yahweh or Allah is "everything." So what I'm trying to do is present the perspective that it's necessary for us to not focus so much on the God of Abraham Isaac and Jacob, but... look over ..... to the look over somewhere else..... look over..." let's have a look....... let's see what Mars is doing. You know one can see historically, the correlation between the planet, Mars and the geopolitical events in Israel. One can see. how that would mean that it deserves more attention. In AD 70, when the Jewish people were driven out of Israel by the Roman army...... essentially the God of Abraham, Isaac and Jacob went head to head with the god of the Roman Empire, the military god of the Roman Empire, which was Mars. And judging from the outcome, it was Mars who was successful. Now that's something that makes a case for the power of this Mars phenomenon Another example is how later on during the Roman Empire, the emperor had made Christianity an accepted religion of the Roman Empire. It was precipitated ..... it precipitated the eventual fall of the Roman Empire. In the book "City of God" Saint Augustine addresses a lot of the arguments made by some of the opponents of Christianity that the Roman Empire would still be in place had they not abandoned the old polytheistic outlook—the worship of multiple gods; the worship of Mars as a protective military force for the Roman Empire. If one wants to argue that if the Roman Empire remained with the polytheistic perspective, the perspective in which the Roman army worshiped a designated god "Mars" as the god of war, one can conclude that the Roman Empire could still be intact today. In "City of God" Saint Augustine dealt with a lot of backlash from opponents of Christianity that felt the reason that the Roman Empire fell was because they abandoned the old gods, they abandoned Mars as the protective military force of the Roman Empire. And this is a pretty strong case. It would be all the more advantageous if Christians, Jews and Muslims could spend...-. could take some of that time that they use giving attention, giving reverence to the God of Abraham, Isaac, and Jacob and bring it ....bring it over to Mars, the traditional god of war for the Roman Empire. Now, in the link below I'm going to leave some information regarding how Mars affects the US stock market. I have data going back to 1896 that shows how the Dow Jones performed when Mars was within 30 degrees of the node. Overall. it presents... Overall, it seems to indicate that the Dow Jones performs better when Mars is not within 30 degrees of the lunar node. I'll leave the link at the bottom so that you can view and study this data yourselves but for now as it stands the next time that we can expect another increase in hostilities in Israel particularly as it pertains to the amount of rocket fire from Gaza. The next time we can expect that increase is between February 9, 2021 and May 13, 2021 when Mars will be within 30 degrees of the lunar node....The end

This prediction was also accurate. Here are the stats. See the year 2021

Figure H - Gaza Rocket attacks on Israel
* = Largest amount of Rocket fire for the year

	2007	2008	2009	2010	2011	2012
Jan	28	241	566*	13	17	9
Feb	43	257	52	5	6	36
Mar	31	196	34	35*	38	173
Apr	25	145	5	5	87	10
May	257*	149	1	14	1	3
Jun	63	87	2	14	4	83
Jul	61	4	1	13	20	18
Aug	81	8	1	14	145*	21
Sept	70	1	~10	16	8	17
Oct	53	1	1	3	52	116
Nov	65	125	4	5	11	1734*
Dec	113	361*	4	15	30	1

cont'd
Figure H - Gaza Rocket attacks on Israel
* = Largest amount of Rocket fire for the year

	2013	2014	2015	2016	2017	2018	2019
Jan	0	22	0	6*	0	6	0
Feb	1	9	0	0	7	4	0
Mar	4	65	0	5	2	0	3
Apr	17*	19	1	0	1	0	0
May	1	4	1	2	1	70	600*
Jun	5	62	3	0	1	64	3
Jul	5	2,874*	1	2	2	174*	0
Aug	4	950	3	1	1	8	0
Sept	8	0	4	0	0	0	1
Oct	3	1	5*	0	1	0	0
Nov	0	0	3	0	0	17	455
Dec	4	1	4	0	28	0	4

Note: in 2019, the heaviest rocket fire from Gaza took place in May. 600 rockets were fired from Gaza on Israel

cont'd
Gaza Rocket attacks on Israel
* = Largest amount of Rocket fire for the year

	2020	2021	2022	2023	2024	2025	2026
Jan	6	3	0	1			
Feb	104	0	0	8			
Mar	0	0	0	0			
Apr	0	45	5	66			
May	1	4375	0	1470			
Jun	3	0	1	0			
Jul	3	0	4	6			
Aug	15	1	1100	0			
Sept	13	2	0	0			
Oct	3	0	0	5000+			
Nov	3	0	4				
Dec	2	0	1				

Dates of Mars-within-30-degrees-of-the-lunar node

March 19 2007 - May 30 2007   Apr 28 2008 - Jul 31 2008   Jan 08 2009 - Mar 24 2009   Aug 24 2009 - May 02 2010
Nov 02 2010 - Jan 18 2011   Jun 11 2011 - Sep 01 2011   Aug 24 2012 - Nov 12 2012   Apr 03 2013 - Jun 22 2013
Dec 19 2013 - Aug 28 2014   Jan 27 2015 - Apr 12 2015   Sep 27 2015 - Dec 26 2015   Nov 21 2016 - Feb 01 2017
Jul 11 2017 - Oct 10 2017   Apr 08 2018 - Nov 14 2018   May 01 2019 - Jul 29 2019   Jan 15, 2020 - Apr 3rd 2020

Below are future dates of Mars within 30 degrees of the lunar node

Feb 9, 2021 - May 13, 2021   Aug 24, 2023 - Nov 15, 2023
Nov 4, 2021 - Jan 22, 2022   April 12, 2024 - June 25, 2024
June 22, 2022 - Sept 19, 2022   June 5, 2025 - Sept 4, 2025
Dec 26 2022 - Jan 24, 2023   Feb 4, 2026 - April 19, 2026
                                    Sept. 27, 2026 - June 12, 2027

Here is where I predicted well in advance on May 27, 2022 that Gaza militants would fire an increased number of rockets at Israel between June 22, 2022 and Sept 19, 2022. At the moment, it stands that Gaza militants fired 1000 rockets between August 5th and August 7th of 2022. https://www.youtube.com/watch?v=6EniwV0TWew

Here is the transcript

Hi, this is Anthony, I am making this video because I want to do another prediction concerning whats going on in Israel. You will notice if you look at my last videos, that I was able to make pretty accurate predictions concerning the timeframe of the highest amount of rocket fire from Gaza into Israel relative to the rest of the year. In one of my older videos back in 2020 during the pandemic, I was able to predict that the number of rockets from Gaza into Israel between January 15, 2020 and April 3rd 2020 would exceed the number of rockets fired at any other point during the year and that turned to be the case. I did the same the next year and….well I mean it wasn't the next year….that same year in 2020, I made another prediction for the next year and that prediction, I stated that the number of rockets fired from Gaza into Israel during the year 2021 would be highest during the timeframe between February 9th 2021 and May 13th 2021. And that certainly was accurate because that's the year the Gaza war took place when militants in Gaza over thousands of rockets into Israel starting around may 10 or may 11th just two days before the [end of the]designated timeframe of which it was predicted that the number of rockets fired during that time would exceed the amount fired for the rest of the year 2021. So thats 2 years in a row that I made accurate predictions simply by observing when Mars would be within 30 degrees of the lunar node. So now we're in 2022 and if we look at where Mars is gonna be situated in relation to the lunar node, we can see that between June 22, 2022 and September 19, 2022, Mars will be within 30 degrees of the lunar node and really the main gist of this thesis is that Mars, not just as a god of war that was worshiped during the time of the Roman empire, but as a planetary influence, it still has an effect on things happening on earth today, and in particular whats happening with Israel. Back in AD 70, the Romans basically used Mars to go into Israel and destroy the temple and today based on my thesis, Mars is still trying to exert an effect on the enemies of Israel in order to destroy the state of Israel. This influence is not going anywhere. So this year, I am going to make another prediction about….we already know the thesis I… the thesis is that when Mars is within 30 degrees of the lunar node, militants in Gaza will fire an increased number of rockets or in engage an escalated warfare against the state of Israel during that time compared to the rest of the year. I made this clear in my other videos that this would be the case when it comes to Mars being within that 30 degrees of the lunar node. So this year, I am going to make another prediction. We are already late in 2022, but still I just want to reinforce the basic thesis here. So we can expect that the number of rockets fire this year between June 22, 2022 to September 19 2022 will exceed the amount of rockets fired by Gaza militants into Israel for the rest of the year. So, the whole point of this is to try and get Israel to become of this Mars influence and the negative impact that its had on Israel throughout history and the reason that I asked in another video for Israel to try and make an image to…to make some sort of an image to this Mars force, is largely built around the concept that we can sort of extrapolate from the Book of Numbers when Moses told the Israelites to make an image to a bronze serpent in order to keep serpents from biting and killing them as they wandered through the desert. So this request that Israel make an image is built around that same framework that if they just make an image to this Mars influence, it'll somehow be a solution to the problem of Mars influencing militants in Gaza to scale up, dial up attacks against civilians in Israel which would ultimately provoke or escalate the entire conflict to where Israel ends up going into Gaza launching airstrikes, conducting military operations that endanger and kills many civilians in Gaza. And vice versa, the militants end up firing more and more rockets directly at Israeli civilians which imperils and kills Israeli civilians. So its important that Israel try and give this whole Mars thesis a look. It may be something can lead to a non-violent solution to this on-going war in Israel. So as it stands for the year 2022, the number of rockets fired by Gaza militants and this is due to the influence of Mars the god of war the same god of war that influenced the Romans to go into Israel and destroy the temple. So we can expect because of this influence, Mars will influence the Gaza militants to dial up the number of rockets fired between June 22, 2022 and September 19 2022, relative to the rest of the year. So with the war in Ukraine happening right now and then of course, there has been some tensions in early 2022..there has been some recent tension just prior to this time frame that I am giving. So it is easy to expect that things will dial up between that time frame of June 22, 2022 and September 19, 2022 relative to the rest of the year and of course you can go back to my old videos and see that I made these predictions accurately in 2020 and 2021, so I am expecting this sort of prediction of basically predicting fire coming down from heaven will pan out accordingly in 2022. So there it is I hope the state of Israel can really look into this and see what they can do to keep this god of war, Mars, from taking every every measure to influence people against the state of Israel, Israelis because this seems to be an ongoing thing, As I said before this was the case in AD 70 and its not just the Romans. Mars as a god of war can be said to be an amalgamation of all the gods of war that ever existed. The Babylonians conquered Israel, They came in with a god of war and so did the Persians. The Greeks as well, they has Ares. And Israel stuck with the God of Abraham whom historically has not been very successful in deterring this god of war aspect from coming in and running the Jewish people out of their land and we can see that Mars is really making an effort to get the militants in gaza to at some point to eventually Israeli off their land. And, ya know, for Muslims who don't really know what to make of this sort of Mars thesis. Basically the best way to understand it. Mars is the source of what Islamic discourse would consider the jinn. Whats happening in Gaza is that when Mars goes within 30 degrees of the lunar node seems to be releasing the jinn directly into Gaza militants which is sort of compelling them to upscale their attacks on the state of Israel specifically during that time frame compared to other times during the year. Just keep in mind for this year the time between June 22, 2022 and September 19 2022 when Mars goes within 30 degrees of the lunar node, an increase in the amount of rocket fire will occur between time compared to other times or other months during the year 2022. Thank you...end

Here is proof that the prediction was correct. See stats for the year 2022

Figure H - Gaza Rocket attacks on Israel
* = Largest amount of Rocket fire for the year

	2007	2008	2009	2010	2011	2012
Jan	28	241	566*	13	17	9
Feb	43	257	52	5	6	36
Mar	31	196	34	35*	38	173
Apr	25	145	5	5	87	10
May	257*	149	1	14	1	3
Jun	63	87	2	14	4	83
Jul	61	4	1	13	20	18
Aug	81	8	1	14	145*	21
Sept	70	1	~10	16	8	17
Oct	53	1	1	3	52	116
Nov	65	125	4	5	11	1734*
Dec	113	361*	4	15	30	1

cont'd
Figure H - Gaza Rocket attacks on Israel
* = Largest amount of Rocket fire for the year

	2013	2014	2015	2016	2017	2018	2019
Jan	0	22	0	6*	0	6	0
Feb	1	9	0	0	7	4	0
Mar	4	65	0	5	2	0	3
Apr	17*	19	1	0	1	0	0
May	1	4	1	2	1	70	600*
Jun	5	62	3	0	1	64	3
Jul	5	2,874*	1	2	2	174*	0
Aug	4	950	3	1	1	8	0
Sept	8	0	4	0	0	0	1
Oct	3	1	5*	0	1	0	0
Nov	0	0	3	0	0	17	455
Dec	4	1	4	0	28	0	4

Note: in 2019, the heaviest rocket fire from Gaza took place in May. 600 rockets were fired from Gaza on Israel

cont'd
Gaza Rocket attacks on Israel
* = Largest amount of Rocket fire for the year

	2020	2021	2022	2023	2024	2025	2026
Jan	8	3	0	1			
Feb	104	0	0	8			
Mar	0	0	0	0			
Apr	0	45	5	66			
May	1	4375	0	1470			
Jun	3	0	1	0			
Jul	3	0	4	6			
Aug	15	1	1100	0			
Sept	13	2	0	0			
Oct	3	0	0	5000+			
Nov	3	0	4				
Dec	2	0	1				

Dates of Mars-within-30-degrees-of-the-lunar node

March 19 2007 - May 30 2007	Apr 28 2008 - Jul 31 2008	Jan 08 2009 - Mar 24 2009	Aug 24 2009 - May 02 2010
Nov 02 2010 - Jan 18 2011	Jun 11 2011 - Sep 01 2011	Aug 24 2012 - Nov 12 2012	Apr 03 2013 - Jun 22 2013
Dec 19 2013 - Aug 28 2014	Jan 27 2015 - Apr 12 2015	Sep 27 2015 - Dec 26 2015	Nov 21 2016 - Feb 01 2017
Jul 11 2017 - Oct 10 2017	Apr 08 2018 - Nov 14 2018	May 01 2019 - Jul 29 2019	Jan 15, 2020 - Apr 3rd 2020

Below are future dates of Mars within 30 degrees of the lunar node

Feb 9, 2021 - May 13, 2021
Nov 4, 2021 - Jan 22, 2022
June 22, 2022 - Sept 19, 2022
Dec 26 2022 - Jan 24, 2023

Aug 24, 2023 - Nov 15, 2023
April 12, 2024 - June 25, 2024
June 5, 2025 - Sept 4, 2025
Feb 4, 2026 - April 19, 2026
Sept 27, 2026 - June 12, 2027

Here is where I predicted well in advance on January 25th 2023 that Gaza militants would fire an increased number of rockets at Israel between August 24, 2023 and November 15, 2023. At the moment, it stands that Gaza militants fired 5000+ rockets during this time frame.
https://www.youtube.com/watch?v=IGbNPEO9qS4

Here is the transcript

All right this is Anthony, so three consecutive years I've been able to predict exactly when Gaza militants would fire more rockets at Israel relative to the rest of the year. So back in 2019 using the observation of Mars, I was able to predict in 2020 that Gaza militants would fire more of their rockets during the time frame of Mars being within 30 degrees of the lunar node. In 2020, Mars was within 30 degrees of the lunar node between January 15th and April 3rd and looking back we can see that it happened exactly as predicted. In between January 15th and April 3rd, Gaza militants fired roughly 112 rockets at the state of Israel during that time, and that amount exceeded the amount of rockets fired during any other month during the year. So it went exactly as predicted. I was able to know in advance exactly when Gaza militants would fire their highest amount of rockets for that year simply by observing when Mars would be within 30 degrees [of the lunar node]. In that same year I predicted exactly how Gaza militants would fire rockets in the year 2021. So in 2020, I made a video predicting that Gaza militants would fire more rockets in 2021 when Mars would be within 30 degrees of the lunar node between February and and May and looking back at the year 2021, that's exactly what happened. During that time, Gaza militants fired roughly....they fired.... during that time, Gaza militants fired over 4000 rockets at the state of Israel. So that's the second year that...So that was the second year in a row I got that prediction correct. In 2022 same thing. you can look back at my previous video where I was able to predict that Gaza militants would fire more rockets when Mars would be within 30 degrees of the lunar node between June 22nd 2022 and September 19th 2022. And looking back, that's exactly what happened. In early August 2022, Gaza militants fired 1100 rockets at the state of Israel. So now I'm.....So that's the evidence is right there. You can look back at my previous videos and see that I was accurate for three consecutive years in in 2020, in 2021, and 2022. By observing when Mars would be within 30 degrees of the lunar node, I was able to know in advance when Gaza militants would fire more rockets at the state of Israel relative to the rest of the year. So for this video I'm going to predict when Gaza militants are going to fire most of their rockets in the year 2023. So, in 2023, Mars will go within 30 degrees of the lunar node between August 24th 2023 and November 15 2023. So between that time we can we can expect Gaza militants will fire more of their rockets at the state of Israel than at any other time during the year. So between August 24th 2023 and November 15 2023, expect the highest amount of Rocket fire from Gaza to occur.....expect the highest amount of Rocket fire from Gaza for the year 2023 to occur between that time of August 24th and November 15th. So I'm gonna make the prediction, I'm going to....I'm gonna confirm the prediction right here for the year 2023. Most of the rockets that will be fired from Gaza....that will be fired by Gaza militants at the state of Israel, will be fired between August 24th 2023 and November 15th 2023. So for the year 2023, we can expect the highest amount of Rocket fire from Gaza into Israel to take place between August 24th 2023 and November 15th 2023 when Mars will be within 30 degrees of the lunar node. This will be the fourth year in a row that this prediction is made. So in 2020 you saw it...you saw it......you can see the video from 2019 when I called down fire from heaven....when I called that Gaza militants would fire more rockets at the state of Israel between January 15 2020 and April 3rd 2020, and the amount they fired between that time will be more than the rockets they would fire at any other point during the year.... and that turned out to be exactly what happened. I made that prediction in 2019, and it transpired exactly as I predicted in 2020. And later in 2020 I made a prediction for 2021....that in the year 2021 Gaza militants would fire more rockets relative to the rest of the year between February 9 2021 and May 13 2021, and looking back, we can see during that time, that's when the Gaza War took place. Gaza militants fired over 4000 rockets at the state of Israel when Mars was within 30 degrees of the lunar node. Fast forward to the next year 2022, I did the same exact thing. You can see the video. Look back at my video when I....when I got on video and I said months before it actually happened that Gaza militants would fire more rockets......when I got on video and said that the highest amount of Rocket fire from Gaza into Israel would take place when Mars would be within 30 degrees of the Lunar node between June 22nd 2022 and September 19 2022 and looking back we can see that's exactly what happened. Early August, Gaza militants fired 1100 rockets at the state of Israel during that time, and now I'm doing this again in the year 2023. Gaza militants will fire more of their rockets between August

24th 2023 and November 15 2023. Between that time, the highest amount of rockets fired from Gaza into Israel will exceed the amount of rockets fired during any other month in the year 2023. So that's the prediction. I'm calling down fire from heaven for the fourth year in a row. Thank you

This prediction was correct Here are the stats. See year 2023

Figure H - Gaza Rocket attacks on Israel
* = Largest amount of Rocket fire for the year

	2007	2008	2009	2010	2011	2012
Jan	28	241	566*	13	17	9
Feb	43	257	52	5	6	36
Mar	31	196	34	35*	38	173
Apr	25	145	5	5	87	10
May	257*	149	1	14	1	3
Jun	63	87	2	14	4	83
Jul	61	4	1	13	20	18
Aug	81	3	1	14	145*	21
Sept	70	1	~10	15	8	17
Oct	53	1	1	3	52	116
Nov	65	125	4	5	11	1734*
Dec	113	361*	4	15	30	1

cont'd
Figure H - Gaza Rocket attacks on Israel
* = Largest amount of Rocket fire for the year

	2013	2014	2015	2016	2017	2018	2019
Jan	0	22	0	6*	0	6	0
Feb	1	9	0	0	7	4	0
Mar	4	65	0	5	2	0	3
Apr	17*	19	1	0	1	0	0
May	1	4	1	2	1	70	600*
Jun	5	62	3	0	1	64	3
Jul	5	2,874*	1	2	2	174*	0
Aug	4	950	3	1	1	8	0
Sept	0	0	4	0	0	0	1
Oct	3	1	5*	0	1	0	0
Nov	0	0	3	0	0	17	455
Dec	4	1	4	0	28	0	4

Note: in 2019, the heaviest rocket fire from Gaza took place in May. 600 rockets were fired from Gaza on Israel

cont'd
Gaza Rocket attacks on Israel
* = Largest amount of Rocket fire for the year

	2020	2021	2022	2023	2024	2025	2026
Jan	8	3	0	1			
Feb	104	0	0	8			
Mar	0	0	0	0			
Apr	0	45	5	66			
May	1	4375	0	1470			
Jun	3	0	1	0			
Jul	3	0	4	6			
Aug	15	1	1100	0			
Sept	13	2	0	0			
Oct	3	0	0	5000+			
Nov	3	0	4				
Dec	2	0	1				

Dates of Mars-within-30-degrees-of-the-lunar node

March 19 2007 - May 30 2007   Apr 28 2008 - Jul 31 2008   Jan 08 2009 - Mar 24 2009   Aug 24 2009 - May 02 2010
Nov 02 2010 - Jan 18 2011   Jun 11 2011 - Sep 01 2011   Aug 24 2012 - Nov 12 2012   Apr 03 2013 - Jun 22 2013
Dec 19 2013 - Aug 28 2014   Jan 27 2015 - Apr 12 2015   Sep 27 2015 - Dec 26 2015   Nov 21 2016 - Feb 01 2017
Jul 11 2017 - Oct 10 2017   Apr 08 2018 - Nov 14 2018   May 01 2019 - Jul 29 2019   Jan 15, 2020 - Apr 3rd 2020

Below are future dates of Mars within 30 degrees of the lunar node

Feb 9, 2021 - May 13, 2021
Nov 4, 2021 - Jan 22, 2022
June 22, 2022 - Sept 19, 2022
Dec 26 2022 - Jan 24, 2023

Aug 24, 2023 - Nov 15, 2023
April 12, 2024 - June 25, 2024
June 5, 2025 - Sept 4, 2025
Feb 4, 2026 - April 19, 2026
Sept 27, 2026 - June 12, 2027

After demostrating accurate predictions of rocket fire from Gaza since 2019, Anthony has made numerous requests for an image to be made to the god of war.

Here on April 4th 2020, I advised the state of Israel should build an image to Mars/Ares in order to tame its influence. Same concept as the building of the bronze serpent on the book of Numbers
https://www.youtube.com/watch?v=wwsGqQK7OV4&t

Here is the transcript

This is Anthony. This is a follow-up video to the one made back in November in which I was observing Mars and correlating it with the 666 referred to in the Book of Revelation. Back in November and an observation of Mars I was able to make a prediction and the prediction had to do with escalation events in Israel. When Mars goes within 30 degrees of the lunar node-historically-there seems to be a correlation between that and the number of rockets fired into Israel from Gaza. So in the last video, I had gave the dates in which Mars would be within 30 degrees of the lunar node. Those dates were between January 15th 2020 and April 3rd 2020. Today is April 4th. So that phase has pretty much ended and looking back, we can see that starting on January 15th--as according to the prediction--there was a rise starting on January 15th. There was an increase in the amount of rockets fired from Gaza into Israel. From January 15 to the end of the month, there were about eight rockets fired. In the month of February, there were about 104 rockets fired. In March, there was 1 and that was it. So during that time, February was the month where there was the highest amount of rockets fired from Gaza into Israel. The amount of rocket fire that takes place during the months when Mars is within 30 degrees of the lunar node will exceed the amount of rocket fire for any other month during the year. So with this recent phase from January 15th 2020 to April 3rd 2020, the total number of rockets fired was around 113... with the majority of them being fired during the month of February. So according to what I've been presenting, the amount of rocket fire that would take place for the rest of the year will not exceed the amount of rocket fire that took place during this Mars-within-30-degrees-of-the-lunar-node phase. So with February having about 104 rockets fired, we can expect that there won't be another month of this year that would exceed the number of rockets fired in February. Why? Because Mars won't be within 30 degrees of the lunar node at any other point during the year. So it won't be until the end of the year where it would be affirmed that Mars within 30 degrees of the lunar node was responsible for the escalation in Israel. But in the meantime, I think it's important that we start paying some attention to this energy, this force that seems to be responsible for a lot of tension or a lot of violence here on earth. Even though according to monotheism, there's this notion that there's just one god, but if there's all these forces here on earth affecting how we live as as human beings then we have a right to take responsibility and observe and prevent this energy or deal with this energy in a way... to where...or deal with this force in a way to where it doesn't destroy us. So with that being said, in the meantime since this recent phase has ended, the people of earth should think about getting in touch with this energy... this Mars energy that's responsible for a lot of the problems we have on this planet as far as war, as far as violence, as far as tension. What I'm asking or what I'm requesting is that if we can start the process of getting in touch with this energy in a way that even though we know it's going to be here, we can somehow figure out a way to keep it from destroying us. I'm proposing that we we follow the same model that Moses used in the book of Numbers when he led the Israelites out of Egypt and when they were wandering in the wilderness for 40 years, they had reached a point where they were being attacked by these fiery serpents. These fiery serpents would attack them, bite them, and kill them...and the Israelites asked Moses to intercede on their behalf and ask God for a solution to this problem --to make it stop. And as Moses did do just that, he interceded. He came back to the Israelites with the solution, and he told them.... he ordered them to make an image.... to create an image of a bronze serpent and the next time all these fiery serpents would end up biting them, they could just stare at the image--not worship it--but they could just stare at the image, and if they did that, they would be immediately healed. Well I'm trying to follow.. or what I'm proposing is pretty much the same model. That if we make an image.... somehow form an image to this Mars force that seems to be affecting us here on earth, that it will somehow mitigate the problems associated with its influence. So when we look at not just Mars, but all the gods of war...Ares notably.... Ares was a god who was wounded and healed. He was wounded in battle and he was later healed and because of that, I think it would be appropriate to start coming up with some sort of plan to make an image... build an image to Ares... a representation of Ares to the Greek god of war who was wounded and was healed. Ares and Mars is essentially..... they're essentially the same thing. Ares is the Greek version of the god of war and Mars is the roman version. So we're looking at both. We're observing both as the same. We're observing the planet Mars and in terms of making an image or building a tribute, we use Ares, the Greek version of Mars. So I think it would be a good plan to start coming up with some sort of way we can follow that same model that Moses and the Israelites followed when (they were being attacked by the fiery serpents and solving that problem by actually building an image to the serpent.... building a bronze serpent and then just staring at it as they were bitten and as they stared at it they wouldn't they were somehow healed).... So this...sort of.... this follows along that same line. We are going along that same... or.... following that same path where we are affected by war... war is affecting us.... so in order to keep it from affecting us in a negative way, we're presenting something.... an image of it here on earth, and we're simply staring at it as a way or as a plan to keep this force from breaking us-destroying us. Now if there isn't any human intervention as far as this Mars phenomenon goes, then I should give the upcoming dates for when Mars would be within 30 degrees of the lunar node: February 9th 2021 to May 13 2021, November 4th 2021 to January 22nd 2022, June 22nd 2022 to September 19th 2022......end

Here is the video made on August 8th 2022 where I introduce the Armaaruss as the image that should be built under the same concept as the bronze serpent mentioned in the Book of Numbers. In the video, I also advise that the Mars 360 system and the astrological marking system be applied to commerce(buying and selling).
https://www.youtube.com/watch?v=KgTiALILAGk

Here is the transcript

Hi, this is Anthony again. I once again was able to prophecy when an increased level of rocket fire from Gaza into Israel would take place. We are currently in the phase of Mars being within 30 degrees of the lunar node between June 22, 2022 and September 19th 2022. And between August 5 and August 7th, militants in Gaza have already fired over 1000 rockets into Israel. The last video I made predicted this would happen. This is the 3rd consecutive year that I have been able to warn in advance of escalated rocket fire from Gaza into Israel, proving that Mars still has an influence on events in Israel and in the world today for that matter. The question is, with this influence still largely in effect in today's world, what should people do about it. The answer goes back to the book of Numbers when the Israelites wandering in the desert were being attacked on a regular basis by fiery serpents. Compare this to today when Israel, year after year is being attacked by rocket fire. Well, back during time of Moses when the Israelites were wandering in the desert and being attacked by fiery serpents, he asked god for a solution. The solution to the problem of fiery serpents turned out to be constructing a brass image resembling the attacker, in that case, fiery serpents, and then having the Israelites stare at the image after being bitten so that they could avoid death from the serpent bites. Moses made a fiery serpent and put it on a pole. This new solution to terrorism and war is the very similar and falls in line with tradition. Ares, the Greek version of Mars, was an unpopular deity in ancient Greece because he was considered cruel, ruthless, and barbaric as a terrorist. During the Trojan war, however, Ares was wounded by Diomedes when Diomedes threw his spear at Ares and wounded him. But Ares still lived. It was a wound that would have been fatal for any mortal. Mars, in Roman times, was considered in a more positive light, but Mars backed the Romans and helped them destroy the Jewish temple in AD 70 and is still working to resist the Jewish presence in Israel as indicated by the fact that escalation of rocket fire is coinciding with Mars being within 30 degrees of the lunar node. People in Israel/Palestine should view constructing an image to Ares/Mars from the vantage point of how Moses was ordered by God to create a brass image/statue of a fiery serpent. Hence Moses was not told how to go out and kill the fiery serpents. He was simply told how to keep the fiery serpents from killing the Israelites and solution did not involve striking the fiery serpents. It was simply staring and contemplation. Likewise in making an image to this Ares/Mars influence, we don't go out and fight against terrorism. We simply use an ancient method of staring and contemplation to keep that energy from from destroying people. There is no fighting involved here. This staring and contemplation should also involve staring at the planet Mars itself. This new statue should be named Armaaruss. Its an amalgamation of the gods of war, but notably Ares, who was for the most part, a terrorist god of war that was wounded by the spear and yet lived. His number is Mars 360, which is simply the revolution of Mars around the sun and its influence on humanity. Every person on earth is influenced by Mars in some manner and the Mars 360 system identifies how and comes up with a system in which each person would be assigned a number based on where Mars is located in their astrology chart, in order to facilitate understanding, which a necessary precursor to peace. In order for this system to work, it requires that everyone acknowledge Mars influence. And in such a system as Mars 360, even things like commerce—buying and selling--should revolve around people having outward indication of where Mars is located in their astrological birthchart. They can indicate this on their forehead or simply show it on an ID card. Its a very simple methodology. The demonstration of calling down fire from heaven was enough to convince people that Mars certainly has an influence on events in Israel and events around the world and on individual human beings. From this point after having demonstrated clearly for the last 3 years that when Mars goes within 30 degrees of the lunar node there is an escalation of rocket fire from Gaza into Israel relative to the rest of the year, this will eventually take on a life on its own. And one can say that the last 3 years, I have been instrumental in breathing life into what is Mars influence. Thank you... end

Here is an overview of the Mars 360 system and why it should be a worldwide accord. This video was made on July 19 2020 https://www.youtube.com/watch?v=w_MGptS4HWY

Here is the transcript

Hi this is Anthony. I want to make this video to explain exactly what the Mars 360 system is. The Mars 360 system is calculating your astrological birth chart and taking the information regarding where the position of Mars was located at the time you were born and placing that information on either your birth certificate, driver's license, state issued id, or any other form of outward insignia. The premise behind this idea is to alert others in a human community as to how to deal with you. In Ares Le Mandat, Mars is said to enact influence on human beings through reducing the amount of gray matter in the area of the brain associated with its natal astrological position. So there are six major lobes of the brain: the frontal lobes, the temporal lobes, the occipital lobe, the parietal lobe, the brain stem, and the cerebellum. So in astrology the astrological chart is divided into twelve 30 degree sectors and in Ares Le Mandat, I take that chart as it's divided into the twelve 30 degree sectors and essentially change it into being interpreted as only six 30 degree sectors; one sign and its correlating opposite sign is read as altogether one sign. So if you take a chart that has twelve 30 degree sectors and read it in that manner, it becomes interpreted as all together six sectors. So in Ares Le Mandat, the six lobes of the brain are correlated with the six seals in the Book of Revelation. The first seal would be at the mid heaven and is assigned to the occipital lobe of the brain and is responsible for how we develop our face-to-face communication within our immediate environment and how we feel about other people's property. If we move counterclockwise to the next 30 degree sector we get to the second seal which has been assigned to the temporal lobes of the brain which is responsible for our auditory processing, our hearing, our listening, and our thoughts. If we move counterclockwise to the next 30 degree sector, we get to the third seal which has been assigned to the brain stem/ cerebellum portion of the brain, which is responsible for our breathing, our diet, our movement, and our basic survival skills. Now if we move counterclockwise to the next 30 degree sector, that portion is assigned to the frontal lobes of the brain and this section is responsible for our executive control functions, our ability to make decisions, engage in discipline, choose our words carefully, learn, our working memory, and our indirect communication and attitude to cultures that are not our own. So if we move counterclockwise[again], that portion has been assigned to the motor cortex portion of the brain which is near the top part of our skulls and is responsible for our ability to plan in advance movements. This portion of the brain is responsible for our work ethic, how we deal with authority figures, and our overall view of economics in general. If we go counterclockwise to the next 30 degree sector this is the last seal and has been assigned to the parietal lobe of the brain which is responsible for how we interpret sensory input from our environment, how we display ourselves in view of others, and how we interpret input from others within our environment. Now the premise is that Mars has an influence on the portion of the brain based on where Mars was positioned at the time you were born. So for example, if you were born when Mars was rising in the east, Mars would be affecting the frontal lobes of your brain and therefore causing you to display deficiencies in the designated characteristics that are assigned to the frontal lobe functions because the planet Mars causes a reduction in gray matter to certain portions of the brain based on where it was positioned at the time you were born. We as human beings can now in understanding that provide a certain amount of leeway to other humans as they engage or as they navigate through life in whatever way they see fit in terms of how they express themselves within a given society or within a given community. This element of understanding that comes into play is something that can be a great potential for peace, understanding, and justice here on earth. The idea of every human placing the location of Mars in their astrological birth chart on a birth certificate, on a driver's license, or state issued id or on some outward form of insignia where people in society can see how that person is influenced by Mars, we can thus provide ourselves an impetus to a more utopian society, to a more peaceful more harmonious way of life; something that's missing in contemporary times and something that has been missing going back to antiquity. The idea is that nations can apply the location of Mars wherever it was at the time a person was born to the state issued id, the driver's license, or the birth certificate as a measure of understanding or as a measure of keeping a certain amount of...or as a measure of maintaining a certain amount of equilibrium and understanding within their society. So this Mars 360 system provides an opportunity for people who live in two different nations to maintain a certain amount of connection based on their Mars position. This can be done without any threat to national sovereignty or geographical borders. The main component that should arise from this Mars 360 system is the element of understanding whereas humans knowing how other humans are affected by the planet Mars and vice versa (other humans knowing how the individual is affected by Mars) can allow for humans to forgive or accommodate qualities that would normally be deemed unacceptable. It's not just having a Mars indicator on a birth certificate, driver's license, or state issued id or having some form of outward insignia that shows where Mars was positioned at the time you were born, it's also allowing society to divide itself or to sector itself based on each person's Mars position--meaning all the people in a given society who are affected by Mars in a certain way would would at the same time be accommodated by that society in which the society would create an atmosphere specifically for that group to express itself according to how Mars influences human beings. So for example, if Mars influences a certain sector of human beings within the society to be a little bit relaxed when it comes to face-to-face communication, the society would create environments where those particular humans can sort of act freely or display that tendency to have a certain amount or a certain lack of care regarding face- to-face communication. Society could create situations where this quality would not be looked down upon by anyone else because the environment would be understanding of that particular situation and this would apply not just to that particular Mars influence, it would apply to every type of Mars influence so the outcome would be at the very least a society divided into six sectors where each of the six Mars influences can be allowed to express themselves as Mars influences them to express themselves in a certain way-- to express themselves freely or feel that they don't have to try and overcome this Mars influence. This is essentially the gist of the Mars 360 system. You're in a nutshell allowing humans to be themselves and you're sort of forcing society to accommodate each human to be themselves according to how Mars influences them at birth. The outcome that should arise from the Mars 360 system is a certain amount of balance, harmony, and cohesion between government and people. Now ideally when it comes to the Israel Gaza Palestinian factor, Israel would be wise to set up some sort of observatory that would indicate where Mars is positioned in the sky just to encourage understanding when it comes to the Mars influence. So as spoken before: when Mars enters within 30 degrees of the lunar node there is an escalation in Israel where a higher than normal amount of rockets relative to the rest of the year are fired from Gaza into Israel. In response to this, Israel should create an observatory so that the people can see for themselves that when Mars goes within 30 degrees of the lunar node, it's invoking an influence that precipitates a certain level of violence and a certain level of strife-- a certain level of war. It should also be something that encourages people to understand that in order to remain safe in society, Mars has to be continuously observed; it has to be watched and it has to be noticed based on the statistics that I give in Ares Le Mandat. Not paying attention to the Mars influence will just continue to infect the human race with wars--with conflict without any of us really understanding why. Such problems continue to happen. So this is why I recommend that Israel would create some sort of observatory to the planet Mars to encourage the public to pay attention to its influence and also alert the public when Mars goes within that 30 degrees of the lunar node ....end.

Here is another request from Anthony that an image be made to the god of war. Here, Anthony admits that he is a mouthpiece for Satan and after performing the sign of predicting the Israel-Hamas war in 2023, he proposes going after other gods and serving them. https://www.youtube.com/watch?v=yEsO6kcJxig

Here is the transcript

Hi this is Anthony we are currently under the alignment of Mars being within 30° of the lunar node. The previous video I predicted that when Mars would be within 30 degrees of the lunar node between August 24th 2023 and November 15 2023, Gaza militants would fire the highest amount of rockets during that time compared to the rest of the year. In 2023, the escalation that occurred earlier in the year occurred in May and that was during a time when Mars was not within 30 degrees of the lunar node. Back in May, Islamic Jihad, one of the Gaza militant groups, had fired roughly 1,400 rockets at the state of Israel, and after that happened it would have been easy to conclude that that particular time would have been the escalation period for 2023, but, as I said in the previous video, the time when Gaza militants would escalate rocket fire against Israel is usually when Mars is within 30 Degrees of the lunar node, and Mars didn't go within 30 Degrees of the lunar node until August 24th 2023 and it's going to remain there until November 15th. Today is October 11th and at the moment Israel has currently declared war against Hamas. Since October 7th, Gaza militants began firing a barrage of rockets at the state of Israel and over the course of just a few days. The number of rockets fired exceeded 5,000. This is this is happening exactly as predicted. This is the fourth year in a row that I've done this. So, for people have who have been following me since 2019, this is of no surprise. I've been doing this accurately every year since 2019 and this year is just another example. In the first video in which I predicted the escalation period for the year based on Mars being within 30 degrees of the lunar node back in 2019, you can look at the first video that I did where I was predicting escalation of Rocket fire from Gaza into Israel back in 2019, you'll see how I was able to tie Mars to Satan basically ....um not just Satan but also 666, and after doing that, I demonstrated for consecutive years how Mars and this entire framework of Satan and 666 has direct influence on Gaza militants in Israel. In English Sumeran gematria, each letter is assigned a value that's based on increments of six, where "A" would equal "6", "B" would equal "12", "C" would equal "18"... so on and so forth. So in using this system, I was able to take the word Mars and add up the numerical value of each letter and get the number 306 and since Mars is involved in a revolution around the Sun I simply added 360 to 306 and that's how I got 666. So, that's how I was able to tie Mars to the influence of Satan and 666, and from that, I was able to find a link between Gaza militants and the movements of the planet Mars around the Sun, specifically when Mars goes within 30 degrees of the lunar node. Now I've demonstrated how this influence works. Since 2019, I predicted that Gaza militants would fire most most of their rockets that year when Mars would be within 30 degrees of the lunar node between January 15th 2020 and April 3rd 2020, and if you look at the stats which I'm going to leave below for people to to view themselves, you'll see that that prediction was essentially accurate. You know that most of the rockets fired that year in 2020 were fired when when Mars was within 30 degrees of the lunar Node between January 15th and April 3rd. And later that year in 2020, I made another prediction for the year 2021, and in that video, I predicted that in the year 2021 most of the rockets fired by Gaza militants would be fired when Mars would be within 30 Degrees of the lunar node between February 9th 2021 and May 13th 2021. And that turned out to be accurate as well. That's the year the Gaza War happened when in early May, Hamas and the Gaza militants fired over 4,000 rockets at the state of Israel. So that was a very intense conflict. And I continued forward with pushing...I continued forward with demonstrating this thesis when uh the very next year I was accurate again in observing Mars to predict when Gaza militants would fire most of the rockets most of their rockets in 2022. I predicted that Gaza militants would fire most of their rockets when Mars would be within 30 degrees of the lunar node between June 22nd 2022 and September 19th 2022, and lo and behold, that's exactly what happened. Islamic Jihad fired over 1100 rockets in between that time frame and it exceeded the amount of rockets fired at any other point during the year. And so that, I felt should have been enough....... I felt should have been convincing enough to show that Mars has, you know, very obvious purposes against the state of Israel, but it gained very little traction as far as viewership or acknowledgement. So what I did was for the fourth consecutive year, I decided to do the prediction again and this was in 2023. This year, I predicted that Gaza militants would fire most of their rockets when Mars would be within 30 Degrees of the lunar node between August 24th 2023 and November 15th 2023. And we're still in the middle we're still in the middle of that alignment, but Hamas has already fired 5,000 plus rockets at the state of Israel which exceeds ....by far exceeds the 1100[1400] that was fired back in May of 2023. And what's remarkable.... I mean what's really ominous about this year.....I think this year is an example of what the full brunt of Mars influence looks like when it has a direct influence on Humanity. I mean this is the god of war, Mars, that's acting on ....that's essentially.....this is the god of war, Mars, essentially infusing.....this is the god of war, Mars, infusing the enemies of Israel with all that evil and sadistic power and just bold aggressive sick satanic behavior. It's infusing the enemies of Israel to act out the full brunt and scale of what satanic power looks like. Some of the atrocities that Hamas and Gaza militants have committed during this time frame of Mars being within 30° of the lunar node is perhaps something unlike anything that's been witnessed in this generation. I mean, there have been reports of babies getting their heads chopped off, entire families being shot to death at point blank range, elderly being executed. I mean this is the full brunt of what Mars influence looks like when it's taken to its apex, and Satan is trying to send a message and the message that he's trying to send is that he's looking for some kind of acknowledgement. He wants essentially....he wants to be....he wants to be seen, he wants to be known, and I guess in a way he's he's trying to...he's using me to deliver deliver this message. And for the last four years, I've given people that have watched, I've given you all a sign and the sign being Mars within 30 degrees of the lunar node leading to escalated rocket fire from Gaza into Israel relative to the rest of the year has come to pass. It's played out exactly as I explained it ....as I said it would happen in the last four years. I gave you a sign and the sign came to pass and therefore I propose that we go after other gods, gods that you have not known and look for a way to serve them. So in saying this, I advise that we start making concessions to this god of war, who gets his power from Satan clearly, as we see the atrocious behavior of Hamas and Gaza militants during this Mars within 30 degrees of the lunar node phase. I advise that we begin making concessions to this god of war and give Satan what he wants. So here's how the the plan works if you can just bear with me for a second. Speaking as a prophet that is speaking on behalf of the god of War who gets his power from Satan, it is advised that an image be made to the god of war and this god of war, historically his name has been Aries, Mars, Horus. There there have been other names for him, but in this generation, his name is to be Armaaruss, and what we have to do is..... we need to make an image to him and give him a platform here on the world stage and that image, that platform will be sort of a dwelling place for him. And in exchange for doing this, the god of war will reduce his influence on the enemies of Israel and the result of this would be that Israel will be able to live in peace and not have to deal with the Insidious nature of Mars influence on those who Harbor antipathy against the Jews in the state of Israel. Really, the nature of this is derived from, you know, as I mentioned before, it's derived from....it's derived from the Book of Numbers when the Israelites were wandering through the desert and they came across these fiery serpents that would bite and and kill them, and after repeated suffering caused from this, they eventually went to Moses and asked him to intercede on their behalf and come up with a solution, and Moses was told to make a bronze Serpent and put it on a stick and tell the Israelites that any time that they would be bitten by these fiery serpents, they could simply stare at the image and they would automatically be healed. And what I'm proposing follows along that same line where by making an image to this god of war that has endless antipathy towards Jews in the state of Israel, does not want them there, never has wanted them there. If we make an image to that, the result will be the same as it was for the Israelites, as explained in the Book of Numbers. The result would be an end to violence and antipathy against the state of Israel and the endless rocket fire, the terrorist attacks, and all the other heinous crimes carried out by Gaza militants would come to an end. So there it is. I've explained the whole purpose of my mission here...my mission since 2019 to get people to see that there is another god out there. There is an evil influence and this influence is Mars, but Mars gets his power from Satan. And by tying all of this to 666 using the English Sumeran gematria and adding up the the the value of the letters in Mars and getting 306 and adding 360, coming up with 666 by doing this, I was able to demonstrate that Satan is active in the world and I am serving as a mouthpiece. And the message is this—give Satan .....make some concessions to Satan, make concessions to the god of war. Give him an image give and a platform and the result of that will not only be peace for Israel, but it will be World Peace. I've also in the last four years have devised a system based on how Mars influences people at the individual level. It's called the Mars 360 system and there's a document online. It's called the Mars 360 Religious and Social System. Look up the PDF. You'll be able to find information regarding that system. And so the Mars 360 religious and social system is an entire system there and each person on the planet should be identified based on where the planet Mars was located at the time they were born, and the personality and characteristics that make up what defines that particular position of Mars in the natal chart. So, in another document, I explain how this can be applied in relation to the state of Israel. In a document called The Armaaruss Project, I advise that Israel begin to expand its biometric database to include other nations. With this biometric database system, people would have their Mars.... their natal astrological Mars position recorded into all the other factors that are assigned to their identity. And what Israel would do is get as many nations involved in this sort of a global concession or Global Accord and the result of this would be Global cooperation. It would be Global understanding ......which should ultimately lead to World Peace. So I I've gone through the entire process in leading up to this moment. Since 2019, I started calling fire down from heaven and this was to serve as a sign to convince you that Satan.... he still exists.... he is giving his power to Mars the god of war who is in turn directing the enemies of

Israel to attack the state of Israel and to remove them from the land. This has been the task for Mars since day one and it's still happening today as demonstrated back in 2019. I've demonstrated this four consecutive years now with this year that we're currently in being the most convincing and intense display of satanic Mars influenced behavior that we have probably ever seen in this generation that we're currently in. The fact that I've been able to make this, to perform this demonstration for consecutive years, to be able to give a sign and have that sign come to pass justifies looking looking into this god of war and making concessions towards it because that's the only way that this problem of of violence and savagery and terrorism is going to be settled. We have to look at the source from a cosmic perspective and by doing so, the result will lead to Greater Harmony in the world, less violence toward the state of Israel and just overall prosperity.

Milton Keynes UK
Ingram Content Group UK Ltd.
UKHW050634130224
437765UK00012B/427